During his remarkable career, David Hill has been chairman and managing director of the Australian Broadcasting Commission, chairman of Railways of Australia, chairman of the Australian Football Association and chairman of the CREATE Foundation – a national organisation working to improve the lives of young people and children in the care system. He has also held a number of national and international executive appointments in the areas of sport, transport, TV and radio, fiscal management and public utilities.

He is author of a number of bestselling history books, including *1788*, *The Gold Rush*, *The Making of Australia*, *The Great Race*, *The First Fleet Surgeon* and *Australia and the Monarchy*.

In 2006 he was awarded a Diploma of Arts with merit in classical archaeology from the University of Sydney and is now the project manager of an archaeological survey of the ancient Greek city of Troizen. He has for many years been a leading figure in the international campaign to have the Parthenon sculptures returned from the British Museum to Greece. He li

David Hill

THE FORGOTTEN CHILDREN

Fairbridge Farm School and its
Betrayal of Britain's Child Migrants

ALLEN&UNWIN

First published in Australia by Random House Australia Pty Ltd in 2007

First published in Great Britain in 2017 by Allen & Unwin

Allen & Unwin
c/o Atlantic Books
Ormond House
26–27 Boswell Street
London WC1N 3JZ

Phone: 020 7269 1610
Fax: 020 7430 0916

Email: UK@allenandunwin.com
Web: www.allenandunwin.com/uk

A CIP catalogue record of this book is available from the British Library.

Paperback ISBN 978 1 76063 132 1
E-book ISBN 978 1 76063 877 1

Author photograph by Ian Bayliff
Printed in Great Britain

10 9 8 7 6 5 4 3 2 1

CONTENTS

For Stergitsa and Damian

SONG OF THE CHILD MIGRANTS

There was rumour in the orphanage
For word had got around
That certain little inmates
Were soon Australia bound

With others, not so lonely
'Twas Government intent
They'd have a horse or pony
Like a little English gent

With a largish cardboard suitcase
Up the gangway walked with glee
The ship then headed seaward
Good bye to family

Six weeks long the journey
Where luxury did abound
But then the final landing
With feet on foreign ground

A long and tiring journey
Through country parched and dry
With ne'er a single hedgerow
'Neath a blazing sun and sky

In house with thirteen others
Who snored or cried all night
Just little English children
Too tired to snarl or fight

Then appeared the rosters
Apportioning the work
To scrub and clean and polish
No chance to ever shirk

To till the market garden
With shovel and with hoe
Planting lots of cabbages
And taters in their rows

Harnessing the draught horse
To the single furrow plough
Holding fast the jerking handles
To plough a straight furrow

Sitting on the bucking tractor
Sowing in the wheat
Smothered in both sweat and dust
From the never-ending heat

Training for the future
The farming life ahead
But surely little migrant lad
You should be in your bed

It's fine to look so manly
With all your duties done
But little British orphan
Where has your childhood gone?

Len Cowne, March 1999

Len was in the first group of children to arrive at
Fairbridge Farm School in Molong in 1938.

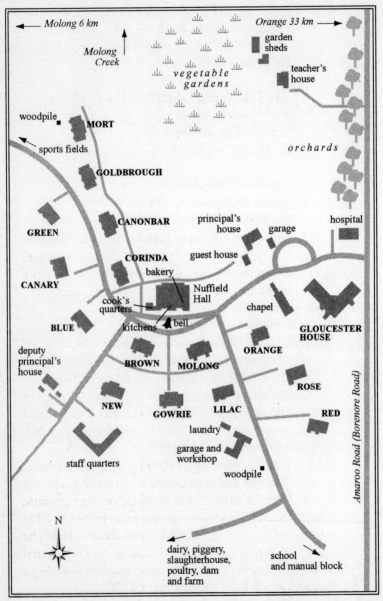

Plan of the Fairbridge Farm School Village

PREFACE TO THIS EDITION

The publication of the book *The Forgotten Children* caused quite a stir in both Britain and Australia, where some of the revelations from hitherto secret files and from the stories of former Fairbridge children attracted widespread media coverage.

The Fairbridge Farm School Scheme was roundly applauded during the 70 years it sent impoverished British children to farm schools in Australia, Canada and Rhodesia. Fairbridge aimed to create worthy citizens for the British Empire by converting boys and girls from English city slums into farmers and farmers' wives, and promised opportunities and an education that the children could not hope for if they stayed in England.

But for many of the child migrants, some as young as four years old and never to see their parents again, the story was very different. Many were denied the promise of a better future, and most were forced to leave school at 15 with no education to work full-time on the farm. The typical child experienced social isolation and emotional privation and spent his or her entire childhood without ever experiencing the love of a parent. When the young migrants left Fairbridge at seventeen years of age, they had nowhere to go and no one to go to. The Fairbridge files in both the UK and Australia that have never been made public show that Fairbridge failed in many of its aims and corroborate most of the experiences the former Fairbridge children relate in the book.

Since the book was released, more former Fairbridge children have come forward wanting to tell their stories. These include the allegation that Lord Slim sexually molested a number of the boys while visiting Fairbridge when he was the governor-general of Australia. Slim was a greatly respected and revered war hero, both in Australia and in Britain, who later became the chairman of the Fairbridge Society in the 1960s when he returned to live in England.

When I was researching the book, one of the former Fairbridge boys had told me that the then Sir William Slim had molested him and a number of others in the back of the governor-general's chauffeur-driven Rolls-Royce. While I believed his story, the boy did not want the allegation recorded and was not prepared to publicly defend the claim, so I thought it was unfair at the time to include it in the book.

However, since then other boys have told newspapers in Britain and Australia that it also happened to them, including Robert Stephens, who happened to be at the Molong Fairbridge Farm School when I was there.

Robert says that he and a number of other boys of eleven and twelve years old were offered rides in the Rolls-Royce up and down the drive along the Amaroo Road between Fairbridge and the main road about one kilometre away. During the ride he was forced to sit on Slim's knee as Slim slid his hand up inside Stephens's shorts.

Other boys spoke of fondling in the back of cars as he toured the farm. How do you explain it? We were innocent kids. I guess we were vulnerable and in a position where no one could really speak out. No adult would believe these things happened, so you didn't talk about it. You think you are the only one. Like so many things that happened at Fairbridge, they don't go away. They live with you all your life.

Ron Simpson is now 78 years old and lives in Sydney. He came out to Australia and to Fairbridge in 1938 as a nine-year-old with his seven-year-old sister Mary and is another who now wants to tell what happened to him.

Ron recounts how his back was broken when he was beaten with a hockey stick because he was late getting in the cows for the early-morning milking when working as a trainee boy on the Fairbridge dairy:

> It wasn't even my fault. The cottage mother forgot to pull out the pin, so the alarm clock didn't go off. The other boys woke me up, and there was a mad rush to get to the dairy and bring the cows in to milk. So we were very late and got down to breakfast at seven-twenty. Principal Woods came over and told me to see him after breakfast.
>
> When I arrived at the principal's house, I knocked on the door, and he said come in, and I had just stepped in, and he was there holding a hockey stick in his hand. He grabbed me by my shirt collar, pushed my shoulder down, then gave me a tremendous wallop across my lower back. I fell into a big black bath opposite the hallway, screaming in pain. He pulled me out of the bath, then he did the same again. This time I flew through the entrance door and hit every step on the way out.

Ron went back to work with constant and worsening back pain. A month or two later he was chopping wood for the village kitchen stoves when he collapsed and had to be carried in a wheelbarrow by another boy to the village hospital.

> I was chopping wood, and as I stooped down to put it into the barrow I felt a terrible shooting pain from my lower back down my legs. I collapsed onto the ground and couldn't move the lower part of my body. I felt no pain, but try as I might I could not stand. Another boy who was with me lifted me into the wood barrow and ran me down to the farm nurse. She put me into a bed and called for the doctor at Molong, who came and checked me out and said I'd be all right in a couple of days. The nurse treated my back with some liniment, and . . . they got me out of bed in three days, and I was in pain, and I couldn't sit on my backside. I was sitting on my spine.

Back at work his condition worsened, and the pain continued until one day the local Molong vicar, who was visiting Fairbridge, noticed him crying in pain and unable to sit properly. The vicar asked to be able to take him to Orange Base Hospital. After some months he was transferred from there on a stretcher by train to Sydney Hospital.

Ron still has some of his old hospital records. For more than a year he lay in the hospital bed with sandbags supporting his back, and apart from being visited by Charlie Brown, a former Fairbridge boy who had joined the army, Ron doesn't recall ever seeing his sister or any other Fairbridge children while he was there. Ron says he told anyone who asked how the injury had occurred, but no one followed it up with any further inquiry.

Eventually, when he was able to walk again, he was returned to Fairbridge and spent the next few years wearing a metal-framed brace around his torso that he only took off at night when he went to bed. After he left Fairbridge, he was found a job on a neighbouring property, and he remembers Fairbridge providing him with a new brace when the old one wore out.

More than 30 years later and after decades of back pain Ron received a message from another Old Fairbridgian that Woods, who was in retirement, was asking after him.

> Tommy Cook, an Old Fairbridgian down at Dapto, saw Woods. Woods kept on asking for me and said, 'If you see Ron Simpson, tell him to please come and see me.' But I never did. I wouldn't go and see him . . . Even just before he died, he asked to see me, but I wouldn't go near the man. I didn't go to his funeral either . . . I think he just felt guilty about what happened to me.
>
> I just couldn't go through and say, 'It's all right, mate.' It's been with me all these years, and it's a dreadful thing to happen to anyone, to children.

Many of the children spent their entire childhood at Fairbridge with no one to turn to and feeling that no one cared anyway. But there were some good staff at Fairbridge who genuinely cared for the kids and who are still fondly remembered.

Following the publication of the book a man came forward to say that his mother had worked for Fairbridge in England and had for many years remained upset about what she saw.

We all knew her as Matron Guyler who ran the big Fairbridge house in Knockholt in Kent where we were all sent prior to being put on the ship to Australia. We all remember her filling our heads with exciting dreams of what Australia and Fairbridge would be like.

What we didn't know is that she had never seen the

place until she went to Australia on a visit in 1961 prior to her retirement. Apparently she was horrified with what she saw and protested, in vain, to the Fairbridge Society in England when she returned.

Her son Mike, who now lives in Australia, described his mother's reaction to the visit in an email he sent to me after the book's first publication:

> My mother was horrified by what she saw at Molong, but really she only saw the surface. What she did see were cold, hungry, unhappy children. All the new clothes that they had when they left England were gone. The cottage was dirty and the cottage mother . . . defensive. The thing that most affected my mother was the look in one of the children's eyes. I don't know if it was a boy or a girl, but my mother told me that she never saw such a pleading look, and it went straight to her heart.

Michael was not a Fairbridge boy himself but he has been in touch with a number of Old Fairbridgians in recent years. He said his mother was now 98 years old 'but still talks of her horror at what Fairbridge allowed to happen in Australia'. He said she was living in a nursing home near Epsom in England and asked if one of the former Fairbridge kids might be able to visit her to reassure her that it wasn't her fault.

> I wonder if there is any Fairbridge boy or girl who now lives near Epsom who might be able to visit her and tell her that she was not to blame. I know that she still feels betrayed by what she discovered. (She really has no idea of the full extent of what went on.) Her mind is still pretty good, and I think it would comfort her. Of course I am aware that there are many

Fairbridge children for whom there is no comfort, and
it troubles me that I have known many of the children
who were subsequently beaten, starved, abused and
denied love.

The Fairbridge organisations in both Britain and Australia still deny any failings of the Fairbridge scheme, as
they did when giving evidence before parliamentary
inquiries into child migration in both countries in 1998
and 2002.

A former Fairbridge girl, Claire B, now living back in
England, said the book had prompted her to ask for her
records from the UK Fairbridge office, where she was told
The Forgotten Children 'was full of tales and lies told by
small children'. In Sydney the Fairbridge Foundation said
it still wanted proof of what went wrong at Molong, even
though much of the evidence came from the files that
remain in its Sydney office.

Some locals from the Molong district and even some
former Fairbridge children were upset by the media coverage and reviews that followed the release of the book, and
a number have been critical of what they perceived as the
negative picture the book painted of Fairbridge. The
strongest criticisms have come from those who are so upset
or disgusted by the book that they have publicly declared
their refusal to read it. The chairman of the Old Fairbridgians' Association, John Harris, who was interviewed
for the book, said he was 'annoyed' by the publication.
'It will be everyone's own decision whether they purchase
the book, and in my case it will not happen,' he said.

For many of the former Fairbridge children the
recounting of their stories is the first time they have told
anyone about their experiences. They have revealed in
the book what they have been unable to tell even their
loved ones and their families. I feared that some would be

traumatised when they read about themselves for the first time, particularly about being sexually abused. However, most have said they have now been able to draw strength from reading that many other children at Fairbridge went through similar experiences.

And many of the families of the former Fairbridge children have said how they have found the book useful in understanding their parents. Many former child migrants never talk about what happened to them, which has left their families with little knowledge or understanding of their parents. 'Thank you,' said one woman. 'I've never really liked my father, but now I can see why he is like that. I had no idea how much he suffered as a child.'

Following the original publication of this book in Australia a number of former Fairbridge children began a legal class action for the abuse they suffered during their childhood at Fairbridge. The defendants in the legal action included the Fairbridge Foundation, the Australian Government (which was our legal guardian at the time) and the New South Wales Government, whose Department of Child Welfare was responsible for the protection of the children.

The case was bogged down with legal technicalities by the defendants for seven years in the Supreme Court until 2015, when nearly two hundred former Fairbridge children were finally awarded damages of $24 million – the largest ever pay-out of its kind in Australia.

Gratifying though it was, no amount of money can ever compensate for a devastated childhood. The sad reality is that many of the children who spent their entire childhood in an abusive environment have never recovered from the experience.

PREFACE TO
ORIGINAL EDITION

In 1959, when I was twelve years old, I became a child migrant. With two of my brothers I sailed from England to Australia, to the Fairbridge Farm School outside the country town of Molong, 300 kilometres west of Sydney. My mum, who later followed us out to Australia, sent us because she believed we would be given an education and better opportunities in Australia than she could provide as a struggling single parent in England.

Britain is the only country in history to have exported its children. Fairbridge was one of a number of British child-migrant schemes that operated for over a hundred years from the late nineteenth century, and altogether these schemes dispatched about 100,000 underprivileged children – unaccompanied by their parents – to the British colonies, mainly to Canada, Australia and Rhodesia. About 10,000 went to Australia. By the mid-1950s twenty-six child-migrant centres were operating in the six states of the country. About 1000 children were sent to the Molong Fairbridge Farm School, which opened in 1938 and closed in 1974.

The child-migrant schemes were motivated by a desire to 'rescue' children from the destitution, poverty and moral danger they were exposed to as part of the lower orders of British society. By exporting them to the colonies, it was thought they might become more useful citizens of the Empire. Contrary to popular belief, barely any of the children sent out under these schemes were orphans.

In an age before the state took responsibility for the welfare of poor children, the child-migrant schemes were operated by the Protestant and Catholic churches, and a number of children's charities, including Dr Barnardo's. Some of the schemes, including the Fairbridge Farm Schools, were created and operated by people from the upper classes. Such emigration programs enabled Britain to deal with its large population of poor children without addressing the massive social inequality that had created widespread poverty in the first place.

The Fairbridge Farm School Scheme was based on a simple proposition first presented by Kingsley Fairbridge in a pamphlet published in 1908, titled 'Two Problems and a Solution'. The two problems were, first, how to open up the lands of the Empire's colonies with 'white stock' and, second, what to do to with the large and growing problem of child poverty. The solution was to put them together.

Fairbridge promised that children who were sent to Australia would get a better education and more opportunities than they would in their deprived environments in Britain. His vision was simple: for boys from the slums of the cities to become farmers and girls to become farmers' wives.

Children were sent to Fairbridge on the condition that their parents or custodians signed over guardianship to the Australian Government, which then effectively delegated responsibility for the children to Fairbridge until they were twenty-one years old. Fairbridge felt it had rescued these children from failed or irresponsible parents, so they did not want children reuniting with their families. They deliberately targeted parents who were unlikely to want to get their children back. But many parents did not fully understand what was involved when they signed away their custodianship, and those who did wish to be reunited with their children found it practically impossible.

By the late 1950s the traditional source of poor British children was declining and Fairbridge was forced to introduce the One Parent Scheme, whereby children were sent unaccompanied to Australia but their single parent followed them out later, found a job, established a home and was eventually brought back together with their children. This was the scheme under which we emigrated.

None of our family knew at the time that Fairbridge had been forced to radically change its rules and introduce this scheme in response to increasing opposition from the British Government and child-welfare professionals. The postwar years in Britain had seen some dramatic improvements in child welfare: the passing of the Children Act in 1948 heralded a more enlightened era, and child migration and large children's institutions such as Fairbridge were falling out of favour.

Nor did we know that fewer than three years before, the British Government had secretly placed the farm school at Molong on a black list of institutions condemned as unfit for children. Fairbridge was able to mobilise its considerable influence in the upper echelons of the British political system to have the ban lifted, and children continued to sail.

Those of us who went to Fairbridge under the One Parent Scheme were far more fortunate than the Fairbridge children who were already there, and our experience was not typical of the majority of children. We were older when we arrived – my twin brother, Richard, and I were nearly thirteen years old, and our brother Dudley was fourteen. We would each spend fewer than three years at Fairbridge and, most importantly, our mother would follow us out, so we would eventually reunite as a family.

In contrast, children unaccompanied by their parents typically arrived at Fairbridge aged eight or nine years old. Some were as young as four. They would spend their entire childhood and youth at Fairbridge, where they would attend the local school till the minimum school-leaving age, then work on the farm for two years until they turned seventeen. The boys were then usually found work as farm labourers on remote sheep stations; the girls as domestic servants on farms. Many of these children would never see their parents after leaving England, and would spend their childhood suffering emotional privation and social isolation.

Few of the Fairbridge children were provided with the education they had been promised before leaving the UK and half would leave school before completing their second year of secondary school. Many left school without having acquired basic literacy skills and would struggle through life unable to properly read or write.

I had not planned to write a book about Fairbridge. In 2005 I completed a Diploma of Classical Archaeology at Sydney University, as I have for a long time been interested in the archaeology of the prehistoric to classical periods of an area in the eastern Peloponnese in Greece. I have also been involved for many years in the campaign to have the British return to Athens the marble sculptures taken by Lord Elgin from the Parthenon in the early nineteenth century.

Armed with my newly acquired archaeological qualifications, I thought I would first test my skills by conducting a heritage survey of the Fairbridge Farm School settlement at Molong. The old village, which had been home to some 200 people, mainly children, had become almost a ghost town. Having received barely any maintenance, many of the buildings had fallen into disrepair. A number of the cottages the children had lived in had been sold off and moved to other towns to become country homes.

With several other people, I formed the Fairbridge Heritage Association and we set about compiling the historic record of the settlement. The New South Wales Migration Heritage Centre and, later, the New South Wales Heritage office backed the Fairbridge Heritage Project and asked that we also record the oral histories of some of the children who had passed through the farm school.

I conducted about forty audiotaped interviews over the first three months of 2006, travelling to meet former Fairbridge children who lived throughout New South Wales, the Australian Capital Territory and southern Queensland. In March 2006, at the biennial reunion of Old Fairbridgians at Molong, I arranged for three camera crews to film interviews that we plan to use in a TV documentary.

During the interviewing process I realised that while a lot has been written and said about Fairbridge, the stories of the children who lived there have never been told – and the picture their stories paint is very different and much more disturbing than the records of academics and historians. It was then that I decided to write a book about Fairbridge from the point of view of those who lived there.

I found myself both disturbed and angry about some of the revelations of former Fairbridge children, many of whom were speaking up for the first time. I wondered why seventy-five-year-old women would talk on the record of regular sexual abuse at Fairbridge when they had never discussed it with their husbands, children or grandchildren. Nearly every woman and most of the men openly talked about physical or sexual abuse. When asked why they were now prepared to tell of their experiences, some said they had never previously had the opportunity to set the record straight. Others said they did not have the strength or courage to speak out before, but now, as they were reaching middle age, found it easier to confront the ghosts of their past. A number who initially had declined to be interviewed heard that others had spoken and then came forward to say they now wanted to tell their story.

There are many others for whom it is still too difficult. One former Fairbridge girl, Susan, who was at the farm school when I was there and whose brother was in my cottage and later committed suicide, phoned to say she wanted the book to be written and wanted to tell her story but that it was still 'too painful to open those doors that took me years to close'.

In another case, the wife of a man who was at Fairbridge when I was there wrote to explain why her husband would not be telling his story:

> There are too many hurtful memories there. He arrived when he was barely seven years old. He really can't remember any good things to say. He often talks about going to bed in the dormitory alone at seven years old, with the lights out and no one else there; scrubbing floors every afternoon from this age and only having a couple of hours off a week; working in the dairy at 3 am in the cold frosty mornings with no shoes on. Public thrashings, etc. This sort of discipline and loveless routine sets a person up for an untrusting and confused life.

Another former Fairbridge boy, Allan, whom I remembered as an interesting and colourful character, rang and asked me not to send any more letters asking for an interview. 'I've forgotten a lot of it. I don't want to remember,' he said. 'I'm happy now I have my eleven grandchildren around me. Please don't write to me again – it's too upsetting.' I told him I wouldn't bother him again and asked when his life had turned around. 'It hasn't,' he said. 'It never turned around.'

Almost all those I interviewed insisted their stories were ordinary and unlikely to be of interest to anyone. Yet every single one is special – even more so because nearly all of them experienced deprivation and disadvantage, and were denied the nurturing, love and support afforded to most other children.

Much of this book is based on my own experiences and the stories of others who spent part or all of their childhood at the Fairbridge Farm School at Molong. I was also able to access rather limited personal files about myself from the Fairbridge Foundation offices in Sydney and the London Fairbridge Society archives, which are now held at Liverpool University in the UK. A number of other Fairbridge children who accessed their personal files from Sydney and Liverpool have kindly made them available to me.

I have been given notes, letters, diaries, photographs, unpublished autobiographies and assorted other material by former Molong Fairbridge children in Australia, New Zealand and England. Altogether, I have used material from over one hundred people who were at Fairbridge from the day it opened in March 1938 till it closed in January 1974.

In addition to the children's stories, I accessed material from the Fairbridge Foundation in Sydney, the Fairbridge Society archives in the UK, British and Australian parliamentary and government files, the National Library in

Canberra and the State Library of New South Wales. I also accessed Department of Education and Department of Child Welfare files from the State Records office of New South Wales.

However, I encountered a number of difficulties when trying to access or use material from the Fairbridge organisations in Australia and the UK.

The Fairbridge Foundation in Sydney is the successor body to Fairbridge Farm Schools of New South Wales, which was responsible for running the Fairbridge school at Molong. When the foundation sold off the Molong site in 1974, it invested the proceeds. It donates the profits and dividends from the investments to other children's charities. The Fairbridge Foundation supported the Fairbridge Heritage Project and contributed $10,000 toward the recording of the history of the Fairbridge settlement and the hiring of film crews for the interviews of former Fairbridge children.

The foundation is the custodian of the old Fairbridge Farm School files, which are kept in its Sydney office in a number of un-catalogued boxes. The records, which include farm production reports, principals' reports, staff pay sheets and a limited amount of correspondence, are far from comprehensive. While the foundation allowed me to access the material in some of the boxes, it did not allow me to access the minutes of the Fairbridge Society Council meetings, which are also stored in its office in Sydney. This was despite the chairman of the foundation, John Kennedy, telling an Australian Senate inquiry in 2001 that the files would be made available to 'bone fide scholars and researchers'.

I wrote to Kennedy in July 2006 asking that the foundation reconsider their decision to deny me access to the minutes. Four months later he told me the board had considered my request and decided that I could have limited access to the minutes, but I would not be allowed to use material that identified any child or staff member who had been at Fairbridge. I said that I already had extensive testimony and evidence from other sources that identified improper and illegal acts by a number of staff members.

In July 2006 I was able to gain access to the London Fairbridge Society files, which are in the Liverpool University archives and include the minutes of meetings of the Fairbridge Society. (I did not seek access to the individual files of Fairbridge children.) Before I was allowed to see the material, I was asked to agree to a number of restrictions that the UK Fairbridge Society had imposed. I had to sign a declaration that 'I will not in any way by any form of communication reveal to any person or persons nominal information or individual details which might tend to identify individuals or their descendants.' The rules stipulate that I cannot identify any Fairbridge child for one hundred years and any Fairbridge staff member by name for seventy-five years from the date of the lodgement of the files. I was obliged to 'agree to abide by the decision of the director' as to what might identify individuals. In the event, I did not need to use any confidential information from these archives to identify individuals as the names of children and staff set out in this book come from either my own knowledge, from information given to me by those I interviewed, or from a variety of other sources.

While I was in the UK researching at the Liverpool University archives, I was contacted by the chairman of the UK Fairbridge Society, Gil Woods, who had been tipped off about my research by the university and wanted to talk to me about the project. He explained that while Fairbridge no longer operated a child migration scheme it was still active in child welfare in the UK.

I told him that I had come across material in the Liverpool University archives that corroborated some of the more disturbing oral histories and asked that Fairbridge allow me to use this material in the book. Woods agreed to consider my request but said he was concerned that any adverse publicity about Fairbridge would make its ongoing public fundraising more difficult. 'My highest priority is to protect the reputation and name of Fairbridge,' he warned.

I found the papers of Professor Geoffrey Sherington of Sydney University very helpful. Sherington co-authored an excellent book titled *Fairbridge, Empire and Child Migration* with Chris Jeffery and also helped me access his papers (other than personal files), which are lodged with the State Library of New South Wales.

Finally, there are the records from the Department of Education and the Department of Child Welfare in State Records NSW in western Sydney. There are restrictions that prevent the naming of individuals in Child Welfare Department files. While some child-welfare records confirmed the maltreatment of children, it appears investigations by the department were rare as the children had no way of initiating any inquiry. The Education Department has a simple thirty-year restriction, which made their files more accessible. However, I could not find any records that shed light on the reasons why Fairbridge children failed to receive the same standard of schooling as other Australian children in the state school system.

Most of the information about Fairbridge in these files has never been made public. In many cases it reflects very badly on Fairbridge.

It has always been accepted that the Fairbridge Farm School Scheme, as with all the child-migrant schemes, was well-intentioned and that the Fairbridge organisation could not have been expected to be aware of the dreadful experiences of some children.

However, the hitherto secret files confirm that the Fairbridge hierarchy, and the British and Australian authorities, knew about many of the flaws and failures of the scheme, and the maltreatment of children, for decades. They reveal that Fairbridge consistently rejected criticism and resisted reform, even when changes would have improved the welfare of the children in its care.

Most importantly, the files confirm much that's contained in the former Fairbridge children's accounts, which may otherwise have sounded too far-fetched to believe.

BOOK 1

1

JOURNEY OUT

One morning early in 1959 two well-dressed and nicely spoken ladies from the Fairbridge Society came to see us in our small council house on the Langney estate outside Eastbourne in Sussex. A few weeks before, we'd had a visit from the local Fairbridge 'honorary secretary' and she had now brought down a very important person from the Fairbridge Society in London.

Sitting with Mum, we three boys were wearing our Sunday best. We were very poor: my mother was a single parent with four sons. Our oldest brother, Tony, was twenty and in the RAF. My twin brother, Richard, and I were twelve and Dudley had recently turned fourteen. The three of us were attending the local secondary school but Mum was finding it increasingly difficult to make ends meet, so there was little prospect of us staying on at school beyond the minimum school-leaving age.

The ladies from Fairbridge told us wonderful stories about Australia, and showed us brochures and photographs. The picture they painted was very attractive: we would be going to a land of milk and honey, where we could ride ponies to school and pluck abundant fruit from the trees growing by the side of the road.

They explained that Fairbridge had recently introduced

a new plan called the One Parent Scheme whereby Mum could follow us out to Australia and we would be back together as a family in no time.

They were good salespeople. By the late 1950s Fairbridge had become a slick organisation with almost seventy 'honorary secretaries' spread throughout the UK, recruiting more children to its scheme.[1] For a poor family like ours, the offer of free transport to Australia, then free accommodation and education once we got there, sounded almost too good to be true.

The ladies told Mum that however much she loved us, she couldn't provide us with the opportunities we would be given at the Fairbridge Farm School in Australia. They gave us brochures, one of which read:

> In Britain many thousands of children through circumstances and the bad environment in which they are forced to spend formative years of their childhood are deprived of the opportunity of a happy, healthy and sound upbringing and are allowed to go to waste.
>
> We believe that a large number of these boys and girls (plus a parent where there is one) would have a far greater chance in life if they are taken out of the wretched conditions in which they live, and given a new start in life in the Commonwealth at establishments like our existing Fairbridge Farm Schools.
>
> ... Here they can exchange bad and cheerless homes set in drab and murky surroundings of the back street ... for a clean and well kept home, good food and plenty of it, and fresh air, sunshine and myriad interests and beauties of the countryside.
>
> ... Here they are given the love and care which many of them have never known.[2]

They told us we qualified for Fairbridge.

We were almost the perfect catch for them: three healthy boys, all above average intelligence, from a deprived background. We were, however, a bit older than the ideal age, as Fairbridge preferred children no older than eight or nine. They felt there was a better chance of turning younger children into good citizens because they'd had less exposure to low-class society.

Ironically, the Fairbridge children who would do better in life tended to be those who entered when they were older, and stayed there for the shortest period of time. The ones who would struggle through life tended to be those who spent their entire childhood in the care of the farm school.

We were like most other Fairbridge children in that we came from a deprived background. Our mother, Kathleen Bow, was born into a modest, working-class family during World War I in Bruxburn, about twenty-four kilometres from Edinburgh, in Scotland. Her father went to war in 1914 and was gassed in the trenches of France before being pensioned out of the army. Her mother worked as a nurse in the Bangor Hospital, to which the wounded were brought, usually from the hospital ships that berthed on Scotland's Forth River. It was said that many of the men were so terribly wounded that they were brought from the ships to the hospital at night so as not to panic the civilian population.

Mum was illegitimate and when her mother moved to Glasgow to marry a badly wounded soldier she had nursed – her second marriage – Mum was left to be brought up by her grandmother with two children from the first marriage. Mum used to say that she thought her gran was actually her mother, and she only learnt the truth after Granma McNally died when Mum was about fourteen years old.

With nowhere else to go, Mum went to work in one of

the big houses in Surrey, in the south of England, living very much 'below stairs' as a domestic servant. Within a couple of years she had married local builder Bill Hill and in 1937 she gave birth to Tony, who was to be the first of five sons. In 1940, Billy was born but died of meningitis within months. Dudley was born in 1944.

By the time Mum was pregnant with me and Richard she was separated from her husband and had been abandoned by her partner. At that stage, she was working in a big house in Hertfordshire, but as her pregnancy developed it became clear she would have to leave. She was taken in by a vicar in Eastbourne, Sussex, and lived in the basement of the vicarage till we were born.

So, we were born in 1946, when being a single mother or a divorcee still carried a stigma. Throughout our childhood we were instructed to tell people that Mum was a widow, even though we, along with everyone else in our village, knew it didn't ring true.

For the first six or seven years of my life we survived on charity, welfare and the small income Mum generated working whenever she had the chance while caring for four children. We lived in three rooms on the second storey of a small terrace house in Dersley Road, Eastbourne. It was a very poor and rough neighbourhood with a sullied reputation. The local council, in an effort to tidy up the street's image, changed its name from Dennis Road shortly after we moved there.

The three-room flat had a coal-fired stove, which was used for cooking and heating. There was no bath, but in the kitchen there was a large stone sink, which for all our early childhood doubled as a bath for Richard, Dudley and me. We would sit on the draining board with our feet in the water and wash ourselves as best we could. Mum and Tony would bring the tin bath in from out the back of the house, lug it up the stairs, heat water on the stove and take a bath in the tiny living room. We didn't have a toilet so we paraded down the stairs and through Mrs Symes's flat on the ground floor below, carrying our potties though her living area and kitchen to the toilet out the back.

In the early postwar years we still had gas street lamps. Every night the gasman came with a long pole to ignite the flame, and he returned early the next morning to douse it. Everyone around us was poor. We were all still issued with ration books full of coupons to go toward paying for food. An old lady across the road used to give us her sweets ration coupons, even though we didn't have enough money to use them anyway. It was a common occurrence just before payday for a child to go to their neighbour's house with an empty cup to borrow half a cup of sugar, flour or milk. Seldom did you ask for a whole cupful for fear the neighbour wouldn't have enough – or that you wouldn't be able to pay it all back. Shearer's, the little grocery store on the corner, would run up a slate for each family so they could buy food between paydays, but on more than one occasion they had to halt our credit because Mum was continuing to run up a tab though she was unable to pay anything off.

From a very early age we learnt how to get ourselves to school and care for ourselves in the afternoons, because Mum took any work she could get. From the age of about ten, Tony had to help look after us, and at eleven he got a job at weekends and during the school holidays in the local fishmonger's. He would come home smelling so strongly of fish that Mum would insist he change his clothes outside our little flat – but we had more fish to eat than any of our neighbours, even if it was the leftovers they couldn't sell in the fish shop.

Dudley, Richard and I were all doing reasonably well at Bourne Junior School. Tony had already sat for his

Eleven Plus exam and won a place at the Eastbourne Grammar School. Dudley and Richard always managed to be in the A classes, but I tended to lag behind in the B classes. Our school, like most in those days, was a dark and oppressive building with equally severe, bleak teachers. School was not much fun, but it wasn't designed to be.

As all the other kids did, we played in the streets or on one of the many bombsites in the neighbourhood. Eastbourne had not been a major target during the war but it was said that after raids the German bombers would drop off any bombs there that they had left on board, before returning over the English coast.

One of the more popular games played by the kids in the narrow back lanes of the terrace houses was a form of badminton, using an old shuttlecock and hardcover books for racquets. Eastbourne has always been a popular beach resort so we spent a lot of time during the short swimming season up near the Eastbourne Pier. The tourists created job opportunities for Mum, who worked at different times as a domestic in one of the hotels, in beachfront tourist shops, and as a waitress in a coffee shop or in one of the better hotels. Sometimes she came home to tell us she had seen someone famous at work. Once it was the Duke of Edinburgh, whom she had seen at the top table of a banquet at the Grand Hotel up near Beachy Head, while she was working as a waitress on the bottom tables. Another time it was Billy Wright, the then England football captain, whom she served coffee to in the café at Bobby's department store. We were terribly upset that she didn't get his autograph, and even more upset when she said she hadn't known who he was until the other waitresses told her.

When Mum was sick or there was some crisis, we would be put into children's homes, but would always come back together as a family as soon as things stabilised. As we got older it became increasingly difficult for the five of us to live in three tiny rooms. When we were six years old, Richard and I were put into a giant Barnardo's children's home in Barkingside, Essex, while we were found slightly bigger accommodation. It was a tough and traumatic experience. I can remember being teased and bullied by the other children when we tried to write a letter to our mum – it seemed they didn't have mums to write to.

After some months we were reunited with the rest of our family in a new home. We had a five-room flat in a big, dilapidated old Victorian house in Terminus Place, Eastbourne that had been converted into a number of smaller welfare apartments. I can still remember the day Mum came to get us from Barnardo's, her excitement on the train trip back to Eastbourne, and our arrival in the early evening to see Tony and Dudley cooking up a pan of bacon and eggs for our tea. There were a number of families living in the grand old house. Years later I would be reminded of it while watching the David Lean film *Dr Zhivago*: when Zhivago came back from the war he found the large house owned by his father-in-law's family had been broken up into small apartments for fourteen families.

When I was about eight years old we moved into a new house on a council estate outside Eastbourne. The new village had been built on land reclaimed by the government from the estate of an old aristocratic land-owning family, the Austins. At last we had a home with an indoor bathroom and toilet. It had a large living room, kitchen and coal shed downstairs, and three bedrooms and a bathroom upstairs. There was one fireplace and chimney in the centre of the living room that heated upstairs and downstairs, and also heated the water.

Our improved circumstances were part of the marvel of Britain's postwar welfare state, initiated by the British Labour Government. It was much maligned in later times, but this phenomenally successful social experiment meant that for the first time all classes of people were assured of basic food, shelter and clothing, and some level of health care and education. Prior to the welfare state most Britons lived and died poor, in a land of appalling class rigidity and social inequality where there was virtually no prospect of social mobility.

By now Tony had left school and was working and paying Mum a big part of his wages, which helped a great deal. We were still very poor but most of our neighbours in Langney village were only slightly better off. In those days you paid for electricity as you used it, by putting a shilling in the meter under the stairs. Often we went to bed early on a Wednesday night because the last shilling ran out or we had no more coal to put in the fireplace until payday the next day. Despite a lack of money, Mum somehow always managed to put food on the table.

Being on the edge of Eastbourne, Langney village was a pretty good place for kids. We lived in a semi-rural environment and spent lots of time playing in the fields or on the 'crumbles', a vast stretch of pebbled beach between Eastbourne and Langney, where the pillboxes and concrete tank blocks built in 1940 in anticipation of Hitler's invasion of Britain were still standing. A little over a mile from the village was Pevensey Castle. On the site there was an outer Roman wall built in 300 AD, a Norman keep and a medieval castle with drawbridge and moat. It was a favourite location for playing and camping with the Boy Scouts, and has remained a favourite spot for me throughout my life.

Television had already been in Britain for a few years but no one in Langney could afford to buy one until the late 1950s, so community activity survived. It seems everyone was either in the Boy Scouts, Civil Defence Corps, the drama club or one of myriad other communal activities. Throughout the year the village would turn out for special and festive occasions, including the annual fete. On Guy Fawkes Night we would all march in a torch-lit procession around the village before lighting a huge bonfire in the park at the bottom of Priory Road and letting off fireworks.

Christmas was especially good as people helped one another as best they could. Mr Fry – who lived down on the next corner, had five kids and drove a vegetable truck for a living – would always leave a basket of fruit on our front doorstep. Mrs Austin, one of the landed gentry who still lived in the big family house on nearby Langney Rise, used to leave a sack of potatoes. She didn't mind when her son Philip came round to play with us lower-class kids when he was home from his exclusive boarding school.

We finished our primary education in a school built as part of the Langney village, then went on to Bishop Bell Secondary Modern, which was also built to cater for the increasing number of postwar baby-boom children.

By the time Dudley, Richard and I reached secondary school our eldest brother, Tony, was in the Royal Air Force. Britain still had conscription in the 1950s and Tony, who as a boy had been a member of the boys' Air Training Corps, decided to do his national service in the RAF. He signed up for five years instead of the standard two. Conscripts were paid only a tiny allowance, but by signing up for a longer period, Tony was able to earn enough as a regular to continue to send money home to help Mum. Nevertheless, as the rest of us boys were getting older it was becoming increasingly obvious that Mum would not be able to afford to keep us at school beyond the minimum school-leaving age of fifteen.

Some years before, a woman who lived out the back from us in Dersley Road and who was struggling on her own had sent her three boys out to Australia with one of the child migration schemes. She was able to boast that her sons had done well for themselves: the eldest had become a policeman and where we came from that constituted considerable social mobility.

Several things were weighing heavily on Mum's mind. There was a recession in Britain in the late 1950s and jobs were hard to get, so she was concerned about our poor prospects if we stayed in England. At the same time, Australia was promoting itself as the land of golden opportunity where jobs were plentiful. Years later she would reveal that she was also concerned about conscription and the risk that we would have to go to war. In the mid to late 1950s Britain was involved in the 'troubles' in Malaysia, the Suez crisis, and one of the boys we knew had been killed while a national serviceman in Cyprus. Mum's family had been split up in World War I, her own family fell apart during and after World War II, and she didn't want to see further family disruption.

When the day came for us to go around the village and say our goodbyes to all our friends and neighbours, it was very sad. It was the first time I recall having to say goodbye to people I was close to, knowing I would probably never see them again.

Then I was on the train with Mum and my two brothers to Knockholt in Kent. Fairbridge owned a house there, at which children would gather in a group before sailing out to Australia. We were a little anxious about our journey into the unknown, but as young boys we were also excited about embarking on an adventure, sailing to the other side of the world. I remember Mum being filled with sadness when she left us that night to go back home.

She would remain unsettled until our little family was back together three years later.

We were all amazed at our magnificent new home in Kent, as we had never experienced such fineness and luxury. We were told that Fairbridge had bought the house with money donated by a woman whose son had disappeared after being parachuted into German-occupied France in World War II with the British Secret Service. It was presumed he had been captured and executed. His mother had wanted the house named in his memory, so it was called John Howard Mitchell House.

It was an imposing two-storey mansion, with an attic and cellars, gardener's lodge, squash court and stables. There seemed to be countless rooms, including a large library, banquet room, billiard room and bathrooms upstairs and downstairs. Outside there were orchards and vegetable gardens and rolling green fields that seemed to go on for ever.

There was a matron and her assistant, a cook, a gardener and a cleaner who came every day. Between them, they catered for our every need. They cooked our meals, ran our baths, bathed the smaller children, laundered, ironed and laid out our clean clothes, and made our beds. We spent three weeks at Knockholt in beautiful springtime weather. We played all day, as we were not sent to school and not assigned any work.

Ian 'Smiley' Bayliff was at Knockholt in 1955 as an eight-year-old, with his three brothers, and remembers it as the best time of his life:

> I remember it very, very well. Lovely place, something out of a book. The food was absolutely beautiful, you know. We'd come from a very poor family; we were just as poor as church mice. We were that poor the church mice moved out. So coming down to

> Knockholt . . . there was food, there was three meals
> a day – breakfast, lunch, tea – there was afternoon
> tea, there was room to move – almost had your own
> bathroom there were so many bathrooms in the place.
> It was warm; you always had plenty of clothes.
>
> . . . We were there for two months and really loved it
> and it was the best Christmas of my life. It was sort of
> what you would expect at a big, rich country mansion.

Richard, Dudley and I were joined by eight other children. At fifteen, Paddy O'Brien was the oldest in the
party. His sister Mary was thirteen and his sister Myrtle
was eleven. Billy King from Cornwall and John Ponting
from west London were about my age. Beryl Daglish was
about eleven and Wendy Harris ten. Wendy's six-year-old
brother, Paul, was the youngest of the group. We were all
a bit older than the average children going to Fairbridge
and most of us were going to Australia as part of the One
Parent Scheme.

Once all the children in our party had arrived at John
Howard Mitchell House we were taken up to London by
bus for the day and fitted out with wonderful new
summer and winter clothing, the likes of which none of us
had ever seen before. The girl's kit included a raincoat, a
'pixi' hood, a linen hat ('for journey'), two gingham
frocks (one 'good enough for best dress'), a coat, one
tunic, a pair of grey flannel shorts, a woollen jumper, a
woollen cardigan ('colours should blend with each other
and with skirt'), skirt with bodice, two aertex blouses,
two pairs of lightweight knickers, two woven knickers,
two lightweight vests, two interlock vests, a pair each of
best shoes, sandals and plimsolls, a pair of best socks, a
pair of fawn socks, three pairs of pyjamas, a bathing
costume, face flannel, sponge bag, brush, comb, toothbrush and paste, and a Bible.[3]

The boy's kit included a raincoat, a woollen coat, khaki, flannel, corduroy and sports shorts, two khaki shirts, a white shirt, tie, belt, black shoes, three pairs of socks, three summer singlets, a winter singlet, three pairs of pyjamas, a dress jumper, a play jersey, a pair each of sandals and plimsolls, a pair of bathing trunks, a drill sun hat, brush, comb, toothbrush and paste, face flannel, sponge bag and a Bible.[4] Interestingly, the standard boy's kit did not include underpants. This otherwise wonderful outfit, which was provided to us by the London Fairbridge Society, had been a feature of the Fairbridge scheme since the beginning in the 1930s. Len Cowne remembers as a ten-year-old being taken and outfitted in London in late 1937 before sailing to Australia in the first party of boys sent to the Fairbridge Farm School at Molong in early 1938.

> I was kitted out by the Society with an enormous fibreboard suitcase filled with brand new clothes – three of everything – shirts, cotton shorts for the summer and corduroy shorts for the winter, as well as pullovers, socks, towels, underwear, shoes and sandals, even a new toothbrush, toothpaste and face flannel. Whilst I had never gone short of clothes or footwear, I had never seen so many new clothes at one time in my short life.

On the last Sunday before we left, Mum came to Knockholt to spend the day with us. It was one of the saddest days of my life. It was wet and miserable. We went in to the larger town of Sevenoaks, where we sat silently in a Lyons teahouse drinking tea and eating cakes before going to a cinema to see Rosalind Russell in *Auntie Mame*, which was supposed to be fun but in my eyes was a very sad movie. We hardly exchanged any words that

day and I remember walking slowly in the rain back up
the road to John Howard Mitchell House as it was getting
dark, to say goodbye amid uncertainty as to when we
would see each other again. We loaded Mum up with
more daffodils than she could carry – we had picked them
in the fields below John Howard Mitchell House for her.

A couple of days later the bus came to take us to
London and to the ship bound for Australia. We were all
excited and a bit anxious. Mary O'Brien says she remembers as a twelve-year-old feeling the anticipation of the
bus trip to Tilbury Docks as we drove under the Black-
wall tunnel and through parts of the East End of London,
where she had lived.

We arrived late on a wet and miserable April afternoon
at Tilbury Docks. None of us had ever been in a tall building before and we were overawed by the sight of the
eight-decked S.S. *Strathaird*, which was to become our
home for the next six weeks.

There was no band or streamers or cheering crowds
and no family to wave us goodbye. I felt the excitement of
the adventure giving way to sadness as I began to grasp
the significance of leaving. During the evening one of our
two adult escorts, a New Zealand nurse, came into our
cabin with her guitar. While she had every intention of
cheering us up with a singsong she made us all even
sadder when she sang 'Botany Bay' and the words, 'We're
leaving old England forever . . .'

The S.S. *Strathaird* was a grand old P&O liner built in
1932. After being used as a troopship to carry Australian
and other Allied soldiers in World War II, it had been
beautifully restored to its original splendour, which
included oak-panelled walls, stained-glass windows,
ornate ceilings, parquet floors, Persian rugs, and antique
furniture and artworks.

None of us kids from poor backgrounds had ever

been near the luxury we were to experience on the
S.S. *Strathaird*. At home the food was very basic: most of
the meat was minced; a big cooked meal was likely to be
sausage and mash; and our evening meal might consist of
a fried-egg sandwich. All of our furniture was second-
hand. Our bedside tables were made of upturned wooden
orange boxes; our floor coverings were mostly offcuts of
linoleum; and almost all our clothes were hand-me-
downs. Having already spent the previous three weeks in
Fairbridge's grand country mansion in Kent and been
taken to London to be outfitted with the finest summer
and winter wardrobes, we were to spend the next five and
a half weeks being treated like royalty.

The *Strathaird* had been converted from a three-class to
a one-class ship for the carriage of migrants to Australia,
but many of its first-class features remained. We were
assigned two former first-class state cabins on the preferred D Deck. Both of these large cabins had six bunks
and an ensuite bathroom. The girls in our party and the
youngest boy, six-year-old Paul, who was to commit
suicide a few years after he left Fairbridge, were in one
cabin. The older boys were in the other. We were lucky
to have ended up on the P.O.S.H. side of the ship: in the
days before air conditioning you paid extra to travel on
the port side travelling out and the starboard side home –
Port Out, Starboard Home – thus avoiding the hot afternoon sun of the Red Sea and the Indian Ocean.

Our other escort for the journey was an Australian
primary-school teacher. The Fairbridge Society in London
would have recruited her and the New Zealand nurse
because they came from good families and had excellent
references. Having completed their customary 'grand
tour' of Europe the young women were given a free trip
home in return for being our carers on the journey to
Australia.

After leaving Tilbury we headed across the North Sea to Cuxhaven in northern Germany, where we picked up around 600 German migrants also destined for Australia. Almost as a reminder of who won the war, they were allocated the less inviting cabins on the lower decks because the British migrants had already been allocated most of the former first-class sections of the ship.

After Cuxhaven we steamed back through the English Channel and south through the Bay of Biscay with its huge waves and gale force winds, which made most of the passengers seasick. I recall going to the front of the top deck with my brothers and we could lean almost forty-five degrees into the strong headwind without falling over. Ten-year-old Wendy Harris kept a diary of our voyage out:

> The sea is very rough and very cold out on the deck . . . Along the corridors I have to hold onto the rails otherwise I would fall over . . . The boat is very rocky and making me feel sick.

After a couple of days we passed into the relative calm of the straits of Gibraltar in the early dawn, and we entered the beautiful, sunny Mediterranean.

Of course we missed our mum. We were able to send postcards home from the ship, and posted the first one when the mail boat came alongside us as we sailed past Gibraltar. Not until we reached Australia would we receive our first letter from home.

I was fascinated by the deep blue Mediterranean Sea, which some years later would become one of the great loves of my life. Wendy's diary records the day we approached Egypt and the Suez Canal:

> The sea is quite calm and the boat is a bit rocky. For breakfast I had fish and mashed potato. It was lovely.

I have been sun-bathing this morning. All today we
will be passing land, we will be passing Egypt. This
afternoon I played for two hours in the swimming
pool. I can float with a rubber ring on but not without
one on. The sea is very blue and you can see through
it if you look very carefully. Just before tea I changed
from my shorts in to my frock. For tea I had some
sausages with potato and then some lovely ice cream.
I am in bed now and I am going to sleep.

The *Strathaird* was a fabulous adventure for a boy and we
spent days exploring, and uncovering all of its secrets: its
eight decks from A to H, its lifeboats, games rooms,
cinema, swimming pool, sundecks, library and reading
room, smoking rooms, lounges and staircases.

We had our own cabin steward who woke us each
morning with an orange juice, or a cup of tea and a
biscuit, in bed. He did everything for us, including making
our beds, and organising the washing and pressing of our
clothes.

It is unlikely that any of the migrants coming to Australia with us on the ship had ever experienced anything
like the sumptuous cuisine provided on the *Strathaird*.
The ship's bell rang for breakfast, luncheon, tea and
dinner – in that order, which caused some initial confusion as we were accustomed to meals in the working-class
order of breakfast, dinner and tea. When we had boarded
in Tilbury it had been 'teatime'. Where we came from
'tea' was the term for the evening meal so we were pretty
unimpressed by the bread and jam and buns on offer,
wrongly thinking that was all we would have to eat until
the next day. Then at eight o'clock the bell rang for dinner
and we were introduced to a five-course silver-service
meal the likes of which we had never seen before.

Very proud waiters from Goa, dressed impeccably in

stiff, starched, white uniforms, served our meals in a splendid dining room. Our waiter told us that Goans had worked on P&O ships for over a hundred years and that for several generations his family had worked in the service of the line. Before the *Strathaird* our only restaurant dining had been egg and chips in the café behind the Gaiety cinema in Eastbourne, Mum trying to teach us how to hold a knife and fork properly when eating in company.

The breakfast menu on the *Strathaird* included tea, coffee and cocoa, steamed peaches, fish kedgeree, eggs to order, grilled breakfast bacon, lamb's liver with brown gravy, snow potatoes, bread and butter, and toast, jam, golden syrup, honey and marmalade.[5]

Here is an example of one of our luncheon menus: Potage Windsor, Fried Fillets of Pamphlet Tartar, Hamburger Steak and Fried Egg, Malay Curry and Rice, Potatoes Creamed or Berrichronne, Marrow and Portagaise or a Cold Sideboard of Roulade of Veal, Ham Loaf or Ox Tongue plus a salad of lettuce, tomato, potato and caper, followed by Rusk Custard or Neapolitan Cream Ices and cheeses, including Danish Blue, Wensleydale, Kraft and Greyers.[6]

This is an example of a dinner menu, which was changed daily and was always printed with a pleasant still-life painting on the front: Cream Pompadour, Fillets of Plaice, Romoulade, Medallions of Veal Jardinière, Roast Quarter of Lamb with mint sauce, Potatoes Roasted or Maitre d'Hotel or from the Cold Sideboard, Roast Beef or Savoury Brawn and Salade Polonaise, followed by Plum Apple Tart or Coupe Alexandra. Adults also had a selection of fine French and German wines, and the children an unlimited supply of ice-cream.[7]

Mary O'Brien remembers the opulence:

Being served orange juice in bed in the morning. The fabulous meals in the dining room, being waited on, the tablecloths and the lovely silver cutlery. It was classy and I had never experienced anything so classy in all my life. I loved it . . . It just opened my eyes to a world that I just didn't know existed, and travelling to those places and being treated like little lords and ladies. It was just incredibly wonderful.

We had never seen food so beautifully presented and in such quantities. It was little wonder that I put on a lot of weight. On arrival at Fairbridge the children already there immediately gave me the nickname of 'Faddy'. While I quickly lost the excess weight (no one at Fairbridge was fat), the nickname would stick so that even decades later many Fairbridge kids knew me as 'Faddy 'ill' rather than by my real name.

On most afternoons we would sit in giant armchairs in the first-class lounge learning to play chess and being served by waiters who put ice and straws in our drinks, while a string quartet dressed in tails played Brahms and Tchaikovsky. It was the first time I had seen a violin or heard live classical music. The quartet would play requests but we and most of the other British migrants had no knowledge of classical music so it was the German passengers who did most of the requesting.

As we sailed south, the weather warmed and the officers switched from navy blue to white uniforms. We began to spend more of our time in the swimming pool or playing deck sports with the young Germans, mainly single men who were going out to Australia to work on the Snowy Mountains hydro-electric scheme or other construction projects. We made friends with a number of them and were surprised how polite and friendly they were – we had been brought up in an environment where the memory of two bitterly fought wars in the past forty years was still strong. They were very patient with us and would play chess with us in the afternoons. I recall them being puzzled at the idea of a group of British children being sent to the other side of the world without any parents.

In the tropics I suffered from prickly heat and my body was completely covered in a blotchy red rash. On instruction from the ship's doctor I was confined to our cabin for several days. I lay all day, painted head to foot in calamine lotion, on top of a cabinet to catch the breeze coming through the portholes.

The ship's crew worked hard on providing entertainment and practically every night there was a party or a concert, including the customary Neptune party as we crossed the equator. Much of what was on offer was too adult for us – but it wasn't too adult for our escorts, who were both single and in their twenties. As the voyage progressed we saw less and less of them. By the time we were approaching Australia our general cleanliness, hygiene and discipline had deteriorated. No one was even checking that we washed and bathed regularly.

Like most Fairbridge children I found the voyage a marvel. My brothers and I had never even seen a big city like London before our proposed emigration. Now we were seeing the world: the Rock of Gibraltar, the Suez Canal, elephants in the main street of Colombo. It was all like something out of a picture book: giant palm trees, pyramids through our cabin portholes, the desert, and the Union Jack flying from the highest point to remind us of the great British Empire.

Mary O'Brien has similar memories:

> Going through the Mediterranean and how the colour
> of the Mediterranean struck me, it was just so beauti-

ful. Going through the Suez Canal. I can vividly recall standing on the side and saying to one of the other boys: 'I really would like to come back here one day and visit this part of the world.' And all the places we stopped at – I thought the whole journey was very exciting and loved it.

At our first port of call, Port Said on the entrance to the Suez, we were not allowed ashore because it was thought to be unsafe for passengers to wander unprotected around the city. It was, after all, only three years since the Suez crisis and the British were not popular in Egypt. While we were in Port Said little boats came alongside to sell toy camels, leather photograph albums, clothes and assorted other memorabilia. The vendor would throw one end of a rope up for a passenger to tie to the railing on the upper deck; on the other end they would tie a basket so their wares could be pulled up on deck.

Wendy Harris wrote about arriving at Port Said in her diary:

> Today I feel very excited. The sea is calm and very blue . . . This afternoon I played and also watched the shore of Egypt . . . After tea I watched us draw up at the dock, there are lots of palm trees, I never knew they had such long trunks and very small green leaves. Hundreds of little boats have been selling clothes and hundreds of other different things. They throw ropes up in the air and someone has to catch it then the passengers ask for something. The clothes and other things are dreadfully dear.

We were allowed ashore in both Aden and Colombo, which were both great outposts of the British Empire. We were treated extremely well by the resident senior P&O

managers who appeared to have attained almost vice-regal status and were living in huge houses with scores of local black, turbaned servants. It was the first time we ate abundant tropical fruits and we became sick eating the coconuts.

When everyone was getting a little bored – as you do toward the end of the long school summer holidays – we reached the West Australian coast. The weather cooled when we landed in Fremantle harbour on a wet winter's day at the beginning of June. I realised that in all the photographs I had seen of Australia it was always bathed in sunshine. Of course we knew that it rained in Australia, but this was not what we were expecting. While in Fremantle we were taken on a picnic and a tour of Perth. This happened in Adelaide and Melbourne, too. Local charities were happy to give a good time to the kiddies destined for the 'orphanage'. Meanwhile, at each port a steady stream of migrants departed the ship for their new lives in Australia.

Finally, we arrived in Sydney in the early dawn. Full of excitement, we rushed to the front of the top deck as we sailed under the Sydney Harbour Bridge. We were convinced that the funnel of the ship would not fit under the bridge, but of course it did. We docked safely at Pyrmont's pier thirteen, where so many migrants and Fairbridge children had landed before us.

Waiting for us at Pyrmont was a huge man we were to come to fear and respect. Mr F. K. S. Woods – 'the boss' – was the principal of Fairbridge. Woods's immediate no-nonsense manner signalled to us that the fun was over. We spent the morning being ordered through a variety of medical checks, then were marched around Taronga Zoo and taken to Sydney's Central railway station.

After a meal of baked beans on toast in the Railway Refreshment Rooms, we took our seats in the second-class passenger compartment of the steam-hauled, unheated Forbes mail train for the 300-kilometre overnight journey across the Blue Mountains to Molong. We had enough compartments to spread out along the bench seats and were able to have at least a little sleep.

Like many other Fairbridge kids before us, the harsh thud of reality hit as we disembarked after a fitful night's sleep into the cold pre-dawn darkness of a deserted Molong railway station. The memory of the luxury of the *Strathaird* was quickly beginning to fade.

The temperature was close to freezing as we stood huddled together out the front of the station, across from the main street of this little country town. The Mason's Arms pub on the corner still had a hitching rail for horses. We were all frightened and anxious. I heard Paddy O'Brien and my older brother, Dudley, already whispering together about how we might plan our escape. The transport to take us out to Fairbridge Farm School was late and Woods was angry when his wife Ruth finally arrived in a canvas-covered truck.

Paddy's sister Mary vividly remembers arriving at Molong:

> About six o'clock in the morning and it was dark and cold and we were tired and there was nothing. There was this old country train station in the middle of Woop-Woop and we were greeted by the truck with a canvas back and a couple of long benches and we were herded in and driven out to the farm. And the honeymoon was over.

A number of other Fairbridge children have similar recollections. David Eva had arrived five years before from Cornwall, as a ten-year-old:

We got on the train and it was so bloody cold . . . I can remember old Woods giving us a blanket. There were kids sleeping in the luggage racks and on the floor and across the seats . . . We got to Molong and it was freezing . . . I can remember getting off the train and someone came in this blue truck . . . it was like a bloody cattle truck. When we arrived at Fairbridge I just wondered what the hell I'd let myself in for.

I remember the cold six-kilometre ride with the wind blowing through the back of the truck. We sat in the darkness saying very little and exchanging anxious glances. The levity was gone and we all felt fear and apprehension about what lay ahead.

2

ORIGINS

The Fairbridge Farm School Scheme was the brainchild of Kingsley Fairbridge, who was born in South Africa in 1885, a member of the upper middle class of the Edwardian era and a 'child of the Empire'. His great-grandfather James William Fairbridge left England in 1824 to become a surgeon and physician in the Cape. James became a member of the Children's Friend Society, which failed in its attempt to start a scheme to have destitute British children migrate to British South Africa. Kingsley's grandfather Charles Aken Fairbridge became a lawyer, politician and famous book collector. A wing of the South African Library in Cape Town was named in his honour. Kingsley's father, Rhys Seymour Fairbridge, moved the family from the Cape Colony in 1897 to Umtari in Rhodesia, which is now on the border of Zimbabwe and Zambia. He built a new family home and called it Utopia.[1]

As he got older, Kingsley Fairbridge was struck by what he believed was the unrealised potential of the farming land in Rhodesia for want of white settlers. In his autobiography, he notes that his dream of increasing white settlement was formed long before he travelled to England and became aware of the needs of destitute English children.

Like his great-grandfather, grandfather and father before him, Kingsley Fairbridge was educated in England. In 1906 he cashed in his insurance policy, sailed to England and went to stay with an aunt in East Grinstead in Sussex, where he met Ruby, whom he would later marry.[2] He would never return to Africa. Fairbridge was no great scholar but was fortunate in that his cousin administered the Rhodes scholarship scheme in Rhodesia. While Rhodes scholars usually have at least two years' university before arriving at Oxford, Fairbridge had none. Nor did he have any formal secondary school training. He had to sit the prerequisite Responsiones, or 'smalls' exam, four times at Oxford before passing. Once admitted, he chose to study forestry because he believed it would be an easier course than law, which he had initially chosen.

In 1908, while he was at Oxford, the young Kingsley Fairbridge first published his views on child migration, in a pamphlet titled 'Two Problems and a Solution'.[3] The two problems were: how to extend white settlement of the Empire's colonies, and what to do with Britain's poor and destitute children. The solution was simply to combine them.

The following year, at a meeting in a Japanese restaurant on Oxford's High Street, he addressed Oxford's Colonial Club, a formidable group of supporters of Empire.[4] In a speech titled 'The Emigration of Poor Children to the Colonies' he called for the establishment of a child-migrant scheme:

> I propose to establish a society in England for the furtherance of emigration from the ranks of young children, of the orphan and waif class, to the colonies.
>
> I propose, therefore, to take out children at the age of eight to ten, before they have acquired the vices of 'professional pauperism', and before their physique

has become lowered by adverse conditions, and give them ten to twelve years' thorough agricultural education at a School of Agriculture.[5]

'I told them I believed in Imperial Unity,' he wrote later in an account of the speech. 'Great Britain and Greater Britain are and must remain one.'[6]

Fairbridge went on to explain that Britain should not continue to send out to the colonies its upper classes, which it needed in Britain. Rather, it should send out its poor children. 'The best emigrant farmers have been the aristocracy of English Yeomen, such as England can ill afford to lose,' he said. 'The colonies should take something England does not need . . . if both sides are to profit.'[7]

Fairbridge placed great emphasis on the interests of Empire, and that would be a feature of the Fairbridge scheme for nearly the next seventy years. Britain would be rid of a problem and the colonies would be opened up by the availability of white labour. Both sides would profit.

Fairbridge also stressed the importance of sending poor children out to the colonies at a young age: 'Adult paupers are useless to new countries but the children of the Poor Laws have in them the makings of excellent citizens.'[8]

The fifty men at the Colonial Club meeting passed a motion that 'We should declare ourselves the Society for the Furtherance of Child Emigration to the Colonies.'[9]

Fairbridge, who by now was a handsome, sociable twenty-four-year-old, was accepted into the higher echelons of British society and managed to attract considerable support for his scheme from influential people, including Earl Grey, the governor-general of Canada, the bishop of Kingston and the mayor of London. In May 1910 an article he wrote on child emigration was published in the Empire day edition of *The Times*. In it he argued that the farm school system would create 'patriotic, capable and self reliant citizens'.[10]

As Kingsley Fairbridge was to admit later, he didn't plan to start the scheme in Australia. He intended to launch it in Canada, and secured a commitment from the Newfoundland Government to support a local farm school there. But that commitment fell through.

In 1910 some Australian friends at Oxford arranged for Fairbridge to meet with Premier Frank Wilson of Western Australia, who was in London for the coronation of King George V, and his London-based agent-general, Sir Newton More.[11] Wilson offered Fairbridge 400 hectares of land at a peppercorn rent, and £6 for each child toward assisted passage on a boat to Australia.

In designing the first Child Emigration Society Farm School, Fairbridge recognised two necessary requirements for the success of the scheme. The first was the need to appoint qualified staff. He wrote: 'Our chief care must be to entrust training of these children only to men and women truly and fully able to undertake it.'[12] Second, he noted the need for capital if children were to become farmers. He planned that each boy would leave the farm school with a certain amount of money and a land grant from the dominion or colonial government.

With the help of his wife Ruby, in 1912 Kingsley Fairbridge opened the first Child Emigration Society Farm School in Pinjarra, eighty kilometres south of Perth, Western Australia. Fairbridge spent the next few months preparing the school for the first party of thirteen boys, aged eight to thirteen, who arrived in January 1913. They initially lived at the farm in tents.

Ruby Fairbridge would later write a book about Pinjarra and in it she describes the arrival of the first party:

They arrived about sundown – a more incongruous desolate little bunch of humanity it would be hard to imagine. They stood in the hot evening sunlight, in their dusty thick nailed boots, cheap woollen stockings, cheap smelly suits with the trousers half mast to allow for growing, with tweed caps, each boy clutching an evil looking overcoat and a dirty white canvas kitbag. There was practically nothing suitable to wear in that climate, and everything was dirty, having been worn indiscriminately on ship. The Guardians had just fitted them for life in an English workhouse.[13]

In the early days, Kingsley Fairbridge laid out the routine of the Pinjarra Farm School in what he called 'Orders of the Week'.[14] The older boys would be up earliest to work at the dairy and on other parts of the farm, while the rest of the children would be assigned household and other work around the village before and after breakfast. Schooling followed, and after school more work at the farm and village before the evening meal and then bed. Almost every waking hour at the Fairbridge farms in Australia, Canada and Rhodesia would be governed by a similar routine for the next seventy years.

The Pinjarra Farm School did not get off to an altogether good start. In July 1913, six months after the first children arrived, a further twenty-two boys came from England. Mr A. O. Neville, an official from the West Australian Colonial Secretaries Department, inspected the centre and, though he described the scheme as 'excellent', he reported critically on the condition of the farm school.

On the whole the arrangements are very primitive and some of the premises would doubtless be condemned were it a Government institution. As a training farm, in order to render the boys fit to undertake farm work in Western Australia when they grow older, the place is quite unsuitable, in my opinion, as there is no real farming carried on, though, until the boys are beyond the school stage it is sufficient. It is quite certain that there is no room for any more boys until additional buildings have been erected, the premises, in my opinion, being already overcrowded.[15]

The report caused considerable consternation, leading Ruby Fairbridge to later complain that in England 'the report did us incalculable damage'.[16] Nevertheless, the scheme continued, as it had strong support in high places in England. Children kept coming until the scheme was interrupted by World War I. After the war there was little interest in child migration, leading Fairbridge's friend Lady Talbot to write 'all over England is against emigration for anyone – except perhaps tired soldiers who want a change'.[17]

Kingsley Fairbridge reinvigorated support for the scheme, first with a letter-writing campaign and then by returning to England in September of 1919 to meet with important and influential supporters. He made an address to parliamentarians, including Prime Minister Lloyd George.[18] He also addressed meetings of potential financial supporters in England and Scotland, and secured a commitment from the British Government's Overseas Settlement Committee.

Fairbridge was politically conservative and had become a member of the Western Australian Country Party. He believed child migration would discourage the spread of communism, which was becoming an increasing threat to the Empire following the revolution in Russia. In 1919 he wrote to a good friend and supporter, the British Conservative MP Leo Amery, to say:

> These children under the poor environment and their
> class in England are just the recruits that aren't into
> Bolshevism and destitution . . . The average London
> street Arab and workhouse child can be turned into
> an upright and productive citizen of our overseas
> Empire.[19]

Amery, the Secretary of State for the Dominions, was a
significant supporter and played an important role
throughout the Fairbridge story. He was a confidant of
Kingsley Fairbridge, and wrote the foreword to Fairbridge's autobiography.

In August 1920 Fairbridge returned and immediately
purchased a farm of 1250 hectares on the north side
of Pinjarra, to replace the sixty-five-hectare site that
had been the school since 1912. In 1921, three parties
totalling fifty-eight children who were all under ten
years old went to Pinjarra. It was the first year that girls
had been sent. The new farm school was officially opened
by the governor of Western Australia in April 1923. The
children's cottages bore the names of heroes of the British
Empire: Nelson, Livingstone, Clive, Rhodes, Wolfe and
Haig. Fairbridge remained loyal and committed first and
foremost to the British Empire. He was to name his first
son Rhodes, having been in awe of Cecil Rhodes when he
had met him as a boy in Rhodesia.

Fairbridge was attracting financial support from the
governments of Australia and Britain, and from the local
Farm School Society in Perth, but the scheme was admin-
istered and financed principally from London, where the
Child Emigration Society shifted its headquarters, from
Oxford, in 1920.[20]

In 1922, Pinjarra received more criticism – this time
from Miss Williams Freeman, a former matron at the
farm, who alleged maltreatment of the children. Again

Kingsley Fairbridge sailed for London, where he successfully addressed his critics and secured more government and private funding. He returned home to Australia ill and exhausted. He struggled on for another eighteen months, then died in the Perth hospital of a lymphatic tumour on 24 July 1924. He was only thirty-nine years old.

After his death the Child Emigration Society increasingly referred to itself as the Kingsley Fairbridge School, and officially changed its name to the Kingsley Fairbridge Farm School in 1935. It would eventually come to be known as the Fairbridge Society. [21]

Throughout the 1920s and into the 1930s the Fairbridge model was regarded as a highly successful emigration scheme and was increasingly embraced by the British establishment. By the late 1920s the Duke and Duchess of York, the Duke of Gloucester, the governor-general of Australia, Lord Stonehaven, and the governor of Western Australia had all visited Pinjarra.

Fairbridge and child migration attracted further attention during the Depression. Its many upper-class supporters saw the scheme as a vehicle for rescuing destitute children and providing them with greater employment opportunities than existed in Britain. Fairbridge received a further boost in 1932 when the British Government's Interdepartmental Committee on Migration Policy reported to the parliament:

> In our opinion the 'farm school' system inaugurated by the [Fairbridge] Child Emigration Society is beyond question the most successful method of establishing young children overseas and we think the establishment of similar farm schools in other states and other dominions should be encouraged. The system is comparatively expensive but we believe the expense has been justified by the results.[22]

The chairman of the Fairbridge Society for most of the 1920s was Sir Arthur Lawley, later Baron Wenlock.[23] Lawley had earlier served as governor of Western Australia, lieutenant governor of Transvaal and governor of Madras. Following the retirement of Lawley, Sir William Edward Goodenough, former aide-de-camp to King George V, became chairman. He was replaced in 1932 by MP Lawrence Roger Lumley, the Earl of Scarborough. Lumley, who had fought with the 11th Hussars and the Yorkshire Dragoons in World War I, remained chairman of Fairbridge for five years before resigning to become the governor of Bombay and Bengal in 1937.

With the departure of Lumley, Sir Charles Hambro became chairman of the London Fairbridge Society and remained in the position for the next twenty-six years, until 1963, the year he died. Hambro was born in 1897 into a Jewish family, and his father was the founder of the Hambro Bank. After being schooled at Eton he attended Sandhurst Military College. He served in France in World War I and was awarded the Distinguished Service Order. Hambro would later serve as a governor of the Bank of England and chairman of the Great Western Railway. As a friend of Winston Churchill's, he was appointed head of Britain's secret service agency, the Special Operations Executive, during World War II.

In the early 1930s the Fairbridge Society began to seriously plan for the expansion of the farm schools to other British colonies and dominions.

In June 1934, the Prince of Wales, who would later become King Edward VIII before abdicating the British throne, started the ball rolling. At the launch of an appeal to raise £100,000 at Grocers Hall in London, he committed £1000 and echoed the words of Kingsley Fairbridge when he said: 'This is not a charity. It is an Imperial investment.'[24] *The Times* reported that His Royal Highness described Fairbridge as 'the only completely successful form of migration at this time' that would give orphans and poorer British children the chance of happiness and successful careers, contribute to solving the problem of unemployment and provide a steady flow of good citizens to the dominions and colonies.

The launch was supported by a four-page lift-out in *The Times* on 21 June 1934 carrying the headline 'FARM SCHOOLS FOR THE EMPIRE' and the subheading 'These pages are paid for by a reader of *The Times* as a gift to the £100,000 appeal.' On the front page of the supplement was a large photograph of His Royal Highness, the Prince of Wales, and a picture of a Coutts Bank cheque written out to the Child Emigration Society for £1000 and simply signed 'Edward'. The remainder of the front page contained the text of the prince's speech.

The inside pages contained photographs of children at Pinjarra at work, school and play. The caption under a photograph of a group of children standing around a cottage mother read 'Homely scene at Haig Cottage'. Another photo of two boys working in a field read 'Where labour is a delight', while another, of a boy with bare feet chopping up a felled tree, read 'In Training for the clearing of his own block of land'.

On the back page, for contrast, there was a photo of a large group of children crowded onto the back stairs of an old house in Britain, with the caption 'Slum warrens'. Below was a list of the patrons of the appeal, including a selection of marquises, earls, countesses, ladies and lords, knights of the realm, and the famous actress Dame Sybil Thorndike.

The next Fairbridge farm school was opened in 1936 on Vancouver Island, Canada. The village was designed to eventually accommodate 250 children.[25]

A child-migrant centre that was to be closely connected to Fairbridge opened in 1937 at Bacchus Marsh outside Melbourne, Victoria. The scheme was launched by the Northcote Trust with the help of a donation of land from a wealthy pastoralist, William Angliss. The late Lady Northcote was the wife of Lord Northcote, the governor-general of Australia from 1904 to 1908. Two years before her death she had established a trust to:

> . . . enable and assist poor children of British birth of either sex and in particular orphans to emigrate from any part of Great Britain to any part of the Commonwealth of Australia and there to establish and equip themselves for life.[26]

The Northcote centre secured a commitment of funding from both the British Government and the Australian Government. While independent, it had a very close relationship with the Fairbridge Society in London, which effectively acted as Northcote's agent by recruiting British children to the scheme.

The Fairbridge Farm School that was to be opened in Rhodesia was to be different from the others. In 1936, Rev. A. G. B. West of the London Fairbridge Society travelled extensively throughout Rhodesia, meeting with the prime minister and others before recommending the building of a farm school capable of housing 250 children.[27] However, the Fairbridge Society in London was concerned that British children from poor backgrounds would not be suitable for farming in Rhodesia, where unskilled farm work was usually undertaken by poorly paid blacks. At the same time, it was felt that working-class British children would prove incapable of filling leadership roles expected of white Rhodesians.

Consequently, the Fairbridge Farm School in Rhodesia

was designed along different lines to the others. The children were to be recruited from a better class of family, and were to be trained for white-collar and leadership roles, and their parents were to contribute financially to their upbringing. The children were also going to be older – between ten and fifteen years of age.

The Rhodesian scheme was officially launched at the Rhodesian High Commission in London in August 1939 but then war broke out. In May 1945 the scheme was re-launched, with a commitment of funding from the British Government, and of funding and land near Bulawayo from the Rhodesian Government. The first party of children arrived in 1946. The London Fairbridge Society did have some misgivings: perhaps the different design of the Rhodesian farm school would create confusion in the public's mind at a time when the society was trying to recruit children in Britain for its other farms.

In Australia a group of former Rhodes scholars, some of whom had known Kingsley Fairbridge at Oxford, had become enthusiastic about opening new farm schools. Fairbridge's widow, Ruby, spoke at the biennial conference of Rhodes scholars in Melbourne in January 1935. She was keen to have the memory of her husband promoted in new schools, and the former Rhodes scholars resolved to establish Fairbridge farm schools in each of their states.

About six months later, the New South Wales Rhodes Fellowship met in Sydney and began raising money to build a Fairbridge farm school in New South Wales. They had the support of Scottish-born Andrew Reid, who committed substantial funds to the scheme.[28] The first meeting of the provisional committee of the Fairbridge Council was held in the University Club, Phillip Street, Sydney, on 30 July 1936. The meeting voted that a cable be sent to the Fairbridge Society in London, 'intimating the launching of the scheme in New South Wales' and that the executive were 'empowered to carry on enquiries for the land for the Farm'.[29]

Initially there was a decided lack of enthusiasm in London about the prospect of a Fairbridge school being opened in New South Wales. The London Fairbridge Society had been happy to leave New South Wales to Barnardo's, who had been operating a farm school at Picton, outside of Sydney, since the early 1920s. London had been looking at other spots in the British Empire that might be suitable, including Queensland, where there was considerable support in the upper echelons of the state government. New Zealand was also considered but the plan fizzled out.

In advice to the Dominions Office, the London Fairbridge Society said: 'Mrs. Kingsley Fairbridge's efforts to start a new farm school in New South Wales were entirely uninspired by this Society and made without our knowledge.'[30] The Dominions Office replied that 'The Society runs the risk of being overwhelmed by the enthusiasm of its supporters.'[31]

There was to be ongoing tension between the local Fairbridge Society in Sydney and the Fairbridge Society in London regarding their respective powers and responsibilities. (This was also the case with the Fairbridge farm schools at Pinjarra and Rhodesia.) The local Fairbridge Society in Sydney was to organise much of the funding to start up the farm but would need ongoing financial support from London to cover its operating costs. London would be responsible for ensuring the continuing support of the British Government and the ongoing recruitment of British children. London would also retain the power to hire and fire the school's principals.

The building and opening of the Fairbridge Farm School at Molong happened very quickly: there was only a year between the acquisition of the land and the arrival of the first party of children.[32] On 8 February 1937 the society bought Naragoon, a 650-hectare farm six kilometres east of the town of Molong in New South Wales. At the time there was only one timber house on the site, which was to become the farm supervisor's house.

On 24 February 1937 a public subscription campaign was launched in *The Sydney Morning Herald*. The target – £50,000 – was quickly reached and passed.[33] By the end of 1937 a windmill, water pipes and water tanks had been installed on the farm and by January 1938 the first of the children's cottages was completed. The cottage was used by Commander R. R. Beauchamp, the school's first principal, and his family until the big two-storey principal's house was completed a couple of months later.[34]

By March 1938, when the first party of twenty-eight boys arrived, three children's cottages – named Brown, Green and Molong – and the principal's house were completed. The boys were split between Brown Cottage and Green Cottage. Molong Cottage was used for cooking, dining and schooling until the dining hall, kitchens and school were built over the next two years.

Len Cowne recalls the Fairbridge Farm School he saw when he arrived in March 1938 in the first party of boys. The design of the cottages was to stay essentially the same for the life of Fairbridge:

> When we, the first party, arrived, the school consisted of the beginnings of a settlement which – probably because we were English – became known as 'the village', and was to become the main domestic and communal area of the farm school.
>
> Three very large wooden bungalows, the principal's two-storey house and a small guesthouse had already been completed; and about half a mile away stood the original farm and dairy buildings. The

cottages were to be the homes of the child migrants, and were solidly built of timber standing on brick piers for both ventilation and to discourage termites; these were roofed with heavy-duty red corrugated asbestos sheets. Apart from the bathroom, which was open to the roof, all rooms had ceilings and upper walls made from a sugar cane waste product called 'Canex', that looked like compressed straw but was a good insulating material. Some of the later cottages had the upper walls and ceilings lined with asbestos sheets.

Each cottage consisted of a large dormitory at one end separated from the matron's quarters at the other end by a locker room, a dining/common room, a bathroom, and a kitchen complete with wood-fired black iron range.

There was no main drainage or main sewer, so domestic waste water went into soakaways via a grease trap, and sewage went into large septic tanks.

Our beds were made of metal tubing, somewhat like the frame of a farm gate, with unsprung diamond wire mesh stretched between; there were no pillows, one end of the frame being angled slightly upwards instead. This took some getting used to, as did having to depend on oil lighting for several months until the electricity was connected. Using oil lamps for lighting and having our meals cooked on a Victorian-style wood-fired range seemed, at least to me, like being transported back into the days of my grandmother's youth.

But these were our living conditions and we had to get used to stepping back a century or so – at least for the time being.[35]

The official opening of Fairbridge took place in November 1938 and was an opportunity for the Sydney Fairbridge

Council to demonstrate the strength and breadth of its support. *The Sydney Morning Herald* reported that over 700 guests arrived to witness the official opening by the governor-general of Australia, Lord Gowrie. During the ceremony his wife officially opened Green Cottage, which was renamed Lady Gowrie Cottage in her honour.[36]

By the outbreak of World War II most of the village's buildings and roads had been built. There were ten children's cottages (an eleventh was finished during the war), the village hospital, village school, schoolmaster's house, staff quarters, farm supervisor's houses and the deputy principal's house.

The last party of children to arrive at Fairbridge before child migration was halted due to World War II had to sail from England to Canada and then across the Pacific, via Honolulu and New Zealand, in order to avoid the conflict. They arrived in Sydney in May 1940. No more child migrants would come to Australia until shipping became available again in 1947. In the meantime, the Fairbridge Farms at Molong and Pinjarra, and the Northcote Home in Victoria, shrank in size as children progressively left the schools to take up jobs outside. In 1944 the smaller Northcote home closed for the duration of the war and its forty-two children were transported by train and truck to live at the Fairbridge Farm School at Molong.[37]

In 1948 Princess (later Queen) Elizabeth donated £2000 to start a fund to help former Fairbridge children establish themselves in life. A very grateful Fairbridge Society in London proposed to rename the Molong farm school the Princess Elizabeth Fairbridge Farm School. After all, the Prince of Wales had allowed his name to be used for the Fairbridge farm school that had been opened in Canada in 1936.

The princess declined with a very diplomatic 'deferral' of a decision, as noted in the society's minutes:

The chairman reported correspondence he had with Her Royal Highness the Princess Elizabeth Comptroller with regard to using her name for the Molong Fairbridge Farm School. The Comptroller has advised Sir Charles that the Princess wished to defer granting the request until such time as she herself might visit Australia.[38]

The school was never to be renamed after Elizabeth. When Queen Elizabeth II visited Australia in 1954, Her Royal Highness declined an invitation to visit Fairbridge when she was touring the west of New South Wales.

More buildings were constructed at Molong after the war, including cottages for the farm supervisors and their families, a laundry and a garage for an old World War II bus that Fairbridge bought in 1948.

In that same year the giant pastoral company Goldsbrough Mort donated £15,000 for the building of four new children's cottages as part of the commemoration of its centenary celebrations. Goldsbrough Mort was a great beneficiary of the Fairbridge scheme. Many of the unskilled farm labourers produced by Fairbridge were employed on the company's sheep stations in the most remote areas of the west and north-west of the state.

The building of the four new cottages – named Corinda, Canonbar, Goldsbrough and Mort – was controversial. Fairbridge began construction without consulting the New South Wales Government or the Australian Government, who were still committed to providing financial assistance under an earlier capital funding agreement. Building materials were in short supply after the war, construction costs escalated and it would take almost four years for the cottages to be completed. Nor could it be established that Fairbridge needed the additional accommodation, and at no stage in the future did it ever use all of the cottages in the village.

In the early 1950s Fairbridge abandoned its earlier plans for a much larger village capable of housing and supporting 300 children; it was decided that the number of children living in the village was never to exceed 200 at any one time. In 1952 the Sydney Fairbridge Council said:

> The Society now has fifteen cottages for the children. The original intention was to build a village of twenty cottages. In view of the very high cost of maintaining the children and the difficulties being experienced, both here and in England to raise sufficient funds to meet these costs, the Society has decided to temporarily defer the full completion of the development plans.[39]

The final layout of the village was similar to other Fairbridge farm schools. Each of the cottages was designed to house about fifteen children and they were built around the centre of the village: the large communal dining hall, Nuffield Hall. The hall, built in 1939 with money donated by Lord Nuffield, the founder of Morris Motors, was designed to seat more than 300 children and staff. Next to Nuffield Hall were the village kitchens and bakery. The village had its own school, hospital, the big two-storey principal's house, a number of other staff residences, and a number of other buildings and facilities including garages, laundry, workshops, school, chapel and sports fields. The vegetable gardens and the orchards were planted below the village down toward Molong Creek and up behind the village was the dairy, poultry farm, piggery, slaughterhouse, shearing sheds, grain silos and four houses for the farm supervisory staff and their families.

In the late 1950s Fairbridge opened Tresca House in the Tamar Valley of Tasmania and Drapers Hall in

Adelaide, South Australia, but the single dwellings each housed only fifteen children and operated for only a few years.[40]

By the late 1940s there were already a number of changes occurring in child welfare in Britain that would make it more difficult for Fairbridge to attract children to its scheme. In 1946 the Curtis Report into child welfare became the foundation of the Children Act of 1948, which gave responsibility for child welfare to local government in Britain and placed greater emphasis on foster care rather than institutions.[41] The childcare professional was replacing the philanthropic amateur and the inherent failures of children's institutions were being recognised. Child migration and children's institutions such as Fairbridge were rapidly falling out of favour. Fairbridge resisted change and rejected the growing criticism of its schemes. In 1957 it changed its rules to allow a single parent to follow their children out to Australia. And that is how I came to find myself at Molong, so very far from home.

3

A Day in the Life

It was still dark when we arrived at the farm school on our first winter's morning in Molong. We got out of the truck and were ushered into the kitchen of the principal's house, where we were given a welcome mug of hot cocoa. Nobody spoke as we stood in a circle wondering what was to happen next.

The first bell of the day had been rung and, unknown to us, out there in the darkness the village had begun to stir. One after another a child arrived to escort a boy or girl from our party to the cottage we had each been assigned. The sight of these Fairbridge kids appearing on the back porch of the house was frightening. They were mostly barefoot, wore rough, old clothing and had awful haircuts that, as we found out later, had been done by other Fairbridge children.

Gradually our little group that had been together for the past two months since coming together at Knockholt was broken up, until only my brothers and I were left standing silently in the kitchen of the principal's house.

Woods was angry that no one from our assigned cottage, Canonbar, had come for us. The cottage mother was away on leave and the boys, left unsupervised, had slept through the first bell. Woods grabbed a big cane and, sternly ordering us to follow him, strode down from the house and across the lawn to Canonbar Cottage, which we couldn't see properly in the dark. He led us through the back and ordered us to stand in the locker room – I noticed a lot of dirty clothing hanging out of shelves and lying on the floor – while he went into the dormitory and closed the door.

Next we heard yelps and screams as he went around the dormitory whacking the sleeping boys in their beds. It was a serious offence to be in bed after the bell. The children scurried out to the locker room in ill-fitting and un-matching pyjamas, rubbing their eyes and the places where Woods had hit them. The big man was shouting at them to get under the shower, get dressed and get to work.

A short time later a bell rang and we were told this was the signal for the children to finish their work, make their beds and prepare for breakfast. About fifteen minutes later another bell rang and we went across to Nuffield Hall, where the whole village breakfasted each day. We saw the other children from the *Strathaird*. We stood out because we were wearing different clothing to the khaki, blue and grey shirts and shorts worn by everyone else. Later we were to be issued with the same clothing as the other Fairbridge children and we never again saw our London wardrobe. Those beautiful clothes all disappeared after coming out with us on the back of the truck that morning from Molong train station.

In Nuffield Hall each cottage had its own long wooden dining table. There were no tablecloths; instead, each table was covered with a strip of lino. All the bowls and plates were made of steel. We sat on long wooden benches, seven or eight children down each side, ranging from the biggest at the top of the table to the smallest at the other end. One of the children went into the kitchen and brought out a big steel bowl of porridge, which was doled out into individual bowls from the end of the table. The porridge was followed by a piece of bread with honey and a mug of milk.

We weren't sent to school that first day. I was instructed to work in the village vegetable garden with a fifteen-year-old boy called Max. My first impression of the country-side was how drab and unappealing it looked. It was still recovering from a severe drought, which had left the grass dried out and brown – very different to the deep green of the English countryside. I spent most of my first day with Max shovelling chicken manure that we hauled from the village poultry farm to the garden by horse and cart. Max was wiry and tough, like most of the Fairbridge kids, and was unimpressed with my work, making no allowance for the fact that I was only twelve years old and had never done a day's labouring before.

We had lunch back at Nuffield Hall and at the end of the day returned to Canonbar Cottage for a shower and our evening meal. In addition to me and my brothers there were a dozen kids in Canonbar, who displayed little curiosity about us new boys. I remember being frightened and lonely, and missing my mother. I was also drained and physically exhausted from my first full day of manual labour.

Billy King, who came with us to Fairbridge on the *Strathaird*, remembers his first days at Fairbridge:

> I felt terrible. I cried for a week. And I still wanted to go home. Even then, I wanted to go home. And then I realised, like when I was on that boat, how far I was from home.

Derek Moriarty has similar recollections. He had been in institutions in England since he was three years old and has no memory of family life. But he still recalls being frightened when he first arrived at Fairbridge in 1951 as an eight-year-old, with his six-year-old brother, Paul.

> We eventually arrived at the village I think around about five in the afternoon. It was just coming on sundown and apprehension started to creep up on me then. He [Woods] stopped the truck and we were climbing out. That's when I started to get scared. And I mean really scared . . . and funnily enough, I got homesick. I felt homesick from that moment, the moment I put my feet on the ground. And I thought, Why am I homesick? I didn't come from a home, I've come from another orphanage.

Despite being tired, I did not want to go to bed that first night. There was no way I could talk to either of my brothers because there was no privacy and, besides, I didn't know what to say. Eventually, deeply sad and very frightened, I went into the dormitory to the bed I'd been allocated, the second along on the right, with strangers either side – my brothers were across the room and up the other end. Much as I tried not to, I sobbed myself to sleep – but I was as quiet as possible for fear one of the other children would hear me.

On cold winter's mornings after the breakfast bell rang we sat or lay on the big wooden cottage verandah, warming ourselves in the early morning sun. Sometimes up to a dozen boys were there, having worked in the cottage or around the village for the best part of the past hour before coming back after the second bell to wash up and make the beds.

All the other children in the village were already lined up outside the big dining hall, which was across the lawns, waiting for the principal to come down and let them in. But as our cottage was close to Nuffield Hall we could see the boss leaving his big two-storey house up on the other side of the village and we could race across before he strode down to let everyone in for breakfast and closed the doors on latecomers.

The wake-up bell went at six a.m. when, in winter, it was still dark. As soon as we got up we were expected to have a shower, which was always cold because the fire in the 'donkey' water heater had petered out the evening before. In Canonbar we usually managed to avoid the cold shower because our cottage mother was not an early riser: we would quickly dress and go off to work before she came down to our end of the cottage. We dressed in the locker room. The cottages had no heating and in the winter we learnt to take off our shirt and pullover together at night so that in the cold the next morning we'd be able to quickly pull both over our heads in one movement and be dressed in a matter of seconds. In other cottages, where the early-morning shower rule was enforced, most kids learnt to dance in and dance out of the freezing water, but some cottage mothers were particularly nasty and forced them to stand under it for longer.

Each child was allowed four shelves and a small area of hanging space for clothes in the locker room. Shoes and socks were not to be worn inside the cottages and were stacked inside the back-door porch, but most kids went around the village barefoot anyway and we were actively discouraged from wearing shoes. The bathroom had two toilet cubicles, two sinks, two showers and a bath, which was never used. We each had a numbered hook on which to hang our towel, and a numbered slot on the shelf above the sinks for our toothbrushes. There was no personal privacy in the cottage, which didn't bother most of us boys once we got used to it, but upset many of the girls.

Each cottage had a kitchen with a wood-fuelled stove, on which our evening meals were cooked, and a dining room with a long table where we would eat them. There was no lounge room, no lounge furniture and no floor coverings anywhere in the cottage. A door at the end of the cottage led into separate quarters for the cottage mother, which contained a lounge, bedroom and bathroom.

The cottage mother, who for some strange reason we called 'Sister', was a key figure in the lives of children at Fairbridge. She was the closest thing to a parent many would ever see again. Michael Walker, who arrived at Fairbridge as a six-year-old with his five-year-old brother, Jimmy, in 1950, believes the title 'Sister' had some religious origins:

> It probably stemmed from the religious orders and their respect for females working in the service of God. We used it as a form of address, which was often shortened to 'ster', such as when replying to a request one would answer, 'Yes 'ster.'

All the children between four and fourteen were assigned work around the village or farm before breakfast every day except Sunday. The smaller children usually worked inside their cottages, cleaning, sweeping, scrubbing and polishing under the supervision of the cottage mother.

For a while I had the job of chopping wood for the girls' Lilac Cottage. I'd join other boys on one of the two village woodpiles, swinging our axes in the pre-dawn light, racing to fill our wheelbarrows, often in bare feet, before the bell rang to tell us to get back to the cottages. There we'd stack the chopped wood under the water tank, then wash up, make our beds and go to breakfast when the next bell rang.

For a while, my twin brother, Richard, was assigned to the milk run, which involved going up to the dairy, harnessing the horse and cart, and, with one of the boys who had finished the morning milking, bringing down the milk and delivering it around the village. Other jobs included setting fires for heating and cooking, and cleaning a number of staff houses, the tiny Fairbridge Hospital and the village guesthouse.

Another job I had was to make the sandwich lunches for the children going to secondary school. Two of us would be assigned to make two sandwiches each for about sixty children. Making two sandwiches for each kid was relatively straightforward – if the bread had been properly baked. Our bread at Fairbridge was cooked in a bakehouse behind the village kitchens by fifteen- and sixteen-year-old boys, who were rotated on different jobs each month around the village and farm. Some of the boys had a natural talent for baking, but on many occasions the dough was close to being uncooked, and on others it was almost burnt to charcoal. Whatever the standard, there was no choice but to try to slice it, and put some butter and filling in each sandwich. We were told only to butter one of the slices of bread and use whatever fillings the cook gave us, which on the whole were very limited and lacking in nutrition. Sometimes they'd be pickles – not cheese and pickles, or ham and pickles, just pickles. At other times we'd get cucumber, or devon, or Vegemite or, occasionally, lambs' brains.

Most of the children at Fairbridge left school at the minimum school-leaving age, which was fifteen, or a little before. For the next two years they became what were called 'trainees' and worked on twenty-eight-day rosters, rotated through different jobs around the farm. When they turned seventeen they were found farm jobs, and left Fairbridge.

The boy trainees worked on rotation in the dairy, slaughterhouse, poultry farm and piggery; the vegetable gardens and orchards; the village kitchens, bakery, laundry and principal's house; and on general village maintenance. For the last few months at the farm school they usually worked up on the wheat and sheep farm, learning to use farm equipment.

The girl trainees worked in the village kitchen and as serving staff at mealtimes, helped in the laundry, or worked as domestic servants in the principal's house or one of the other larger staff quarters.

Breakfast was the same almost every day I was at Fairbridge. The principal would open the door of the hall and we would all march in single file as he inspected us to make sure our hands were clean and our shoes polished – if we were wearing shoes. When prayers had been read and grace sung and we were all seated, one child from each cottage would go into the kitchen and bring out the big bowl of porridge, which the cottage mother would ladle out into each child's metal bowl. David Eva, aged ten when he arrived at Fairbridge, recalls:

> And I never forgot – they took us down and we had breakfast, and I couldn't believe it when they gave us steel plates ... In England we were poor, but you never ate off bloody tin plates. I couldn't believe it.

The porridge was often too watery or thick – 'splodge' we called it – and frequently it was contaminated with weevils. But we still had to eat it. The porridge was followed by a slice of Fairbridge bread with a small pat of butter and a small spoonful of honey, which we mixed together before spreading it on the bread, so none would be wasted. Finally, we had a metal mug of milk, which in winter was heated and had cocoa added to it.

The trainee boys – but not the trainee girls – were also given a 'cooked' breakfast, which usually meant simply a single mutton chop, a boiled egg or some of the previous day's leftovers from dinner reheated. Each cottage mother, who sat in a straight-backed chair at the head of her children's table, ate a full English breakfast – a choice of cereals, eggs, bacon, tea, coffee, toast and jams, set on a little tablecloth by a trainee girl acting as a waitress.

The other village staff members sat at a long table up on the stage at the end of the dining hall, with the boss at the head, and were also served a full English breakfast by the trainee girls.

During my first eighteen months at Fairbridge I was one of a few children sent to the high school in Orange, some thirty-four kilometres away. The handful of us who were sent to Orange High School had to leave breakfast early and walk hurriedly about a kilometre down the Amaroo Road to the Mitchell Highway to catch the overcrowded school bus. The bus came from Molong and carried children going to Orange High and an assortment of private schools, including the Catholic De La Salle School and the exclusive Wolaroi Boys College. By the time the bus picked us up it was already full so we usually spent almost an hour standing on the trip to Orange.

We qualified for the same cooked breakfast that was given to the trainee boys, which was lucky because from 7.30 a.m. till the evening meal back at Fairbridge more than ten hours later, we had to survive on the two-sandwich ration given to all the Fairbridge secondary school kids.

While we were on the bus to Orange, the other Fairbridge school-age kids either went back to their cottages to wash up their breakfast utensils or back to work, before getting ready to go to the local schools. The primary-school children normally went barefoot to school but the secondary-school children wore shoes.

The primary-school children walked to school over the hill at the back of the village to a small four-room construction built in 1939, shortly after Fairbridge was opened. At lunchtime they walked back to Nuffield Hall for a cooked lunch with the village staff and some of the trainees, then went back to school for the afternoon. As with breakfast, a child from each cottage went into the kitchen and brought out the lunch on a metal tray, which the cottage mother served onto a steel plate for each child at the table. The cottage lunch tray had three sections: one for the meat, which was invariably mutton, one for potatoes, and one for other vegetables grown in the village gardens.

The secondary-school children assembled at about a quarter to nine outside the principal's house to catch the bus for the six-kilometre trip into Molong. One or two were responsible for carrying a big basket containing the sandwiches wrapped in greaseproof paper, and sometimes a sugarbag of shrivelled oranges that had been donated to Fairbridge. It would all be left under the stairs outside the classrooms until lunchtime.

The Fairbridge children disliked their school sandwiches and envied the nice lunches the other kids brought to school. Daphne Brown recalls how Fairbridge children scrounged leftover food from the town pupils:

> The girls that came from private homes would be eating lovely sandwiches. They would have an apple and we used to say 'Bags your core.' And they gave us their cores and we would eat the rest of the apple because any fruit we got was seconds.

Fairbridge was not geared up to care for the very young children, some of whom were only four. These little ones, who weren't old enough for school, were sent out after breakfast on their own to pick up small twigs, called 'chips', to help light the cottage fires and boilers.

Stewart Lee arrived at Fairbridge in 1955 as a four-year-old, with his three older brothers. He recalls being left each day as the older children went off to the little school at the back of the village:

> I don't remember a great deal . . . like, it's bits and pieces . . . I used to follow them up as far as the wood-pile, then they'd have to go on to school and I'd go home and start picking up chips . . . So, you're four years of age and there's nobody looking after you and you just go out all day collecting chips of wood . . . Or sitting down on the septic tank just looking down the road. There was nothing else to do.

Daphne Brown remembers she had to pick up chips with the other small children when she arrived at Fairbridge in 1948 as a seven-year-old girl:

> One of the worst jobs I can remember was for the little kids, when we first went there, in the winter you had to go and pick up chips for the fire. And it was all frosty and your fingers were frozen. It was dreadful.

After school all the children changed into work clothes for assigned labour around the village or the farm. On Monday and Friday afternoons we all had to present ourselves for 'village muster' behind the Nuffield Hall kitchens, near the village bell.

The bell dictated our lives. It rang to wake us up, to tell us it was time to make our beds, to signal breakfast and lunch, when to assemble, when to go to church, and when it was time for evening showers and the night-time curfew.

It wasn't actually a bell – it was a piece of steel railway line about a metre long that was suspended by a steel chain from a wooden crossbeam. One of the boys, usually a trainee working in the village kitchens, was assigned to ring the 'bell' by striking it with an iron bar. Most of us boys liked to ring it because it meant you could make a sound that would be heard for miles around. Fairbridge did own a proper big bronze bell, but it would have been broken if beaten regularly with an iron bar. For years it sat next to the piece of railway line before eventually being put into the Fairbridge chapel, which was built in 1961.

Village muster was physically hard maintenance work around the village and farm. It could involve planting trees, cleaning drains, clearing roads, repairing fences or periodically cleaning out the septic sewerage systems around the village. We also spent a lot of time weeding, and painting the rocks bordering the village roads and paths with white paint. At harvest time we would all be taken up to work on the farm.

On Tuesday afternoons we worked under the guidance of our cottage mothers on the cottage gardens, which were judged once a year by the Fairbridge board of directors. The Cottage Garden Competition was fiercely fought out, particularly among some of the longest-serving cottage mothers: children in their cottages dreaded spring, when they would be ordered out at every available moment to clear, plant, mow, prune and weed the gardens.

In an otherwise totally regimented week we all looked forward to our 'free' afternoon on Wednesday. If you were on the discipline list for some offence, though, your privileges were withdrawn and you had to work. During the couple of hours' free time after school the kids enjoyed playing or simply hanging around. There wasn't a great deal to do, but most of us enjoyed the little time when we weren't being ordered around.

Thursday afternoon was sport, which, depending on the time of year, meant cricket, soccer, rugby league, hockey, swimming or the annual inter-cottage Fairbridge athletics carnival. Most of us loved sport as much as we enjoyed our free time but for those children who were not good at sport it could be a nightmare, as the boss would run after the boys he thought were being slack and whip them on the back of the legs to force them to try harder.

Before the evening meal we all had a shower in the cottage bathroom, usually with hot water because the boy who was assigned to clean the bathroom in the cottage each morning was also responsible for relighting the 'donkey' heater before going off to school.

The quality of the evening meal varied from cottage to cottage. The cottage mother was responsible for 'tea', as we called it, which might be some of the lunch leftovers brought back to the cottage and reheated. Some of the cottage mothers would take the trouble to cook an interesting meal for the children, while the lazier ones served up little more than bread and milk. In other cases, the cottage mother ordered one or more of the secondary-school kids to do the cooking for the whole cottage.

After tea, the Orange High School kids normally did the washing up because we had missed a lot of the cottage and village work during the day. It was an awful job because all the hot water was used up with the evening showers. Cleaning mutton fat off steel pots and plates in tepid or cold water was hard work and seemed to take for ever.

After dinner we just hung around until it was time to

go to bed, because there wasn't much else to do. Unless there was some ordered activity, we were not permitted to leave the cottage after the evening meal. In our cottage there was no radio or TV and no books, except for the odd comic or Zane Grey western.

On winter's evenings we were allowed to light the one fire in our cottage, and up to fifteen children would crowd around it before going off to bed in the freezing cold dormitory at the other end of the building. The farm rules dictated the dormitory windows always stayed open – in summer and winter – and there was no heating. A number of Fairbridge children recall they were only permitted by their cottage mothers to light a fire on rare occasions. Talking after lights out was always forbidden.

The weekend was as regimented as the rest of the week, but it usually involved sport and free time, which most of us loved. A regular feature was the Weekend Notice, which was roughly typed on pink or yellow paper by the boss on his old manual Olivetti typewriter and pinned up on one of the entrance doors of Nuffield Hall every Friday afternoon. A surviving example of a Weekend Notice begins with orders for Friday afternoon village muster, and on this particular Friday, arrangements had been made for some of the children to go to the cinema in Molong.[1] This was a special occasion, as normally a trip to the cinema was limited to the trainees over fifteen years of age.

> Friday: 4 pm. Muster for all Children not needed for Cottage Duties. (The work will be in and around the septic tank at Red Cottage and the Shetland Pony Paddock and the Sheep Paddock there.)
> Members of the Pony Club to get harnesses & Ponies ready.

7 pm. Bus to Molong with children for Pictures. Primary and Secondary Children can be granted special Picture leave by their cottage mothers if they have earned the privilege – Trainees may go with the normal Picture Leave. School children will be paid for by Fairbridge – Trainees will pay for themselves.

After breakfast on Saturday some of us were put to work on jobs such as picking up meat and vegetable rations for the evening meals or collecting wheelbarrow loads of coke for the cottages' hot water systems. Everyone else worked on the big Saturday-morning village muster.

Saturday: 7.15. Cottage meat dishes to Main Kitchen and all covered please. Cottage Vegetable orders will be also taken during Breakfast.
8.30 to 9 am. Cottage Coke Supplies from main coke yard – Keith Prince to take charge of loading and to tidy coke yard afterwards.
10 am. Muster of all Children not needed for Cottage Duties.

During the summer months there might be other events woven into the weekend schedule, including pony club for the few children who had access to the handful of horses at Fairbridge:

10 am. Pony Club Members to start riding into Molong for Pony Club meeting. They must take their project books for examination and marking by the judges. (All members wishing to attend the Meeting must arrange with Mrs Woods for Ponies and Harness.)
11 am. Sunday School Children to be ready to go to Sunday School Picnic. Paul Suret and Eric Fowler to go with them as Supervisors and act as life guards

when they go swimming. The following Children are to go from Fairbridge: R. Henderson. R. Hillman. B. Piercy, M. Marsh, L. Lipscombe, A. Bingham, G. Scott, R. Battley, D. Parker, D. Attwood, P. Wilcox, S. Wilcox, C. Wetherall, N. Edge, P. Harris, H. Battley, J. Connell, S. Hillman, P. Wells, S. Wells, R. Elliott, J. Bannerman, S. Wugman, M. Gunther, R. Boutler, Each child to take a Swimming Costume, Towel and a Stainless Steel Mug.

After a busy morning the village had lunch, at the end of which pocket money was handed out. The base pocket money when I was at Fairbridge was threepence for the little kids, sixpence for the secondary-school-age kids, a shilling for the fifteen-year-old trainees and two shillings for the sixteen-year-olds. The tuckshop would be open for half an hour and we'd be able to buy a few sweets with our pocket money.

12 noon. Staff Dinner.
12.30 pm. Children's Dinner (Sunday School Children absent).
1.15 pm. Tuck Shop.
2 pm. Swimming for all School Children and trainees who are Free.

Saturday afternoon involved organised sport for everyone, except trainees who were working in the dairy, the farm or the village kitchens. In summer we usually played cricket or went swimming in the big dam at the back of Fairbridge Farm, but during droughts or when the water level was low we were taken into the little town swimming pool in Molong.

In winter we were relayed in an old bus or in the farm truck or station wagon into Orange or Molong to play rugby league or hockey against 'town kids'. The transportation of multiple sporting teams of boys and girls by Principal Woods, his wife Ruth and perhaps one or two other staff members was a logistical marvel. On more than one occasion, Woods, who was a very large man, squeezed an entire team of thirteen of us rugby league players, covered in mud, into the one station wagon for the trip back to the farm.

Most Saturday nights were like any other night of the week. We were confined to our cottages, although every couple of months an old movie would be shown on the antiquated Fairbridge film projector in Nuffield Hall. Sometimes Fairbridge would hire out the large and impressive Nuffield Hall on a Saturday night for banquets and balls and we would be the waiters for the evening, or we might host a dinner and a social for the Junior Farmers Club, or some other local community activity.

> 5.30 pm. The following children to report at Dining Hall to set out tables for dinner . . . After setting the tables, they will go back for their own tea at 6 pm. and return for duty at Dinner at 6.30 pm.
> 7 pm. Dinner for all Members of the Junior Farmers Club, and guests from Visiting Clubs and Official Guests from Molong. The boys who are serving and Washing up may stay for the Social afterwards.
> 8.30 pm. Social to follow the Dinner. J.F. Members will be selected to help serve Supper at 11 pm.

Sunday was the one day we did not work before breakfast; the whole village, except the working trainees, slept in until 7 a.m. Attendance at church was compulsory and on most Sunday mornings the Anglican vicar came out to Fairbridge to conduct a service in the Fairbridge dining hall. But on the first Sunday of each month we crowded on to the old Fairbridge bus and went to the service in Molong. My brothers and I had been to church regularly at school in England, and I found the services at Fairbridge every bit as tedious and boring as the ones I remembered in Langney.

> Sunday
> 7 am. Rising Bell
> 7.45 am. Bedmaking
> 8 am. Breakfast.
> 9 am. Bell. Get Ready for Church.
> 9.30 am. C. of E. M[olong] C[hurch]. Service.
> 11 am. Sunday School for all children aged 9 years and Under.
> 12 noon. Dinner for all.

Sunday afternoons consisted of more sport, usually for the trainees, who normally worked all day on Saturday.

> 2 pm. Cricket for Trainees and Older School Boys.
> 3.30. Bus to Molong with those children who have to be Baptised at the St. John's Church of England (Such child being Baptised may invite a friend or brother or sister to attend the Baptism as well.)

Sunday night back in our cottages was usually an empty time when we would sit around after the evening meal and talk, or perhaps write a letter home – for those of us who had someone to write to. For me, a slow Sunday night was a time to reflect on how it was that I had gone from living happily as part of a family in a village in the south of England to being with almost 200 other children in a tough farm school in the Australian bush.

4

SETTLING IN

Almost every child who went to Fairbridge Farm School still vividly recalls the day they arrived. I remember having to adjust to a regime that was much tougher than anything I had expected. There was no induction on arrival, and no one to show us the ropes, so we all quickly learnt to tag along with the others whenever the village bell tolled.

The adjustment was even harder for many other children. I missed my mum but I was nearly thirteen years old and I knew she was following us out to Australia. Most of the other kids were not so lucky. They were much younger than me when they arrived and were unlikely to see their parents again.

Linda Gidman was only five when she arrived at Fairbridge. Her older sister and brother were already there, but she was still unhappy:

> I kept asking for my mother and I was saying, 'My mother will come through the door any time,' and 'Mum wouldn't leave me here,' you know. 'I'm waiting for Mummy to take me home,' and all that sort of thing . . . And they were saying, 'Well she's not coming: make the most of it.'

Laurie Reid arrived as a seven-year-old in 1950 with an older brother and two older sisters. He remembers crying for his mother:

> After just a couple of days I started to cry, 'I want my mother, I want my mother.' . . . And she [the cottage mother] said, 'I'll give you something to bloody well cry about.' And they did, they strapped me and I found every time I cried I got the strap. So hey, I'd better cut this out and grow up fast, you know.

Within a fortnight of arriving at Fairbridge, Billy King wrote to Dorothy Watkins, the social worker who had arranged for him to be sent from a children's home in Cornwall, pleading to be allowed to come home:

> I do not like it hear [sic] it is nothing like you said . . . I wish I could come back to England than stay in this place until I am 17 and I still won't have enough money to come back . . . They at least could have told me the truth about the place instead they told lies . . . We do not ride horses to school.[1]

Watkins responded by writing to Woods asking him to calm down Billy:

> I can remember Woodsie taking me down to his office and . . . him threatening me with a hiding if I didn't stop my blubbering and get back to my cottage . . . As time went on . . . I sort of knew that I couldn't do nothing about going home. I had to sort of put up with it.

Being forced to adapt to life without parents was difficult enough, but many of the children were also split up from their brothers and sisters as soon as they arrived. My two brothers and I were lucky: we were put in the same cottage. We later learnt it was because there happened to be three beds available in the dormitory when we arrived, since three boys had left the cottage in recent months, having reached seventeen years of age. Being together gave us greater security. On our first morning in the cottage, one of the older boys started picking on my twin brother, Richard. Dudley quickly moved in and made it clear he would fight the bigger boy if necessary. From then on the message was clear: if you picked on one of the Hill boys, you might have to take on the others as well.

Not all the children were so fortunate. Siblings who had never been apart were sent to live in separate cottages, as Fairbridge simply allocated children to the available beds, making no attempt to keep families together. Boys lived in separate cottages from girls, which meant sisters and brothers were separated within an hour of arriving at Fairbridge. This could be especially traumatic for the smallest children, who were already yearning for their parents.

Wendy Harris and her little brother, Paul, came out in the same party of children as us. On the ship coming over Paul was allowed to sleep in the same cabin as Wendy, so she could look after him. But immediately after arriving at Fairbridge they were separated: Wendy was sent to live in the girls' Molong Cottage and Paul to the boys' Blue Cottage. Wendy remembers that Paul kept coming over to her cottage crying for his older sister, until the Molong cottage mother banned Wendy from seeing him and told Paul he couldn't come over to his sister's cottage any more.[2]

When Stewart Lee arrived with his three older brothers, the four boys were split up and put into three cottages. Nine-year-old Sid went into Red Cottage, eight-year-old

Ian into Blue and ten-year-old Graham went with Stewart into Mort Cottage. He says: 'Well, the worst memory is . . . when I was split from my brothers . . . I was only four. Always, even in England, where my brothers went, I went.'

Six-year-old Peter Bennett and his nine-year-old sister, Marie, were in the last party of Fairbridge children to leave England before World War II, and arrived at Molong in 1940. They were plucked from Middlemore Homes just outside Birmingham. Marie was to have been sent ahead of Peter to the Fairbridge school in Pinjarra in Western Australia, but she was delayed with tonsillitis and then the threat of war. By then it was thought Peter was old enough to go with Marie, so together they were sent to Molong. Peter often wonders:

> If Marie had gone to Canada, or Pinjarra, and I ended up in Fairbridge Molong, would we have ever met again? Possibly never.

Because of the war, Peter's party came via Canada:

> We left up in Newcastle on the east coast in the *Duchess of Richmond*. We couldn't come down the Suez because the war was on; we had to go up around the Atlantic and across to Quebec, up the Lawrence River to Montreal, five days by train across Canada and we got to the Canadian Fairbridge Farm School [on Vancouver Island] and stayed there for a month.

Margaret Watt was a ten-year-old travelling in the same party as Peter in 1940 and remembers the excitement of the wartime convoy leaving England: 'We went right up north to escape all the submarines and we went past ten icebergs and two merchant ships were sunk and some other damaged but we weren't touched.'

Peter described the trip across the Pacific:

> Then we boarded the *Orangi* and came down to Aus-
> tralia through Tahiti and Honolulu. At Honolulu we
> couldn't get off the boat because they had twenty-
> eight names on one passport. So they had to get in
> touch with Washington and by the time the reply
> came, it was time for the boat to leave. So we never
> got off the boat.
> . . . We were able to land in Fiji and they took us
> around the island and we saw coconuts and bananas
> and pineapples. The kids didn't even know what they
> were; we'd never seen anything like it. And we left
> Suva and came down to Auckland, where they took us
> to see a movie, and from Auckland we came across to
> Australia . . .

As soon as Peter and Marie arrived at Fairbridge they
were split up and saw little of one another in the village
after that: 'Very seldom did I see my sister, or she see
me, or very seldom did we talk to each other . . . because
we just weren't allowed to mix with the girls. That
was it.'

Peter recalls his difficulty settling in at Fairbridge:

> I was a very timid, scared, frightened little person
> . . . I had a lot of time and trouble settling down in
> Fairbridge . . . I used to wet the bed and you were
> made to hang out your clothes and sheets every
> morning and, I mean . . . a six-year-old child that's
> come out of an orphanage. I mean, when I look back
> on it, it's just unbelievable that you could be treated
> like that.
> I really didn't have a happy childhood and it was
> only . . . the friends that we had and the mates and

everything within the cottages, the camaraderie that we'd got between each other, that sort of helped you through.

Malcolm Field arrived at Fairbridge as a nine-year-old in 1952 with his fourteen-year-old brother, Laurie. Their six-year-old sister, Jane, was already at Fairbridge, having arrived more than a year earlier. When they were finally reunited they were to see very little of each other:

> My sister says to me that the only time she saw me was on Sunday at the church, which was in the dining hall in those days before the chapel was built, and she'd say to her friends, 'That's my brother, Malcolm, he's the server.' That's the only time. We hardly ever spoke.

*

The Fairbridge village was very beautiful and well maintained, largely by the children. The village was built on typical Australian harsh and sparse bushland. By the time we arrived in the late 1950s, the shrubs and trees that had been planted when Fairbridge first opened in the late 1930s had matured, and each cottage garden was well cared for by the children, under the supervision of their cottage mother.

Like many others, I was surprised to find it so cold when I arrived. In all the photographs and brochures we were given by Australia House and by Fairbridge in London the sun was always shining. We simply weren't prepared for the winters to be so cold. Joyce Drury, who arrived in Australia in 1939 aged ten, recalls:

> I came in June to Molong – and I have never felt the cold as I did that first night . . . And getting up in the morning! And there was frost, and even though

I came from England, it's a wetter kind of climate up
in Lancashire in the north-west and I'd seen snow but
I hadn't seen frost on the ground, and that surprised
me.

Suffering such temperatures was made worse by having to
go about the village barefoot most of the time and not
being allowed to put your hands in your pockets. David
Eva, who arrived at Fairbridge as a ten-year-old, remembers his first morning:

Of course I had no shoes on, and all these other
bloody kids had no shoes on, and there were two
heaters in this massive great hall and these two little
heaters ... and I mean, they wouldn't heat up that
hall if you had a furnace there, the size of it.

Peter Bennett recalls how, aged only six, he was forced to
run around in bare feet in winter, and wasn't allowed
to put his hands in his pockets, so both his hands and
feet bled:

You couldn't have any shoes. And Molong was the
coldest place in the world. And I used to get these
chilblains on my fingers and they would bleed and
my feet would bleed ... And hands in pockets!
Woods said to me, 'Hands out of your pockets,
Bennett.' So he said, 'Come down to the machine.' So
I had to take my pants off, and he sewed the pockets
on the leather-working machine he had down at the
end of the hall. So, I'm smart, I undid them. And I got
caught again. So he sewed them up again and got an
assistant to cut the pockets out and said to me, 'Now
open them up.'

Laurie Reid describes how our feet eventually toughened up:

> And the only time we used to wear shoes was if you went to church or to secondary school. Now when I left the place it took years and years for me to get all that hard skin off the bottom of my feet. I could walk on bindies or anything and wouldn't even feel them.

On our first day at Fairbridge we were issued with clothing to replace our London wardrobe. We were given two sets of clothing: one for work and for wearing in the village, and another for school. We also wore our school clothes to church on Sunday, with a grey jacket that was worn on special occasions. The work clothes were khaki, blue or grey shorts and shirt, with a pullover in winter. The school clothes were khaki or blue shorts and shirt, with a Molong school grey pullover for winter and a pair of shoes and grey socks. It was 'sissy' to wear socks pulled up so they were worn rolled down around the ankle, however cold it might be, and boys did not wear underwear until they were twelve years old.

Lennie Magee arrived at Fairbridge in 1954 aged seven and was nicknamed 'Moon' because of his round face. He remembers his fine English wardrobe vanishing and being issued with rough Fairbridge clothing:

> When we first arrived at Fairbridge, each of the boys was wearing a brand new pair of shorts and a blue shirt, a gold and brown tie, a blazer, long grey socks and black leather shoes. They were taken from us the moment we arrived and we were never to see them again ... With few exceptions all of the clothes we were issued at Fairbridge were hand-me-downs. Someone else had worn them to a frazzle before us.

My first trousers were short, grey and hairy, with buttons, worn with a threadbare T-shirt and bare feet, except on Sunday mornings when we wore shoes. Generously, we were given an extra blanket in winter and a pullover to wear, but it wasn't until I was twelve years old that I was given my first pair of underpants. Thankfully they were new.

My brother, Dudley, then fourteen, remembers being ordered to the sports field for rugby league practice on our first afternoon at Fairbridge. At that stage he had no clothing other than a pair of khaki shorts and what he'd arrived in, including the black shoes and socks that he had been wearing all day. When he complained that he had no sporting gear, Principal Woods said, 'Don't worry, play in what you're wearing.'

There were fifteen children's cottages in the Fairbridge village, though not all of them were occupied. For most of the time there were three girls' cottages and eight boys' cottages in use, each housing up to fifteen or sixteen children, ranging in age from four to seventeen. For some periods a separate cottage was opened exclusively for trainee boys aged fifteen and sixteen, but the experiment was not very successful, largely because there was no one to keep the cottage clean, as the boys were working long hours around the farm.

Our cottage was fairly typical. There were three boy trainees who were fifteen or sixteen years old, about six of us who were under fifteen years old and attending secondary school, and five more who went every day to the local primary school at the back of the village. Our cottage was named Canonbar after a great sheep station way out in the remote west of the state owned by the Goldsbrough Mort pastoral company.

Those Fairbridge children who were lucky enough to have good cottage mothers are likely to remember their time at Fairbridge far more positively than those who weren't so lucky. Unfortunately most Fairbridge children remember that from the very beginning they received little love and care from their cottage mothers. Henry McFarlane, who was an eight-year-old when he arrived at Fairbridge in the first group of boys, in March 1938, recalls: 'There was no love, nobody if you felt a bit down; nobody came around and put [their arm] around [you] and said, "Come on – we're here for you."'

Margaret McLaughlan arrived in Australia as a five-year-old in 1939 with her six-year-old brother. They went to the Northcote child-migrant school in Victoria, but were sent to Molong when it was merged with Fairbridge in 1944. Nearly seventy years later Margaret says the cottage mothers were unsuited to their jobs and provided no love or affection to the children:

> I think they were sadists and a lot of them were very cruel and you never got a cuddle. No one in my whole life there put their arm around me and said, 'You're a good girl, Maggie,' or 'Margaret, we do care for you, and we do love you.' I was never told I was loved until I got married.

David Eva says that when he was at Fairbridge in the 1950s the cottage mothers 'didn't know what love was':

> Nobody gave you any affection . . . a lot of kids wanted affection and they just didn't get it. I can remember at one stage a kid hearing that his mother was sick . . . or something had happened. He was really down in the dumps but there was no affection.

Linda Gidman recalls:

> There was none of the nurturing ... The cottage
> mother would be so up and down, so militant, she
> didn't know how to come and comfort a child in need
> ... So there was none of this, 'Well, don't worry, we'll
> take care of you.'

In Canonbar Cottage we had a German cottage mother
named Ilse Boelter, who had come to Fairbridge with her
husband, Kurt, and their six-year-old daughter, Ulrica.
Kurt, a university graduate in agriculture, was the Fairbridge village garden supervisor. His wife was a graduate
in literature, including English, and we were all amazed at
her grasp of English grammar when we were studying it
at school.

I thought Mr Boelter was terrific. I remember him
showing us dozens of scars all over his body, which were
the legacy of fighting on the Russian front in World
War II. We had been brought up on a diet of tales of how
England beat Germany, and had hardly ever heard of the
far more significant eastern front. I was captivated by his
stories: he had been a captain and a tank commander
until his tank was blown up by the Russians. He had been
left to die as a hopeless case until one of the German
doctors decided to try to save him. After he recovered, he
served out the rest of the war in the Italian campaign. He
was convinced he would not have survived had he stayed
on the eastern front, where German losses were huge.

He was stern but never violent, and while many of the
supervisory staff at Fairbridge hit the children, Kurt and
his wife, who were cultured and dignified, never did. He
rolled his own cigarettes, like a lot of people did in those
days, and, knowing that we all smoked, tried to tell us
how dangerous and addictive it was. Of course, we
wouldn't listen.

Billy King, who was in Orange Cottage, remembers his cottage mother:

> Mrs Hatto was under the impression that the kids were there for her. Well, she did nothing. I never saw her iron anything, or cook a meal. We even each had a turn on cottage mother's quarters – we used to have to clean their bloody quarters as well as our own.

Daphne Brown remembers being one of the other lucky ones when she arrived, being put into a cottage that had a good cottage mother:

> I was quite happy. I can remember Mrs Tampling, she was my cottage mother, came and picked us up and took us from the truck to the gate of our cottage . . . I remember Mrs Tampling being very good to us girls . . . Her husband had died. She'd apparently married an eye specialist when she was in London and she was a nurse, and she had three children to him and he'd died – he was quite a bit older than her. And so she came back to Australia and she couldn't get a job because she had three children, and this job came up where she could have her children with her. So she took the job. She was very, very kind and very strict – I was a bit scared of her because she was so strict.

Mrs Tampling left after about three years and Daphne recalls: 'We had some awful cottage mothers after that . . . They got people who couldn't get jobs anywhere else . . . Some of them were dreadful. Dreadful.'

Joyce Drury remembers having some good cottage mothers, but others who were not so good:

We had one cottage mother – she wore skirts down to her ankles – and she used to cook our evening meal and it was always awful. One night she made, I can't remember what it was, it might have been scrambled eggs, and the oldest girl, Wickens, said, 'Don't eat this, it's rotten,' and then she said to the cottage mother, 'We're not going to eat this,' and the cottage mother got up on a chair and screamed at us.

. . . Then she sent one of the little ones to get the principal, Mr Beauchamp. And Beauchamp came with his little dog and he asked the cottage mother the problem and she told him she'd cooked this and we were refusing to eat it. Then he put some in the dish and said if the dog, whatever its name was, eats it, the children have got to eat it. And he puts the food [down] for the dog and the dog refuses to touch it, and he says to one of the girls, 'Pack it all up,' and to the cottage mother, 'Boil them an egg and toast.' . . . She wasn't there very long.

*

The fifteen barrack-style timber cottages in the village at Fairbridge Farm were all of a similar design. The dormitory at one end of the cottage had fifteen small, metal-framed beds. They were raised slightly at the end, as we had no pillows. Each bed had a kapok mattress, two ex-army blankets in summer and three in winter, and two calico sheets, one of which was laundered each week. There were no bed-side tables and, as I found out on that first night, the windows, which were on three sides of the dormitory, had to be kept open all year round. The reason was that Fairbridge had more beds squeezed into each dormitory than child-welfare regulations permitted. John Ponting, who came with me as a twelve-year-old to Fairbridge, recalls an encounter between a child-welfare inspector and Principal Woods:

I was on boss's duties one day when the child welfare came calling. I remember this joker measuring the dormitory in Gowrie Cottage; he then counted the beds and decided that it would never do to have that many beds in such a small space. Mr Woods asked what was the reason. The guy said it had to do with each child having x amount of space. Woods showed the guy the open windows on the three sides of the dormitory and this guy nearly had a heart attack when he was told that the windows were never closed.[3]

In each cottage bathroom there were two toilet cubicles with short saloon doors. Toilet rolls were rationed out to each cottage and, as Daphne Brown recalls, when they ran out of toilet paper the children had to make do with whatever they could find: 'I can remember we used to get four toilet rolls per month for fifteen children. Four toilet rolls! So we used to use any magazines or anything we had. It was quite horrific.'

The stove in the cottage kitchen was used for the preparation of the evening meal. Again, my brothers and I were lucky for most of our stay at Fairbridge. While our evening meal was often a boring and repetitive version of mutton and vegetables, we were better off than children in many of the other cottages.

David Eva spent seven years in Brown Cottage and remembers some appalling evening meals:

This is true. I'm not making this up . . . I came home from school and it was the cottage mother's day off. And normally they used to cook the [evening] meal the day before their day off and all the boys had to do was put it on the stove and heat it up. Now, this day she made this bloody soup. Now, her soup was just throwing the [mutton] flap in the bowl with a couple of onions floating on the top, and boil the Christ out of it, and leave it on the stove. Well, I came home from school this day and I looked in the bloody bowl and the bloody meat was nearly walking out of the saucepan. I took it to Woods, who was running the village work muster with the other children who had come home from school. And I went down there and shoved it in front of him and said, 'Would you eat this?' And he took the lid off and said, 'Oh, extra meat rations!' Extra meat rations? Maggots were crawling up the sides, they were. She'd just left it on the stove, no cover on it or nothing and the maggots were crawling all up the side and all over the meat and everything.

Before each meal at Nuffield Hall all the cottage's metal plates, bowls and mugs were brought over to the hall by one of the smaller children, who would set the table. The eating utensils were carried in a dixie, which was a four-gallon oil drum cut vertically in half with a piece of fencing wire attached to each end for a handle. After the meal, the remaining food on the plates and bowls would be scraped into the bin in the kitchen, then taken back to the cottage to be washed.

The scraps in the bin would be taken up to the piggery and boiled up for the pigs. If the food they served us in Nuffield Hall was inedible, we would try to eat as little as possible and scrape as much as we could into the pig bins. But Fairbridge did not tolerate wasted food. On many occasions Woods would inspect the pig bins and if too much food had been thrown out, it was immediately taken back to the cottage table to be served up to the children. It didn't matter that the mutton might be mixed with custard, or cabbage with semolina.

Billy King recalls Woods forcing a child to eat contaminated porridge and, on another occasion, ordering the children to eat the scraps straight from the pig bins:

> I've seen him have this kid sit at the table eating the porridge and him vomiting it back up and he had to stay there and spoon it back into his mouth until he ate it. And [another time] Woods went into the pig bins and got a ladleful each because there was too much waste [and] – with all the jelly and custard and rubbish they used to feed us – tip[ped] it all back and made us eat it.

Peter Bennett is one of many Fairbridge children to recall having trouble eating the porridge:

> I remember the porridge. I'll never forget the porridge because the . . . rolled oats used to come in a big 200-pound bag and by the time it got a third of the way down it was full of weevils. And one morning I was having my breakfast and I wouldn't eat it.

Principal Woods's reaction was much the same as it had been to the maggots in the mutton:

> 'What's the matter, Bennett?'
> And I said, 'It's got maggots in it, sir.'
> He said, 'They're not maggots. This is the larvae of the weevils. Good protein. Eat it.'

This 'waste not want not' philosophy extended to all food grown on the farm. Once, Kurt Boelter, the normally competent garden supervisor, planted an experimental crop of kohlrabi, a type of cabbage, and harvested it later in the season than he should have done. The bumper crop had become wooded. It smelt awful and tasted even worse. No one could eat it. All these years later I still feel nauseated by the smell of kohlrabi. For lunch sometimes a sizeable portion was piled on each child's plate. It was so disgusting that we hid it in our trouser pockets, hoping to get out of lunch in time to empty our pockets into the gardens before the gravy seeped through our pants and became obvious to the staff. Throwing out food was a serious offence.

On another occasion we had a bumper harvest of cucumbers. When I was rostered to make the sandwiches for the schoolkids I was instructed to give all the sandwiches cucumber fillings. Nothing else, just cucumber. When we arrived back at our cottages at night for the evening meal we were each expected to eat another cucumber; this went on until the crop had been eaten.

Not all the Fairbridge children remember the food being bad. John Harris, who arrived at Fairbridge as a nine-year-old in 1948, feels the choice of food was too limited, but he says he wouldn't complain about the quality. Joyce Drury also thought the food at Fairbridge was okay, particularly compared with her experiences in the late 1930s in England when she was a small girl and food was scarce:

> I found the food all right, especially when Mr Oates was the gardener and there'd be times when there would be lots of fruit growing on trees, and the strawberries, and we'd go out mushrooming . . . Or someone would say a farmer had rung up to say, 'We've got all these apples that are blown off the tree.' So we had fruit . . . [In] England fruit was a thing I got for Christmas in my little Christmas sock, where we got a few nuts, a comic and a piece of fruit and that was the Christmas stocking.

By and large, Fairbridge children were quite healthy. There were the usual illnesses and injuries that could be expected in a school of 150 children, but kids quickly toughened up when they arrived and it was unusual for us to be off sick.

Most of the children's ailments were treated in the village by a not-always-qualified nursing sister, who lived in tiny quarters attached to the back of the little hospital near the front gate of the school. The surgery opened immediately after breakfast and again every afternoon at 5 p.m., after the work was done, because it was assumed any health problems would not interfere with work. In more serious cases, children would be taken to the doctor in Molong or admitted to the Molong Hospital. Children were not permitted to stay in their bed in the cottage dormitory if they were ill – they had to go to this little Fairbridge hospital, where there was a four-bed ward for those who needed it. On occasions there were more serious health problems in the village, including an outbreak of hepatitis in 1959, which forced Fairbridge to quarantine much of the farm school and prevent children from going to school for several weeks.

There was no regular dental care and we would be taken into Molong if a tooth had to be taken out. But Fairbridge kids generally had good teeth because we ate very little sugar and few sweets.

The basic health care at Fairbridge was adequate for most children, but not for those with complicated medical conditions. Christina Murray, who arrived in Australia in 1939 as a seven-year-old, had serious medical problems that went unrecognised and untreated:

> I was the fruitcake! I was the biggest idiot . . . I had difficulty with everything. If we had sweets, because I didn't know at the time that I had sugar diabetes,

I just went off my rocker . . . I was living in no man's land . . . If I went to the cottage mother and said I had a headache, she'd say, 'You haven't got a headache; it's only in your mind.' So in the end you just suffered.

When I was twenty-three the doctor came back and said, 'You've got sugar diabetes; you've had it all your life.' . . . He asked, 'Do you have headaches?'

And I said, 'Yes, I've had terrible headaches. I've had them all my life – or the last ten years.'

And . . . he said, 'We've checked that out and there's a tumour.' Nobody [at Fairbridge] knew that I had a medical problem, which I think is atrocious.

In England, my brothers and I had regularly attended the local church and Sunday school, and had weekly religious instruction at school, so we were not surprised by the religious observance at Fairbridge – but it did play a bigger role in our daily lives than in the past.

Before eating breakfast in Nuffield Hall Woods would read a prayer and then each cottage would be rostered in turn to provide a boy and a girl to read the same two prayers every day.

We were also expected to say grace before every meal. At breakfast we would all chant: 'For what we are about to receive may the Lord make us truly thankful, through Jesus Christ's sake. Amen.' Before lunch, to a single note struck by one of the girls on the piano, we'd sing, 'For health and strength and daily food we praise thy name, O Lord.'

Margaret McLaughlan recalls the ritual:

The girl read a verse out of the prayer book, then the boy read a verse out of the prayer book, then Mr Woods . . . I think he had about two different prayers he would read. Then we would all have to say grace.

Then, if I was doing prayers – because they would change the children about from time to time – I'd have to walk over to the piano and press the middle C on the piano as a key note for everyone to sing grace . . . Then I would go back to my table and the boy would go back to his table.

When he designed the child-migrant scheme Kingsley Fairbridge said it would be 'non-denominational Christian' and that worship would be optional for the children. In his 1909 speech to the Oxford Colonial Club, he said: 'Priests of any Christian denomination passing through the school area may be permitted to hold meetings', but 'the children will be under no compulsion to attend them.'

In practice, Fairbridge was almost exclusively Anglican and attendance at church was compulsory. There were only a couple of Catholic children at Fairbridge because the Catholic church ran its own child-migrant schemes. We were all ordered to attend the church service in Nuffield Hall conducted by the Anglican vicar from St John's in Molong. After breakfast on Sunday we cleared up, moved the big tables to one side of the hall and put out the benches in rows, as pews for the service. An altar that was kept at the back of the hall was drawn out and covered, and two candles were lit for the service.

Then, on the first Sunday of each month, we went to the Church of England service at St John's, which was up toward the top of Molong. While Fairbridge kids welcomed any chance to get out of the farm school, most of us found these services excruciatingly dull. As Daphne Brown remembers:

And then Sunday was the same as Saturday but we used to have to go to church and I hated it because

they talked about was the resurrection and all that.
They never made it interesting for the children.

The old Fairbridge bus, which took us to church, was
famous in the central west of New South Wales for several
decades after World War II. Built in 1942, it had a normal
steel chassis but because of wartime shortages, its frame
and bodywork above the level of the windows were made
of timber. Only five of these 'austerity' buses were ever
made and Fairbridge bought this one when the government bus service sold them off cheaply in 1948. Although
only licensed to carry twenty-nine passengers, practically
all the children from the village – often over 100 – would
be packed aboard, with most standing or hanging out the
open doorways for the six-kilometre trip to town.

The bus had its own song, which most of us at Fairbridge learnt before we knew the words to the Fairbridge
Farm School song. There were a number of variations but
the most popular version, sung to the tune of 'The Road
to Gundagai', was:

> There's an old-fashioned bus,
> And it's meant to carry us,
> Along the road to Fairbridge Farm.
> It's got water in its petrol tank and sawdust in its
>   gears
> And it hasn't seen a garage,
> For over fifty years,
> Oh my Lord, Oh my Lord,
> Here comes Woodsy and his horde
> Along the road to
> Fairbridge Farm

David Wilson, who spent more than ten years at Fairbridge after arriving as a six-year-old in 1951, recalls

the tedium of going into Molong for the monthly church service:

> Of course, every first Sunday of the month we'd go into Molong to the C. of E. church there. And Ruth Woods would play the piano. And if she ever caught us talking, she'd tell her husband and the boss used to cane us. And yet he was twice as noisy, snoring away.

When the collection purse was passed around some of the more dutiful children put in a few coins, while others, pretending to be putting money in, were actually stealing.

In the original plans for the Fairbridge settlement at Molong it was always envisaged that the village would have its own chapel, but it was not until 1961 that enough money was raised to build one. After many years of fundraising, driven largely by Ruth Woods, an old army hut was bought from the nearby town of Parkes, brought to the village and converted into a chapel. I remember being off school with a skin infection and spending a week giving the little church its first coat of glossy white paint. (After the Fairbridge Farm School was closed down in 1974 the building was sold again and moved to the local town of Yeoval, to be converted into a private home.)

From time to time children from other Protestant religions came to Fairbridge, and they were allowed to attend their own church. Joyce Drury remembers:

> Sunday was funny . . .because I was Wesleyan and those of us that had a different religion to Anglican had to go to the Anglican service in the morning. Then Sunday afternoon might have been free time for everyone else but we had to go into Molong to the Methodist church . . . So I became confirmed in the

Anglican Church and the Methodist Church. And I hated it because we had to stay quiet for church. And we had to get dressed up and walk all the way into Molong for church, I can remember that.

The Miller family – Reg, Doug, Gwen and Kathy – came out to Fairbridge in 1951 from Grimsby in Yorkshire, and their brother Huey followed a year later. They were part of a Roman Catholic family of ten children. When their mother died, their father, who 'hated the nuns', arranged for them to go to Fairbridge. Gwen recalls how they would all attend the Catholic church in Molong:

> We were the first Catholics at Fairbridge and the nuns in England were in touch with the nuns in Molong. They paid for a taxi to take us to the church in Molong and bring us back again. And if we had Holy Communion once a month, the nuns fed us breakfast and it was the best meal we ever had while we were at Fairbridge.

No doubt inspired by the Miller children, the enterprising Paddy O'Brien, the eldest boy in our group that had come to Fairbridge together in 1959, approached Woods to say that he and his sisters, Mary and Myrtle, were Methodists and he wanted the three of them to attend the Methodist service in Molong each week. Like many Australian country towns, Molong, despite having a population of barely 2000, boasted a fine range of stone churches: Church of England, Catholic, Presbyterian, Methodist and Baptist. Not to be outdone by Paddy, my older brother Dudley approached Woods and told him we were Presbyterians and wished to worship in our own church. This was not entirely true. We had never been baptised and as children had attended any number of different

Sunday schools, usually the one closest to where we were living at the time. But it worked and it gave us an excuse to get off the farm every Sunday, when the other kids were obliged to go to the Anglican service in Nuffield Hall.

It wasn't easy to get to the Presbyterian church every week, due to a lack of reliable transport provided by Fairbridge. Eventually Paddy was old enough to get a driver's licence and drive one of the Fairbridge trucks, but this was only any good to us when the timing of the Methodist and Presbyterian services coincided. Mostly we were happy to walk or just hitch a ride.

For all the religion at Fairbridge, only a few carried it into their adult lives, such as Roland Bigrigg, who became an Anglican vicar, and Malcolm 'Flossy' Field, who became a server and deacon of the altar in the Anglo-Catholic tradition.

Lennie Magee left Fairbridge with no religious conviction whatsoever but became 'born again' later in life. While at Fairbridge, Lennie didn't take religion any more seriously than the rest of us:

> On the night I was confirmed into the Anglican church I was with two other kids stealing chocolates from the shop next door ... On Sundays the vicar ... inflicted some of the dullest and [most] tedious sermons ever concocted upon us hapless kids. Unwittingly, these men in white dresses robbed God of any life and personality.[4]

For most Fairbridge children, religious observance was something you had to do at the farm school, and you left it behind when you finally left Fairbridge.

Within a few weeks of arriving at Fairbridge we began to develop friendships with the kids who were already at the farm school. In addition to the other boys in Canonbar Cottage I started to make friends with a few of the boys my age who went with me each day on the bus to school. Apart from the fact that most of them expected never to see their parents again, I wasn't aware of any great differences in our circumstances and within a few weeks I was feeling more settled, and very much a Fairbridge kid.

5

FAMILIES

Contrary to popular belief, hardly any of the children who went to Fairbridge were orphans. Most came from very poor families whose parents – often single or abandoned – had been persuaded that Fairbridge could provide a better life for their children. Further contact with their children was discouraged from the moment kids were put in the care of Fairbridge, even to the extent that parents were asked not to go to wave goodbye when the ship set sail for Australia. This was not, however, made clear to parents when they agreed to hand over care of their offspring to the farm school.

Some children had already been placed in homes in the UK by their parents before they were sent to Australia under the Fairbridge scheme. These children may have been placed in institutions because of economic hardship or some other circumstance that made it too hard for them to be brought up by their mother or father. But some, such as David Wilson, feel they were simply unwanted and are still bitter about that:

> I always remember we got on the train at Newcastle and the lady with the child welfare took us to London and our mother stood on the Newcastle railway

station and that was the last time I've ever seen my mother.

I would never send my children, like my mother did, you know, a five-year-old. Getting rid of kids because you don't want them. Because my parents – not my father so much – but my mother, she didn't want us. Couldn't wait to get rid of us.

Gwen Miller also thought she and her sister and brothers were unwanted by their father, and that being part of a big extended Catholic family, they could have stayed in Grimsby.

My mother died when I was five years old. She left ten children aged seven months to fifteen years old. I didn't ever forgive my father for giving us away . . . We had wonderful family support and we were a close family . . . We felt abandoned. We *were* abandoned. He sent the youngest four children 12,000 miles away to a place somewhere where not one family member could visit. There was no need to send us away. We had a family, we weren't poor yet he still gave us away . . . I hated him till the day he died.

Well, I wish it had never happened. I never forgave my father. He did that to us, didn't he? And it wasn't necessary.

About being sent to Fairbridge, Derek Moriarty says: 'I'm bitter about why I went there. I'm also bitter about the fact that my mother knew where we were the whole time.'

When Derek was three and his brother Paul was one they were placed in different children's homes after his parents separated.

Now, when he was five and I was seven, one day they said, 'Your brother's coming,' and I didn't even know I had a brother. Then, just before my eighth birthday or just after – it might have been just after, I think – somebody came along and said, 'You guys are going out to Australia.' And, even though we were attending school, Australia was just a name. I didn't know anything about it, didn't know where it was. 'Would you like to go?' they asked, and I said, 'No, I'm quite happy here where I am.' Which I was. It was only a small orphanage and it was quite good, although it was very, very strict, and there were things we had to do that we didn't like. But Paul saw it as an adventure and so I said, 'Yeah, yeah, yeah.'

After nearly seventy years, Margaret McLaughlan is still saddened about becoming a child migrant in 1939 as a five-year-old because nobody wanted her or her six-year-old brother. She says her mother was in Scotland while they lived with their father in England, and both children were neglected.

I've got reports – they're in my cupboard there – from when I left England to come to Australia from . . . these orphanages, that we were just little urchins, my brother and I. No one wanted the McLaughlan kids. No one wanted to own, nobody wanted to adopt them. So they might as well go to Australia. And I cry every time I look at them. That's very, very sad. Nobody wanted my brother and I. After reading these reports many years later, it really distresses me to think that we are all God's children, and it can happen to absolutely anyone. And it happened to hundreds – many a thousand children went through what I went through.

Other Fairbridge children have no idea how they ended up in children's homes in England. David Eva has no recollection of ever being in a family and only remembers being in homes:

> I never knew my parents and I was put in this home when I suppose I was three or four . . . I can't remember too much at all. I didn't like it there. It was sort of like a prison camp.
>
> One day somebody came into the home and said to me, 'Do you want to go to Australia?' I think the other place was South Africa, I could be wrong.

The only time David remembers seeing his mother was shortly before he left England:

> We were having all these vaccinations and somebody came into the place and said to me, 'David, we'd like you to go and see your mother, she's in hospital,' and I can remember so plainly going in the car and going to this hospital and seeing this woman in bed. And she said to me, 'I'm your mother.'
>
> Then she asked, 'Do you want to go to Australia?' And I said, 'Oh, yes,' you know, the boat trip, six weeks on the big boat.
>
> And she said to me, 'I'll give you something to remember me by.' And it was a watch. I haven't got it now but . . . I can remember that watch. She also gave me a letter case with envelopes and where I could write. I never saw her again and she never wrote to me, and that was it . . . There was no hugging or anything like that. She was sitting in bed. I don't know what was wrong with her. That was all. Then I went back to Knockholt and then, of course, it was full steam ahead.

While there were many children who came to Fairbridge from children's homes, most were from poor families who had been convinced that Fairbridge would provide their children with a way out of the poverty cycle. For these parents, signing over their children was an enormous sacrifice, made in the hope their children would have a better future than if they stayed in the UK. Daphne Brown's mother turned to Fairbridge in desperation:

> My father left my mother when I was about three, and she had a very hard time because of the war. There was no money and my sister and I were at school and when Mum got work . . . we had to sit and wait or play in the streets . . . So, one day she came and asked us if we'd like to live in Australia, and of course we thought it was great.

Joyce Drury, who was a child of the Depression, says her parents sent her and her siblings to Fairbridge because they loved them:

> I came basically because we were poor, but we had a happy family. I didn't ever hear Mum and Dad have an argument. We always knew that we were loved, and we didn't have that sense of them sending us away, but they were doing this out of caring for us.
>
> Dad . . . was a pianist, and with the Depression they weren't wanting him to play the piano, and he was fixing pianos and never had any money and he ended up selling shoelaces door to door and my mother, who hadn't worked at all . . . found night work, nursing old people. So they really wanted the best for us.
>
> My brothers had to go and find bottles, and they would go and get, like, sixpence for half a dozen bottles, and then they would go to the biscuit factory

and get this bag of broken biscuits . . . And that bag
of broken biscuits would be our meal. There was no
money for food but I can't remember going hungry.

Joyce's mother was one of the few parents to say goodbye
to her children at the wharf when they sailed from
England:

> My mother told me how she felt when she left and
> when the ship pulled out . . . She was very sad, but
> she walked past . . . the church and thought, 'What
> have I done? What have I done?' and went into the
> church and she said she just sat in the back, right at the
> back, crying and crying. And then a real peace came
> over her and she knew she had done the right thing.

Malcolm Field, or 'Flossy' as all the Fairbridge kids knew
him because of his mop of very blond hair, was one of
the few children to come to Fairbridge who was not from
a deprived background. Flossy says that his father was a
university science graduate and a structural engineer who
worked secretly during the war on the development of
jet aircraft. After the war the family went to live in a
seventeenth-century rectory in Dorset.

> In 1946 . . . my parents rented an old rectory. My
> mother had help in the house . . . there were eighteen
> rooms; there were stone floors in the kitchen and the
> scullery . . . We each had our own bedroom. There
> was a main staircase and then there was a servant's
> staircase . . . They were our best years.

In 1949 his father developed a brain tumour and died,
leaving a wife and four children. Laurie was ten; Malcolm
was seven; Keith was five; and Jane was three.

So things suddenly changed. We were scattered among relatives for six months while mother sort of coped . . . So, after she got herself sorted out we came home and she bought a house in Yeovil, took in a lodger, and after some time, the lodger became a boyfriend and he was married so she couldn't marry him, but she changed her name by deed poll to his name, and his name was Wriggler. Not a nice person.

Within a couple of years the family had moved to Southampton and Flossy's mum was driving around in an MG sports car. One afternoon after school Flossy asked why Keith and Jane were not at home, and he was told, 'They've gone to Australia.'

She'd heard about Fairbridge. She wanted to spend more time with the boyfriend . . . She wanted more room for the lodgers . . . this is what she told the social services, the children's officer, 'because I don't have much income'.

Six months later she decided, 'Oh, I'll get rid of the other two.' So, Laurie and I end up in Knockholt, but within two days she came up in her sports car and took us back home.

After the summer holidays, Flossy recalls, his mother decided that they would all migrate to Australia.

Not on the £10 [assisted passage scheme]. She paid her way, first class on the *Strathaird*. Anyway, Eric Wriggler, the boyfriend, and her were to have one cabin and Laurie and I had the other cabin. And when we got to the ship – no sign of Eric Wriggler. He'd dumped her.

Flossy says that within a week of sailing, his mother had forgotten Wriggler and had struck up a relationship with the waiter at their table, who was a good ten years her junior:

> So we arrive in Australia. My mum sends a telegram to Fairbridge to say that she was coming up and Mr Woods had told Keith and Jane, 'Your mother's coming to visit you.' So Jane told all the girls in Rose Cottage, 'My mother's coming to visit me,' because not many children had parents coming out to visit.

Meanwhile, Flossy's mother and Mark the waiter were enjoying themselves in Sydney before he was due to sail back to England.

> After a week, she didn't bother going up to Fairbridge, only 180 miles. Forgot about them. Next thing, we're on the ship, going back to England, because Mark was a steward and had to go back to England, so why shouldn't we go back, first class all the way.

Within a week of arriving back in England, Flossy and Laurie were returned to the Fairbridge house at Knockholt in Kent by their mother. They sailed with a party of children for the Fairbridge Farm School on the S.S. *Chitral* on 19 December 1952, qualifying as probably the only people to have migrated to Australia from Britain twice in the same year.

Before a child was allowed to go out to the Fairbridge Farm School his or her parent or guardian was required to sign over legal guardianship. The form they were required to sign read:

I, being the father, mother, guardian, person having
the actual custody of the child named _____
hereby declare that I consent to his/her emigration to
Canada/Australia through the Fairbridge Society and
I further authorize the said Society and the Officers
to exercise in Canada/Australia all the functions as
guardians, including power to have carried out such
medical and/or surgical treatment as may be considered necessary for the child's welfare.

Few were aware that in signing away guardianship they
relinquished all rights to their children and would find it
practically impossible ever to get them back, even when
the children were dreadfully unhappy at Fairbridge and
their parents made every effort to get them home.

As a British Government report into child migration in
1953 noted:

There have been a few cases in which the parents have
followed their children to Australia, but this is not
encouraged as the child scheme is primarily for those
children who have been deprived of a normal home
life. The Child Immigration Officer in London and the
voluntary organisations have therefore been asked to
do their utmost to select children whose parents are
not likely to follow them.[1]

For most of its existence, Fairbridge adopted the attitude
that it had rescued children from deprived environments
and was taking over where parents had failed or were
irresponsible. Fairbridge took a dim view of parents who
tried to later reunite with their children. At one stage, in
a letter to the British Government seeking further
support, the director of Fairbridge argued that because
the farm school offered fresh opportunities to children, it
was undesirable for the children to ever return home.

> We feel that such opportunities should be given to more children who need a fresh start in life away from an unhappy environment in Britain – apart from the risk of many such children drifting back to their former surroundings by undesirable parents claiming them when old enough to work.[2]

Smiley Bayliff, who went to Fairbridge aged eight, was to learn almost forty years later how his parents fought in vain for years to have the family reunited. (Ian Bayliff, Syd Lee, Graham Lee and Stewart Lee all had the same father, Sydney Lee.)

> The last time we saw them was on 12 December 1954 at Manchester railway station.
>
> They always believed they could get us back and they tried for years but Fairbridge stopped them. Then they wanted to come out but were stopped. There's letters on the file which show they went every which way to stop them from coming out.
>
> We were a large family and very poor. Dad was a labourer and struggled to give us much at all. He asked about migrating and Australia House sent all the information and brochures, including about Fairbridge, which told my parents that we could have a much better life with lots of opportunities than if we stayed where we were in Stretford.

The boy's parents were sold on the idea. Their mother, Dora, wrote to Fairbridge asking if her sons could go: 'Trusting I will get a reply from you to say they could go for I would like them boys to get something I can't give them in life.'[3]

After hearing back from Fairbridge, who sent more information about the scheme, Dora wrote again, full of

The first party of Fairbridge children bound for Molong from Britain in February 1938.

The Fairbridge Farm School, built in an arc around Nuffield Hall.

'Boys to be farmers.' A trainee boy harrowing.

'Girls for farmers' wives.' Christina Murray (right) making butter outside the principal's house above Nuffield Hall.

'This is not charity, this is an imperial investment.' The Prince of Wales, later King Edward VIII, in 1934. He launched a fund-raising appeal in London for Fairbridge with a personal donation of £1000. (Photograph courtesy of APL)

Kingsley Fairbridge, the founder of the farm schools. He believed, 'The average London street Arab and workhouse child can be turned into an upright and productive citizen of our overseas Empire.'

Princess Elizabeth after her marriage, 1947. She donated £2000 from her wedding gifts 'to assist individual old Fairbridgian boys and girls get a start in life'. The loan fund failed. (Photograph courtesy of Hulton-Deutsch Collection/Corbis/APL)

Lord Slim became chairman of the London Fairbridge Society. Slim dismissed Principal Woods when he proposed to remarry a divorcee, but took no action against staff who physically abused the children. (Photograph courtesy of Hulton-Deutsch Collection/Corbis/APL)

David's party of 1959 in front of the magnificent John Howard Mitchell House in Kent prior to leaving for Australia. Back row, left to right: Mary O'Brien, John Ponting, Richard Hill, Paddy O'Brien, Dudley Hill, Billy King, David Hill. Front row: Myrtle O'Brien, unknown, Wendy and Paul Harris, Beryl Daglish, unknown.

Eight-year-old Ian 'Smiley' Bayliff in his new outfit, shortly before sailing with his three brothers to Australia. His parents tried unsuccessfully for years to get their boys back from Fairbridge.

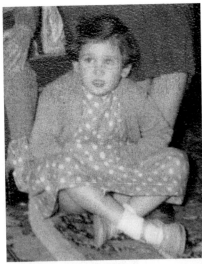

Vivian Bingham arrived at Fairbridge as a four-year-old and was treated badly by her cottage mother, who held her head down the toilet for wetting her bed.

The magnificent first-class lounge of the S.S. *Strathaird*. None of us had ever seen the luxury we experienced on the journey out to Australia. (Photograph courtesy of the State Library of Victoria)

Once at Fairbridge we ate our meals from metal plates and bowls, sitting on wooden benches in front of lino-top tables.

'The boss', Principal Woods, a towering influence over Fairbridge for twenty-eight years, with his former missionary wife, Ruth, on the steps of the Fairbridge chapel.

A 'widow of Empire', cottage mother Mrs Hodgkinson, who had been Lady Routledge in India. 'She was imperious, superior, upper class. We were there to do her bidding; slaves and lackeys on tap,' recalls former Fairbridgian Michael Walker.

Five days on a train across the Rocky Mountains: Fairbridge children who came the long way round via Canada in 1940. A shy six-year-old Peter Bennett is on the left, obscured.

Gwen Miller as a fifteen-year-old trainee girl. She remembers Fairbridge as a 'cold, heartless place' where childhoods were stolen and the word love was never mentioned.

Ten-year-old Lennie Magee (right) at the dairy to pick up and deliver milk.

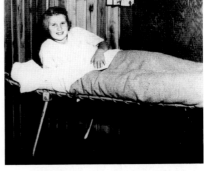

A report on Fairbridge noted that the beds had no pillows and 'consist of wire mesh, which tends to sag, on a steel frame, with very poor mattresses. There is no other furniture in the dormitories and the floors are bare wood'.

Lunch in Nuffield Hall, with the boss silhouetted on the stage at the head of the staff dining table.

The trainee girls were inspected each morning before work on the verandah of Nuffield Hall by the Fairbridge hospital nursing sister.

The village bell ruled our lives.
A kitchen trainee rings the breakfast bell.

enthusiasm for what Fairbridge had offered: 'I have studied your book. The life will be very nice for them. I can't give them the same here.'[4] And later: 'Both Mr Lee and myself made the decision between us; we would like the boys to go together for they will get a good chance in life.'[5]

Within a couple of months the boys were taken into the Fairbridge house in Knockholt, and were in a party of twenty-two children who sailed for Australia on the S.S. *Strathnaver* in February 1955.

Smiley says his parents agreed to the scheme believing that they would be able to get back together as a family, either in Australia or back in England, and would not have let the children go otherwise:

> My parents would not have let us go if they knew they wouldn't be able to get us back. They were encouraged by Fairbridge to believe they would be able to eventually follow us out to Australia and join us but also that if we wanted to, we could come home after two years.

At the time the boys were sent away, a standard condition of all assisted migration to Australia was that migrants stayed for two years. If they didn't they would be forced to repay the cost of the fare.

Smiley says: 'Mum believed if we were unhappy, we could come home.' As it turned out, the boys were not happy at Fairbridge. Smiley recalls he and his older brothers, Syd and Graham, writing to say they wanted to come home:

> We hated it, particularly Syd and me. Our letters home were aerograms and we only wrote a few lines because we were so young but we made it clear we

were very unhappy with the treatment we were getting at Fairbridge.

Within months of the boys arriving in Australia and after receiving letters saying how unhappy they were, Dora wrote back telling the boys she would try to reunite the family: 'Well, boys, what do you think, shall we all come over to Australia to live or would you like to come to Stretford, so write and let us know.'[6]

Smiley remembers the letters from his mother and excitedly discussing the idea of a reunion with his brother Syd and the other boys in Blue Cottage at Fairbridge: 'I was as happy as Larry with the thought I'd be going home. I shouldn't have, but I boasted to the other kids at Blue Cottage that I was getting out of here.'

Fairbridge, which intercepted all the children's incoming and outgoing mail, moved to stop the parents. Principal Woods wrote to the director of the Fairbridge Society in London, W. B. Vaughan, to tell him about the parents' mail to the children. He wrote: 'I hope you will be able to explain to the parents that notions of going back again to England are both impractical and injurious to the children's emotional well being.'[7]

Vaughan, in turn, wrote to Miss E. M. Knight, the regional agent for Fairbridge in Manchester, who had recruited the Lee children to Fairbridge. He asked her to visit the parents and tell them not to encourage the children with any notion they would be getting back together.[8]

Knight went round to the Lees' house and told the parents in no uncertain terms they were not getting their children back, and reminded them that they had signed away their rights when they signed over guardianship. Knight wrote in a letter to Vaughan:

I am quite furious at the very suggestion of bringing them home.

I have replied to Mr Lee's letter reminding him of the statement he signed when the boys went, in which he agreed to leave them in the care of the Fairbridge Society.[9]

The Lees were not the only parents trying to get their children back. At about the same time as this, Julia Buswell's parents wrote to Fairbridge to ask if their daughter could come home because she was unsettled and unhappy. Woods wrote to Vaughan:

So, I hope the Buswells can be made to understand that there is just no question of Julia ever going back – unless she reaches a pitch of unmanageability that we would want to send her back and there is no likelihood of that if the parents will undertake not to unsettle her.[10]

Meanwhile, Smiley's parents continued to agitate to be reunited with their children. In a letter later in the year to Miss Knight, Dora pleaded:

I'm writing these few lines to ask you would it be possible for me to have the boys home for I want them back. They have been away for nearly twelve months and it has seemed like twelve years. So, I trust you will let me know how I go about getting them back home again.[11]

Fifteen months later, Vaughan recorded in a file note that Miss Knight had called to say: 'Mrs Lee wants her children back. I said they were wards of the State.'[12]

Dora didn't stop there. The following year she wrote to the Australian High Commission in London:

> Please could you let me know how I go about getting the four boys home from Fairbridge Farm School Molong, they want to come back so I want them back.[13]

Before the boys had departed for Australia Fairbridge had left open the possibility of the parents following them out from England. They had made it clear, via a local social worker, that they would have to wait two years, though. Vaughan had written to the social worker:

> We do not accept children whose parents plan to follow them shortly, so if Mr. and Mrs. Lee are serious in their intention, we would have to ask them to sign an undertaking to the effect that they would not proceed with the emigration plans until the boys have been in Australia for at least two years.[14]

Nearly four years after the boys had gone to Fairbridge and after many failed attempts to get them back, the Lees applied to migrate to Australia. Their application was rejected:

> This office has recently received application forms from Mr Sydney Lee of 25 Coniston Road, Stretford, Lancs, who states that he wishes to travel to Australia with his wife and four children in order to join the four children who are already at the Fairbridge Farm School at Molong.
>
> You will recall that in 1957 Mrs Lee requested the return of these boys to this country but in view of the cost involved no further action was taken at this time.

> We have written to Mr Lee indicating that it is not
> possible to assist him under a group nomination at
> present, but that it would be helpful if he could obtain
> a personal nomination for himself and his family.[15]

Lee tried again the following year to migrate to Australia
and was told even more firmly that he would not be
accepted:

> This office has advised Mr Lee that he would not be
> considered under a suitable group nomination at
> present and that the prospect of considering him in
> this way in the future is not very good. Mr Lee has
> been further advised that he will not be eligible for
> consideration as a Commonwealth nominee after his
> 50th birthday on 6/7/59.[16]

It was to be more than forty years before Smiley learnt
that his parents had fought for years to get him and his
brothers back.

> For all those years I thought they had abandoned us.
> I felt terrible. I went to see my mother in 1997 in
> England and told her I now had my Fairbridge
> records and asked her why she hadn't told us that
> she'd tried for years to get us back. She turned around
> and said, 'I thought you wouldn't believe me.' And
> you know what? I probably wouldn't, but now I
> know it was true.

Lennie Magee was also to find out forty years later that
his mother had wanted to come out to Australia when he
was nine years old to be with him, but had been told not
to come by Woods. Lennie had missed his mum at Fairbridge and for decades believed she had forgotten him.

I used to ask myself the question, like countless other Fairbridge kids: 'Will I ever see my mother again?' I had no idea that the boss had already firmly closed the door on any such notion. In 1955 he had written to her. The letter, which I still have, was short, poorly typed and gave a rather uninterested impression. After telling her how fabulously I was getting on, in the last paragraph he wrote, 'You speak of selling your home and coming out to Australia. I would strongly recommend you not doing that as housing is even more difficult to get in Australia than in England. Wait for some years at least.'

So she never came. Forty years later when I saw the letter I was dumbfounded. My mother didn't even own a house. Little boys needed love. I would have been happier in a tent in a sea of mud. If I had a mother.[17]

Billy King, who sailed to Australia in the same party of children as I did in 1959, found out decades later when he went back to Cornwall that his mother had changed her mind immediately after signing the authorisation for Fairbridge to send him to Australia.

And I can remember Mum telling me before she passed away that she tried to get me back – like it was only a few days after she signed the paper, a week or something. They told her that I was already gone on the boat to Australia and it was too late. But I was still at Knockholt. Because I can remember how long we were there. I think we were there for about six weeks or something.

*

My brothers and I wrote letters every week to Mum and she wrote as regularly as us. We had been brought up to respect the privacy of other people's mail and it was upsetting to know that every letter from Mum had already been opened and read – Fairbridge intercepted all the children's incoming and outgoing mail. When we wrote a letter we had to hand it to the cottage mother unsealed before it was posted.

Having a mother to write to was a great comfort, as was the knowledge that one day we would be out of that place and back together as a family. But in the meantime I had to face the reality from very early on that I was stuck at Fairbridge, probably for some years, and, like everyone else, I had no choice but to try to fit in and make the most of it.

BOOK 2

6

THE BOSS

The most important person at Fairbridge, the man who ruled over every aspect of our lives, was the principal, and the most prominent of Fairbridge Farm School's principals was 'the boss', Frederick Kinnersley Smithers Woods. He presided over the school from 1942 until 1966 and was the single most dominant figure in the Fairbridge story.

Woods was omnipotent. A giant bear of a man with extraordinary physical strength, he stood over six feet four inches tall and weighed more than twenty stone. He was everything and everywhere at Fairbridge, a part of the lives of almost every one of more than a thousand children who passed through the farm school. He organised our days; hired and fired the staff; rostered every child at work and play; set the rules and enforced discipline; dispensed punishment; and trained the boys and the girls at most sports, including rugby league, soccer, hockey, cricket, athletics and swimming. He was the driver of the old Fairbridge bus, the Boy Scout troop leader and the Wolf Cub pack leader. He ran the Junior Farmers Club and operated the antiquated film projector on the odd occasion we saw a movie. He only rarely took a holiday.

The first principal of the farm school, Richard ('Dickie')

Beauchamp, a retired Royal Navy officer, was appointed shortly before the first party of boys arrived at Fairbridge in 1938. Len Cowne, who was in the first party of boys, remembers him as a 'dapper little Englishman of the old school who met us with his wife Molly' when the boys arrived by ship.

The London Fairbridge Society, which had hired Beauchamp, regarded him as a successful appointment, but after only two years in the job he was suspended by the Sydney Fairbridge Council and immediately resigned. While only the London Fairbridge Society had the power to hire or fire the principal, the local council could suspend him if the circumstances were serious enough. The Sydney council did just this, and offered Beauchamp the opportunity to resign. According to the chairman of the council, Beauchamp had 'failed in his duty' to prevent 'immoral and perverted practices that have been indulged in on a serious scale' at Fairbridge.[1] It seems there had been some nocturnal liaisons between boys and girls, in the cottages and in the principal's house, and even the suggestion of some homosexual activity. Beauchamp was ordered to leave the property within twelve hours. He later moved to New Zealand.

Len Cowne recalls rumours circulating that the principal had been 'fondling some of the senior girls' before leaving 'for New Zealand in what appeared to be indecent haste'.[2]

London had no choice but to accept Sydney's decision, though the society was unimpressed by the suspension of Beauchamp and the appointment of the farm supervisor, Mr E. Heath, to the position of acting principal, over the head of the assistant principal, F. K. S. Woods. The secretary of the London Fairbridge Society reported to his board that they had not received a detailed report of the council's dissatisfaction with the principal, but that

telegrams indicated Mr Beauchamp had failed to control
his staff and sufficiently discipline the children. The secretary also said that the New South Wales council had been
informed that Mr Heath had neither the training nor
qualifications the London committee considered necessary for 'the direction and care of the Fairbridge children'.[3]

In a letter dated 25 September 1940, the chairman of
the London Fairbridge Society, Sir Charles Hambro, made
it clear to Beauchamp that, while London accepted the
decision, they disagreed with it:

> And now, as to yourself, I must tell you that I am very
> unhappy that . . . you have been overtaken by your
> enemies while serving Fairbridge . . . We have lost an
> irreplaceable principal and you have lost the job that
> gave you scope and suited your aims in life. We are
> both, then, in sad case and I see no way of winning
> back the position.[4]

Hambro told Beauchamp they were trying to think of an
alternative way to fit him into the Fairbridge organisation, though it wasn't clear how they would do so.
Hambro was at pains to emphasise that the society would
not forget what they owed him, 'and certainly the
children and their parents will not forget'.

In the end, Beauchamp was not found another job in
the Fairbridge organisation and Heath continued as
acting principal for the next two years.

Heath had come to Fairbridge in May 1938 as the farm
supervisor only weeks after the first party of children
had arrived. He had been the farm manager at the Dr
Barnardo's child-migrant training farm that had been
operating for some years in Picton, New South Wales.

After only two years as acting principal, in 1942 Heath

sought leave from Fairbridge to work during the war with the Red Cross, and Woods was left to run the farm school. In 1944 Heath resigned and became a camp welfare officer with the UN Relief and Rehabilitation Agency.

Woods had started work at Fairbridge in 1939 as assistant to the principal. With his wife, Ruth, he had escorted the fifth party of Fairbridge children from England to Molong on the S.S. *Strathnaver* in August 1939.

Woods was a larger-than-life character whom all of us still vividly remember. I remember him as a person capable of insensitive and even brutal acts, yet on some occasions he displayed remarkable tenderness.

As an eight-year-old, Smiley Bayliff was hospitalised for several months with rheumatic fever. Even years later, when Woods picked us up – shivering, wet and covered in mud – after playing a game of rugby league on a cold winter's afternoon in Orange, he would always remember to order Smiley to sit up in the front of the truck, where it was warmer.

Woods was always gentle with the tiniest of the children. When we went swimming the small children clung to his huge frame as he swam out to the middle of the farm dam. Linda Gidman, who is critical of many aspects of Fairbridge, has fond memories of Woods:

> And the other thing that was lovely about Fairbridge was Woodsy . . . I recall, when it was your birthday he'd come along and say, 'Gee, I know it's someone's birthday.' And he'd be like this – he'd be looking up and down like that, and I'm saying, 'It's me, it's me' – you know, things like that. I do have fond memories of him . . . I think [he] might have been a father figure.
>
> I used to sit behind him in the Fairbridge bus, and he would be the first one when we got to the dam, he

would take me out ... this small child he'd bring down to the water, very gently put me into the water and teach me how to swim.

Woods was physically imposing and we were amazed by his great strength. I recall one Saturday morning on village muster we were replacing an old fence in the Ilkley Moor paddock. We were having difficulty digging out the old corner post: there must have been about five of us with crowbars and mattocks and ropes, digging deep around this wooden post, but we couldn't get it out, however much we tried. Eventually an impatient Woods came over, climbed down into the big hole we had dug around the base, wrapped his huge arms around the post and with a grunt pulled it out. We stood in awe.

We all respected him and most of us feared him. I learnt very quickly at Fairbridge to keep out of his way as much as possible.

Lennie Magee remembers Woods and Ruth:

F. K. S. Woods ... was a giant who loomed over us, filling our horizon in every way ... He loved the outdoors and wore shorts from which protruded muscular legs of Mr Universe proportions. Behind his strong face and Roman nose was a keen and hungry intellect. There was a rocky concreteness about him. He was masculine, even boyish, except his lips. They had a slight hint of feminine softness. There is no doubt that to his own family he was probably the greatest guy in the whole wide world. From the moment I arrived at the farm to the day I left I was petrified and almost speechless whenever I had to stand before him.

His wife, Ruth, had first represented England in hockey and then went off to Africa as a missionary. She still looked and dressed like one. It was rumoured she was the daughter of an Archbishop of Canterbury. Although they were incredibly selfless and benevolent, to me they were both unapproachable and their austerity frightened the life out of me.[5]

A number of the Fairbridge kids liked Woods and some of them remember him with great affection. John Ponting remembers Woods as the 'father I never had'. Gwen Miller has many awful memories of Fairbridge, but she can recall some good times with Woods and was even more positive about Ruth:

> I was caned many times by Mr Woods. It hurt, oh, how it hurt, but I didn't cry once – I looked him in the eye defiantly. But I didn't mind Mr Woods. I remember all the times he took us to sporting things, the pictures and the circus when it was in town. I liked Mrs Woods. I always got the feeling that she liked me. She was the only one that ever told me that I was a good worker and thanked me for doing a heap of ironing for her.

Woods was accountable to two masters. The power to hire and fire the principal rested with the London Fairbridge Society, but on a day-to-day basis he was answerable to the Fairbridge Council of New South Wales. The chairman of the Sydney council was a regular visitor to Fairbridge, but the council as a whole only came once a year, in spring, when it would judge the cottage garden competition.

The visits of the council were quite staged. The cottage gardens had months of preparation and the village received weeks of sprucing up. We were on our best behaviour and were ordered to wear shoes around the village for the weekend. For our midday dinner in Nuffield Hall we put sheets across the tables to give the impression that we normally had tablecloths and, rather than the usual mutton, we ate wonderful dishes that we would not see again till the same time the next year. As Lennie Magee recalls:

> We became unwitting partners and members of the world's biggest con. Gardens were fastidiously weeded, gleaming white sheets were placed on every table, and large pigs and chickens were slaughtered for their succulent white meat. After we worked our butts off to make every floor shine, we polished every doorknob, scoured every sink and toilet, and turned every cottage dining table into a mirror. The whole world became bright, sunny and genial as every child was scrubbed clean until it hurt, dressed in new clothes and made to wear shoes.
>
> When these well-meaning folk sat on the stage at the staff table in the Nuffield Hall and smiled down at us . . . politely eating our lunch, they were a hundred million miles away . . . Eventually, they stood up and waved us all goodbye as they left the hall, clambered into their cars and slowly drove away; no doubt amazed at the impact they were making on the poor and needy. Meanwhile as their dust was still settling, the tablecloths went, the meat went, the clothes and shoes went, and so did the glow and the smiles.[6]

Woods and his wife committed their lives to the Fairbridge scheme, but over the years he increasingly became an anachronistic Edwardian disciplinarian and an overzealous agent of the British Empire – at a time when the Empire was in decline. He upheld the values of a world that had already been swept away by modernisation. In many respects, Woods and the Fairbridge he ran were out of date from the start.

He was born on 23 December 1906 at Bethlehem in Orange Free State in South Africa. Though his father was also born in South Africa and his mother in Argentina, the family always described themselves as British. As well as sharing the same country of birth, there were other striking similarities between Woods and Kingsley Fairbridge. Both spent most of their boyhood on a farm, then undertook rudimentary schooling and received a Rhodes scholarship to Oxford. Both were athletic, strong, outdoor types and married dedicated women who committed their lives to their husband's mission. It is unlikely that the two men ever met, though, as Woods was born twenty years after Fairbridge.

Woods was educated at home until the age of twelve, then sent to St Andrews Diocesan School for boys, Bloemfontein, in Orange Free State, from 1918 till 1923. He became head prefect, second lieutenant in the School Cadet Corps, the school heavyweight boxing representative, and a champion rifle shot and swimmer.

He spent three years at Rhodes University College in the Cape Province and though only gaining a second-class honours degree (majoring in French and Latin) he was awarded a Rhodes scholarship from Orange Free State in 1929. It seems that he was not awarded a degree from Oxford, where he read 'modern greats'. Although he said he satisfied the examiners in politics and economics, he failed in his third subject, philosophy. Like Kingsley Fairbridge, Woods boxed at Oxford. He also played rugby union for his college and represented the university in jujitsu and swimming.

After leaving Oxford at the age of twenty-six he moved to Nyasaland (now Malawi) to work as assistant aide-de-camp to His Excellency Sir Hubert Young KCMG DSO, Governor of Nyasaland. He also tutored the governor's children. He subsequently became aide-de-camp to the new Governor Kiitermaster in 1935 and it was then that Woods decided to apply for the Fairbridge job.

His decision was no doubt influenced by Ruth, who had become ill in southern Africa and was unable to continue working as a missionary in the harsh environment. Many years later Ruth Woods would tell some of the trainee girls that she saw her work at Fairbridge as a continuation of her missionary work. His wife would be a huge source of strength to Woods over the next thirty years.

When they arrived at the farm school, the Woods lived in the assistant principal's house at the back of the village, but they moved into the big two-storey principal's house when Woods became acting principal in 1942.

Woods's reign as the principal of Fairbridge got off to a rocky start. When the London Fairbridge Society officially confirmed him in the top job in 1945 they were unaware that he was under investigation by child-welfare authorities for sexually abusing a Fairbridge girl. The allegations, which never became public, were made by Joy Watt, one of the trainee girls who worked on domestic duties in the principal's house.

Six months after London appointed Woods, Sir Claude Reading KCMG, the chairman of the Sydney Fairbridge Council, wrote to Sir Charles Hambro, the chairman of the London Fairbridge Society:

> One of the Fairbridge girls had made very serious allegations against Woods, of sexual misbehaviour towards her, which were brought to the attention of the Child Welfare Department by a local parson who had heard of the alleged incidents.

He went on to explain that a report recently received from the Child Welfare Department completely exonerated

Woods and that 'The allegations made by the girl can only be put down to the sexual stirrings of an hysterical adolescent mind.'[7]

In December 1945 Ruth Woods, in defence of her husband, wrote to a Miss Hart who worked in the London Fairbridge office:

> I don't think we could have worked harder or with more care for the Watt twins, they have been our most difficult children here, highly-strung and temperamental. I couldn't count the number of nights I have spent sitting on Joy's bed till she was asleep – she seemed a child that needed parental care more than most.

She said that a few days before, they had been confronted by private detectives enquiring about accusations of indecent behaviour Joy had made against her husband.

> They questioned the children and us very closely and are perfectly satisfied that it is the imagination of a distorted mind . . . It is usually rather heart breaking at times, I was so fond of Joy and always stoutly denied to others that she had lied.[8]

Two months later, Ruth Woods wrote again, saying that Joy Watt had been upset with Woods, whom she blamed for the suicide of a fifteen-year Fairbridge boy, Peter Johnson. The death of Johnson upset a number of Fairbridge children and remained an unhappy memory in their lives for decades to come. She wrote of Joy:

> She has a warped mind, we know from a series of notes dealing with unpleasant sex matters, which were discovered at school some time ago written by an external pupil, but aided by Joy.[9]

Mrs Woods believed that Joy's father, who had seen his daughter recently, 'is an unpleasant man, [and] may have aroused her more unpleasant side'.

Less than three years later, in 1948, Woods was again under investigation. A number of serious allegations had been made by the newly appointed bursar to Fairbridge, a Commander Owen. Again, the allegations and the investigation were never made public.

In March 1948, the new chairman of the Fairbridge Council, W. B. Hudson, wrote to Sir Charles Hambro:

> It was felt that the charges were so serious that they required an immediate independent investigation. As the Director of Child Welfare [in New South Wales] is the legal guardian of the children he was asked to conduct the inquiry. He delegated the investigation to the superintendent . . . and it was done with care and a minimum of publicity. So far there has been no publicity in the papers here and I do not think there will be.[10]

The investigation was quickly completed by a Mr V. A. Heffernan of the Child Welfare Department, who concluded that: 'It was not considered that any of the charges made against Mr Woods have been substantiated.'[11]

The report of the investigation listed six allegations made by Commander Owen: that the children were not sufficiently and properly fed; that Woods had employed a cook in the tertiary stages of syphilis; that Woods was a 'sexual pervert'; that Woods knocked down and kicked a boy till his eyes bled; that Woods beat and injured boys with a hockey stick; and 'other matters too dreadful to mention'.

Heffernan did not accept that the children were improperly fed, and reported that Owen could not provide specific details of the matters 'too dreadful to mention'. He discovered that Woods had allowed the cook with syphilis to stay on upon receiving medical advice that she posed no threat of infection to the children. He also dismissed the allegation that Woods was a sexual pervert, because he was satisfied with Woods's explanation for his possession of sex books.

The inquiry did find that Woods had knocked over a boy in the kitchen and kneed him, and that the boy's eyes were 'bloodshot' after the incident. While Woods was 'unwise' to use such a method of punishment it was 'not considered that this action amounted to excessive punishment or serious assault'. The inquiry revealed that Woods had used the hockey stick to beat the boys, but noted 'he has not used it since he was instructed by the chairman [of Fairbridge]'.

Woods survived the crisis and remained principal.

In December 1964, Ruth Woods went with her husband to Sydney to do some Christmas shopping. They drove back to Fairbridge and arrived at around three o'clock in the morning on Tuesday, 8 December. At about two o'clock that afternoon she left Fairbridge and drove thirty kilometres to the town of Milthorpe to keep an appointment as guest speaker at a Mothers' Union meeting. After rising to speak she was seen to falter and then appeared to faint. She was carried to the nearby church rectory, and was pronounced dead at 6 p.m. from what was later confirmed to be a blood clot in her brain.

Her funeral service was held the following Friday afternoon at the little chapel at Fairbridge Farm, which was to be renamed the Ruth Woods Memorial Chapel. The service was followed by a cremation later that afternoon in Orange. Hundreds of mourners attended the funeral, along with Woods, three of his four children – Robert, Raymond and Memory – and a large number of Old Fairbridgians. Woods's daughter Nyassa, who was working as a nurse in England, was unable to be there, but returned to the farm school soon after. More than a hundred mourners were unable to fit into the little church and had to stand outside.[12]

Woods, who had been a towering influence over Fairbridge for nearly three decades, was sacked only six months after the death of his wife. The fact that Woods was sacked, and the reasons for his dismissal, were never made public. Woods may have been under some pressure from the Fairbridge Council in Sydney to retire, but it was the Fairbridge Society in London that dismissed him, without any prior consultation with Sydney.

Within months of the death of his wife, Woods was in a new relationship with a cottage mother, Mrs Wunch, who had recently divorced her husband. Woods quickly proposed. This did not sit well with the Sydney Fairbridge Council, and after discussions with the new chairman of the council, Dr W. L. Calov, Woods agreed to postpone the marriage.

Woods had suggested that remarrying might help solve the housekeeping problem he'd had since his wife's death. In a letter to the secretary of Fairbridge in Sydney, Woods wrote that his daughter Memory had acted as house-keeper at the principal's house for three months after Ruth's death, then had to go back to university. After her departure the housework had been done by trainee girls, but now they hadn't enough trainees to spare for such duties. He asked Fairbridge to consider paying his other daughter, Nyassa, to take up housekeeping duties in the principals' house. 'My original intention to get married again about this time would have obviated this little problem in the most practical way,' he said, 'but after a discussion with the chairman a longer lapse in time is considered wise and proper.'[13]

Unbeknown to Woods, Dr Calov communicated his concerns about the love affair to Lord Slim, who had become the chairman of the London Fairbridge Society in 1963 after the death of the long-serving chairman Sir Charles Hambro. Slim was a war hero. He had been commissioned as a second lieutenant in the British Army in World War I and was badly wounded at Gallipoli before serving later in France and Mesopotamia. After the war he was promoted to captain and spent fifteen years with Gurkha regiments in the British Indian Army before fighting in the Sudan, Ethiopia and finally Burma during World War II. After the war he was appointed commander of Allied Land Forces in South East Asia; and in 1953, with the title of Field Marshal Sir William Slim, he became governor-general of Australia. He served as governor-general till 1959 and became familiar with Fairbridge, visiting the Molong farm school in 1953 and 1955.

At a meeting of the London Fairbridge Society on 2 July 1965 chaired by Lord Slim the decision was made to sack Woods. The minutes of the fateful meeting record that the chairman read a letter dated 21 May 1965 from Dr Calov in which he informed them that Mr Woods had decided to marry the recently divorced cottage mother. Dr Calov went on to say the marriage plans had caused adverse comment in the local community and a hostile attitude in Woods's family.

The society in London had apparently agreed with its chairman, Lord Slim, that Mr Woods had 'created a scandal and had besmirched the good name of Fairbridge'. The minutes also said that:

> For some fifteen years now there had been anxiety about the way in which Mr Woods had been running Molong and some of the major incidents which had arisen are set out in Appendix A.[14]

Appendix A, titled 'Complaints and Anxieties about Molong over the Last Fifteen Years', contained documents that reflected poorly on Woods. One was a copy of a letter from a Fairbridge girl, Margaret Bannerman, to her mother complaining about being physically threatened as a trainee girl by the Fairbridge cook and his wife, and pleading with her mother to be taken out of Fairbridge:

> Mum you don't realise how terrible it is here and how I miss you and dad. Oh, if I was only home. Oh please try and get us home, as I am so unhappy here. Please tell me if there is any news yet of us getting back or even if there is the slightest chance of getting back.

Another document in the appendix was a copy of an investigation by the New South Wales Child Welfare Department that confirmed allegations of child brutality by cottage mothers at Fairbridge. The allegations were made in 1964 by Mrs Jeanette Bradfield, who had followed her son and daughter out to Australia under the One Parent Scheme.

The London Fairbridge Society wanted Woods gone immediately and, while deciding to ask Sydney about a number of financial issues, it was agreed unanimously that the time had come to terminate Woods' appointment. The council resolved that he should be off the property by the end of the month.

On being advised of London's decision, Dr Calov wrote back to register the surprise of the local board at the dramatic sacking of Woods. He professed his 'great shock' at their decision, saying he didn't believe that the complaints were sufficient to warrant 'dismissal of a principal who has had twenty-six years of service in Fairbridge'. He continued:

> We are aware of Mr Woods's deficiencies as an admin-
> istrator and as an office man; but we have balanced
> these deficiencies against his devotion to the children
> and the Fairbridge Movement, and his qualities as an
> outdoor man, a sportsman, a family man, and a
> farmer. He is highly respected in the Molong District,
> and he takes an active part in public affairs.[15]

However, Sydney did not attempt to persuade London to
reverse the decision: most of their communication was
aimed at securing a decent severance package for Woods.
Calov pointed out that Woods had no superannuation,
had not been trained in a profession and would find it difficult at his age – he was fifty-nine years old – to find a
comparable job. Sydney also asked for some financial
assistance for Woods's children so they could continue
their university education after he had left Fairbridge,
which is interesting because the Sydney Fairbridge Council did not provide financial assistance to Fairbridge
children for their tertiary education.

London wanted the cottage mother involved in the
scandal off the scene straightaway and the local Fairbridge Council in Sydney wasted no time following
London's instruction. A meeting of the executive committee decided that: 'the principal of the Fairbridge Farm
School Molong be informed that Mrs Wunch must leave
the employment of the Society immediately'.[16]

Ian Dean was a fifteen-year-old and remembers the
gossip about Woods and Wunch at the time. 'It was
obvious to all of us,' he recalls.

> As a trainee on the kitchens I had to go down and top
> up the stoves with coke late at night and I often saw
> Woods arriving at Molong Cottage just after most of
> the kids were in bed.

> Woods regularly visited Mrs Wunch at night.
> And there was a lot of sniggering around the village
> about it.

Notwithstanding the misgivings of the Sydney Fairbridge Society about their principal's conduct, their intervention on his behalf paid off and Woods was financially looked after. In November 1965, General Hawthorn, the director of Fairbridge London, came to Australia to discuss Woods's departure with the Sydney council. The visit coincided with the news that the last party of British children would be arriving at Fairbridge the following January.

It was all very nicely done. The minutes of the meeting between the Fairbridge Council of Sydney and General Hawthorn record that Mr Woods 'was then asked to retire, which he did'. Hawthorn said that the London council would be terminating his appointment from that 31 December 1966. Woods's appointment was not pensionable, but in view of his length of service London proposed to give him a year's salary when he retired. The minutes detail that the meeting discussed this for a few minutes, agreed with London's decision and 'thought that Mr Woods was being fairly treated'.[17]

Woods was given a splendid send-off, befitting his huge reputation. It was widely reported and universally accepted that he had chosen to retire and there was absolutely no suggestion that he had in fact been dismissed. The major newspaper in the district, the *Central Western Daily* in Orange, gave his departure extensive news coverage and eulogised Woods, describing him as 'a great man'. In Fairbridge's annual report that year the Sydney council recorded:

> The Fairbridge Society of London has announced the
> retirement of the principal of the Fairbridge Farm

School Molong as from 31st December 1966. Mr Woods has rendered outstanding service to Fairbridge and to the children who passed through the school during the 28 years he has been with the Society and for this we are truly grateful.[18]

Woods, with the help of Fairbridge contacts in New South Wales, was able to immediately take up a job as an English and history teacher at the Illawarra Grammar School in Wollongong, south of Sydney. He subsequently married another cottage mother, Mrs Grey, and they lived together until Woods died in 1977. He was seventy-two years old.

Woods's successor was Mr M. A. G. 'Jack' Newberry, who had been the After Care Officer responsible for finding jobs for Fairbridge children when they left the farm school. Newberry, like Woods and Beauchamp before him, would also be sacked, amid allegations of sexual misconduct.

During World War II Newberry had served with the British Army in the Middle East, and after the war he migrated with his wife to Australia. In the 1950s they came to work at Fairbridge, his wife as cottage mother of Canonbar Cottage and he as the supervisor of the village garden. They left Fairbridge and returned in 1959. They wanted their old jobs back but Kurt and Ilse Boelter now held their former positions. For the next couple of years Mrs Newberry was the cottage mother in Brown Cottage, and never let anyone forget her anger at the Boelters, as she believed she and Jack had prior rights to the jobs. No doubt the big drop in the family income fuelled Mrs Newberry's annoyance: the gardener's job paid a lot more than that of cottage mother.

Jack left and went to work as a security guard at the

Port Kembla steelworks, south of Wollongong in New South Wales. Whenever he was back at Fairbridge visiting his wife he was a regular sight after every meal, marching ramrod straight on his 'constitutional' up from the village to the dairy and back. He claimed he had been in the Grenadier Guards, which is where he said he developed the habit.

In 1962, Jack took the job of After Care Officer, which had become vacant because the incumbent, Mr Phillips, had left amid rumours of sexual abuse of children at the farm. Phillips's victims confirmed the rumours many decades later.

When Woods left, Newberry had a shot at the top job. In his application he claimed to have been a captain in the British Army.[19] The director of the Fairbridge Society in London, General Hawthorn, would question Newberry's credentials three years later when he was visiting Molong. In a report to London of his visit Hawthorn wrote:

> Mr Kingsmill, Mr Bennett and Mr George Hitchens (the Commonwealth Immigration Officer) met us at the Airport and after lunch we motored with Mr Kingsmill to Molong. I had not realised that Molong was so far from Sydney. We arrived there about 6 P.M. and were met by Mr and Mrs Newberry. I had Newberry as an NCO in my regiment in Egypt before the war. In fact he was in my company.[20]

Newberry was investigated following a series of allegations of sexual abuse and forced to retire in 1969, three years after being made principal. Stories circulating about Newberry's sexual perversities would be confirmed by a number of Fairbridge girls years later, including Liz Sharp, who said Newberry 'touched her up'.

Again, the allegations against the principal were never made public. In the letter notifying Newberry of his sacking, the chairman of the Sydney Fairbridge Council, Mr H. L. Kingsmill wrote that 'the charges made against you were not substantiated but . . . at 64 years of age [it was] thought you were too old for the position of principal of Fairbridge.' Kingsmill informed Newberry that the council was going to advertise for a new principal immediately, gave Newberry one month's notice of his retirement, and said he would be paid his present salary up to the time that he was sixty-five. The letter finished:

> I am sorry to write this letter, as I have been pleasantly surprised at what you have done for Fairbridge. However conditions there now are such that the decision of Council could not be avoided.[21]

When Newberry was replaced by Mr R. T. Coutts no children had been sent from Britain for four years. By 1970, there were only fifty children living in the village and all but two of them were Australian-born. Coutts was the church army captain from Bathurst in New South Wales and had served in Papua New Guinea and Bougainville during the war, and then with the occupation forces in Japan until 1948. He left Fairbridge in 1971 and later became a church deacon and priest in the diocese of Grafton. The last principal of Fairbridge until the farm school closed in early 1974 was D. W. Aubrey.

One of the most colourful members of staff at Fairbridge was E. T. (Harry) Harrop, the bursar and sometime acting principal from 1953 until he was jailed in 1967 for embezzlement.

In 1966 auditors conducted an investigation and found more than £12,000 missing from the Fairbridge accounts he administered. In April 1966 the New South Wales fraud squad charged Harry with theft. He pleaded guilty before Judge Higgins in the Quarter Sessions Court in Sydney and was sentenced to three years' jail.

The children at Fairbridge knew very little about what was going on. Ian Dean, a fifteen-year-old trainee who had been at Fairbridge for five years, recalls, 'Harry just disappeared.'

Most Fairbridge children were uncritical of Harrop when they later heard about his crime. 'He was the one who treated the kids well,' recalls Gwen Miller. Eddie Baker also remembers Harry with affection, despite the fact that he went to prison for stealing from Fairbridge: 'Well, yes, I know, unfortunately. But apart from that, he was the kindest man with children. Most kindest man.'

Peter Bennett left Fairbridge in 1949, before Harry Harrop arrived, but met Harry when he was back at Fairbridge on a visit with his family years later. Harry asked Peter if he wanted to buy some good new shoes for his children. He said he could offer them at a discount price because Fairbridge bought in bulk and was tax exempt. Peter and his three children followed Harry up to the shoe store, which was located behind the deputy principal's house, and the children were all fitted out with new shoes. 'I've got a good pair for you, too,' Harry told Peter.

'But I'm size ten,' replied Peter.

'That's okay,' said Harry. 'We've got large sizes for the trainee boys.'

Peter left with four pairs of shoes, for which he paid well under half the normal retail price. It was only much later, when he heard of Harrop's conviction, that he realised the money probably went straight into Harry's pocket and not into the Fairbridge coffers.

Later, there was much to suggest that the £12,000 Harry had lifted from the Fairbridge bank accounts was only the tip of the iceberg of corruption at the farm school over many years, involving not only Harry but other members of staff, too.

Harry was a gambler. In fact, he was considered to be the biggest customer of the illegal SP bookmaker who operated out of one of the two pubs in Molong's main street. He was not the only one at Fairbridge with a passion for horse racing. The garden supervisor and then dairyman, Ted Begley, was a punter and the owner of a stable of racehorses that he kept and trained on Fairbridge Farm. He had his own racetrack below the dairy in the homestead paddock.

Begley came to Fairbridge in 1945 and stayed for more than twenty years – longer than anyone else but Woods. His first position was supervisor of the village garden, then he took the higher-paid job of dairyman. Begley lived in the dairyman's house near the dairy with his wife, two daughters and a son. Mrs Begley was the part-time cleaner of the little primary school at the back of the village, and is remembered for her wonderful Christmas cake decorating.

Begley was almost universally loathed and feared by the boys, most of whom he indiscriminately punched and kicked. It seems the only boys not to have been routinely beaten by him were those who loved horses, and rode and trained his racehorses – no doubt saving him the expense of hiring jockeys. As David Eva recalls: 'I got on all right. A lot of people never got on with Begley but because I was "horsy" and he had racehorses, I think that's the reason I got on with him.'

How Begley was able to keep a family and a stable of four to five racehorses, which he regularly raced around the district, on the relatively low farm labourer's wage of around £13 a week should have aroused the suspicion of Woods and the Fairbridge Council. We Fairbridge kids only became aware of it later. One of the Fairbridge children who did notice something amiss was John Harris. He speaks well of his time at Fairbridge and became the president of the Old Fairbridgians' Association, but he says the corruption at Fairbridge was on such a large scale it should have been noted earlier:

> Harry Harrop! How he was not found out sooner is beyond me. How Begley was not found out and prosecuted, is beyond me . . . How he got away with it, how the auditors never picked up on the productivity versus the cost of seed, etc. How they never got on to what happened to all the fruit, vegetables, eggs and poultry. What happened to all that feed – the chaff we used to chop up. The cows can only eat so much. What happened to the rest of it?

While working on the piggery, John remembers Begley selling pigs on the side to a local butcher:

> I saw him do it. I happened to say, 'Where are they [the pigs]?' because I was running the piggery at the time. And he said, 'They died.' If you are on the piggery and a large pig dies of natural causes or whatever reason you are required to get the tractor and front-end loader, dig a hole, put it in, burn it and bury it. And I wasn't asked to do that. So I thought, 'Something strange here.' And there were three Tamworth sows, and they went missing.

Fairbridge generated a wide range of produce, some of which was consumed on the farm. The sale of the rest of the farm produce was a vital source of revenue to Fairbridge. A former Fairbridge boy, Peter 'Stumpy' Maycock, came back to work at Fairbridge in the mid-1960s to manage the piggery because there were no longer enough trainees to do the work. Maycock, who had worked as a trainee under Begley, was amazed at the pig reproduction rate. He calculated that only a small proportion of the pigs had previously been accounted for in the official number of pigs sold by the farm. He then remembered that when he had worked on the piggery as a boy, the local butcher would regularly come out to the farm in his utility truck and Begley would tell Peter and the other boys to help load pigs into the back.

One might wonder whether Woods had any inkling or knowledge of the corruption that appears to have flourished around him for years. He was, after all, responsible for the staff as chief executive. However, no one would ever question his own honesty and integrity. He was totally committed – as was Ruth – to the Fairbridge cause, and the idea of stealing from the farm school would have been beyond his comprehension. He was also a notoriously sloppy administrator and, as we shall see, could not even detect children stealing pocket money from literally under his nose.

But serious questions must be asked of the Fairbridge Council, who was ultimately responsible for the day-to-day running of the farm school, because even the most elementary scrutiny of the management should have revealed something of what was going on.

7

CHILD LABOUR

The Fairbridge Farm School aim of training underprivileged British boys to become farmers and underprivileged girls to become farmers' wives was captured in the Fairbridge school song:

> We are Fairbridge folk, all as good as e'er,
> English, Welsh and Scottish,
> We have come from everywhere:
> Boys to be farmers
> And girls for farmers' wives,
> We follow 'Fairbridge the Founder'.

One of the most unpleasant surprises I had on arrival at Fairbridge was the reality of the trainee scheme – effectively a program of hard labour. Most boys and girls were forced to leave school at fifteen so they could work on a rotating roster of jobs around the farm for the next two years. Although they took on the full-time workload of an adult, they were given only a shilling or two a week in pocket money.

The farm of about six hundred and fifty hectares was about two kilometres wide and ran for five and a half kilometres south from the Mitchell Highway and Molong

Creek, which formed its northern border. Fairbridge was largely self-sufficient, thanks to its sheep farming, grain growing, vegetable garden and orchard, dairy with about fifty milking cows, piggery, poultry farm that produced up to 200 eggs a day, and slaughterhouse, where up to two dozen sheep a week were killed. All the work was undertaken by the children and only a handful of adult farm supervisors.

However, most boys left Fairbridge qualified only to be farm labourers, and the girls to be domestic servants. Though the Fairbridge scheme operated for more than seventy years in Australia – from 1912 till 1980 – practically no Fairbridge child was ever able to acquire and operate their own farm. As Len Cowne recounts:

> Fairbridge Farm School, euphemistically called a 'college of agriculture', was, in reality, an orphanage built to train British migrant children to become farm workers. The advertising said that the Fairbridge scheme was to train boys to become farmers, and girls to become farmers' wives. But in reality things didn't work out like that. Boys were trained in most aspects of agriculture, and the girls learnt all the domestic chores that went with running a house. On leaving our 'alma mater', we boys were found places as farm labourers, and the girls often ended up as skivvies to some wealthy landowner.[1]

When he originally designed the farm school scheme, Kingsley Fairbridge recognised the critical importance of providing capital so that Fairbridge children might eventually be able to own their own farm. In the speech he gave to the Oxford University Colonial Club in 1909 that led to the establishment of the Child Emigration Society he proposed that:

On leaving the School every student, young man and young woman, will have a certain amount of money to start with; the more able of the students may have sufficient to start farming in a small way on their own account.[2]

While there were a number of attempts to create loan funds so that Fairbridge children would have access to start-up capital, none got off the ground. In 1939 at a meeting of the London Fairbridge Society it was decided that, in keeping with the 'ambition of the Founder', a special fund would be established so that Old Fairbridgians might be able to settle on their own small holdings. The minutes of the meeting noted that, 'Augmentation of the Fund was one of the most urgent endeavors of the Society.'[3] Unfortunately, the fund was not augmented and no money from the fund ever reached children of the Fairbridge Farm School at Molong.

Another attempt was made almost a decade later, with the help of Her Royal Highness Princess (later Queen) Elizabeth, who donated £2000 to Fairbridge in 1948 from wedding gifts from readers of the *Recorder* and the *Imperial Review* when she married Prince Philip. The money, to establish the Princess Elizabeth Loan Fund, was handed over to the chairman of the UK Fairbridge Society, Sir Charles Hambro, at a special luncheon in London. He was told how the princess wanted her money to be spent:

To assist individual Old Fairbridgian boys and girls to get established in life. Money received by a young person from the fund would be returned by him at the expiration of the loan period and in this way a very large number of deserving Fairbridge boys and girls in their late teens and early 20s could, in the course of time, be helped to fill their justifiable ambitions.[4]

Her Royal Highness also expressed the hope that the Princess Elizabeth Loan Fund would form a 'nucleus to be enlarged by similar gifts in the future'. The fund experienced no enlargement, and none of Her Majesty's money reached the accounts of the New South Wales Fairbridge Council or the children leaving the Molong Farm School.

The Molong farm school itself established the Old Fairbridgians Grant and Loan Fund in 1940 with £2002, ten shillings and ten pence.[5] The money was not used for the best part of ten years. In its annual report of 1949 the Fairbridge Council announced that it had lent small amounts of money to some Old Fairbridgians:

> During the year, the Old Fairbridgians Grant and Loan Fund, which is shown in the Balance Sheet, was made available for the benefit of those Old Fairbridgians whom the Council considers should be assisted financially, whether by way of allowance or loan.[6]

The following year the fund had barely £1000 after a number of Old Fairbridgians were given small interest-free loans to help buy household furniture. Within two years the fund was exhausted and no further financial capital was made available to the Molong Fairbridge children.[7]

While the Fairbridge trainee scheme was of little benefit to children after they left the farm school, it was a remarkably efficient arrangement for Fairbridge. Within two years of opening at Molong, Fairbridge was able to boast that with the labour of the trainee children and only five supervisory farm staff, the school was already able to produce almost all of its own food.[8]

The trainee boys were on a rotating roster, doing twenty-eight days at a time in the dairy, slaughterhouse and piggery, kitchens, bakery, vegetable gardens, poultry farm and laundry, as well as on general village maintenance and work on the principal's house. For the last three to six months of their time at Fairbridge they were assigned full-time to the farm, where they undertook sheep farming, and ploughing, sowing and harvesting of wheat, oats and barley.

I was lucky in that I was able to skip the two years as a trainee because, after leaving school at fifteen, I left Fairbridge to join up with my mother in Sydney. But, like all the other kids, I was expected to do trainee work in the school holidays from the age of about fourteen. And practically all the children in the village over the age of eight or nine were obliged to help on the farm at harvest time. They would follow the harvester all day, picking up the sheaves of oats and stacking them vertically in piles, or 'stooks'. We bigger lads would also be assigned to lifting the heavy bales and loading them on the truck to be taken to the barn, where they were stored as feed for the livestock during winter.

At shearing time when I was thirteen years old, I was sent up to the farm every day to help. My job was to pick out the burrs from the shorn fleece and cut away the unusable pieces, or 'dags', around the crutch, then pack the wool into a bale using an old-fashioned wool press. The loose wool was manually wound up by turning a big metal handle, then it was lowered and pressed into a tight bale.

One day, when I should have been working, I was playing around with the wool press, and with some great effort wound a full load of wool up but couldn't get it down. It sat suspended until I could work out how to release the safety clip . . . but of course the whole bale came crashing down, the big metal handle spinning around, and catching me in the corner of my left eye socket. I was thrown across the shearing shed, the blow knocking me unconscious, breaking the bridge of my nose and opening up a wound that would forever leave a scar up into my forehead. As I came to and staggered instinctively toward what I thought was a door, dazed by the blow and blinded by the blood, I heard two trainee boys laughing uproariously at the scene. Someone gave me a towel to hold over the wound and stem the bleeding as 'Ripper' Smith, the farm supervisor, came running, screaming in his soprano voice. He drove me at breakneck speed, first to the little hospital on Fairbridge, then to the Molong hospital, where I was stitched up and kept for a couple of days' observation.

But the dairy was the toughest place I ever worked. I found it so exhausting I didn't think I'd survive the experience. Most of the Fairbridge boys dreaded the dairy because the work was unrelenting: more than sixteen hours a day, seven days a week, for twenty-eight days straight. And Begley, the dairy supervisor, was a sadist who regularly kicked and punched boys with the least provocation.

I was rostered on to the dairy shortly after my fifteenth birthday, during the winter school holidays. At around three o'clock in the morning on my first day a boy called Norm 'Goofy' Bannerman came down from Canary Cottage to wake me to go and fetch the cows for the morning milking. It was pitch black, cold and pouring with rain as we trudged up the hill beside the deputy principal's house, through the fence and across Martins paddock to find the cows. We had no wet-weather gear and were getting soaked. I couldn't see a thing but Goofy knew the ropes so I just quietly followed him, slipping and sliding in the mud. It seemed to take ages to get the cows into the milking yard, where the other four boys had set up the machines for milking.

There were about fifty milking cows in the herd, which was one of the biggest in the Central West of the state. The herd had been smaller in the earlier years of Fairbridge but had been increased in size after a donation to Fairbridge of milking machines by the pastoral company Dangar, Gedye and Malloch in the mid-1950s.

There were six milking bails but only four milking machines, so we took turns to hand-milk cows in the two other bails. We also had to hand-milk each cow to fully empty her udder after the machine had taken all it could. If Begley found that you weren't emptying the cows properly he would switch off the milking machines and make you milk the whole herd entirely by hand.

I didn't mind hand-milking in the cold early morning. Sitting on the milking stool and nestling your head into the belly and the udders of a cow was the only way to get a bit of warmth. You could also lean forward and squirt the warm milk straight from the cow's udder into your mouth.

The milking would take a couple of hours. Toward the end, the leading boy of the gang or Begley, who by now had arrived, would begin the separation of the cream from the milk in the separating room, which was next to the milking bails. By sun-up a younger schoolboy would have come up from the village to hitch a cart to the horse. He and an older boy from the dairy would load about three ten-gallon milk urns, a couple of smaller milk urns and the cream onto the cart then head off down the dirt road to the village, delivering milk on the way. The cart's first stop was Begley's house near the dairy, then the two farm assistants' houses, a number of staff quarters in the village, and finally the village kitchens. The horse and cart were left in front of Nuffield Hall during breakfast so the horse could graze.

Smiley Bayliff remembers working as a schoolboy on the dairy cart:

I loved it. It got me out of the cottage early in the morning and away from the cottage mother and the drudgery of cleaning the cottage every morning. It also got me out of village muster and church on Sunday mornings. I managed to get a second stint at it and would have spent about a year altogether on that job. It was one of my best memories of Fairbridge.

Back at the dairy, the rest of us still had jobs to do after the milking and before breakfast. I was assigned to the piggery and had to go across to feed the pigs the slops that had been cooked up the previous day. As was the case with so much of the trainee life at Fairbridge, I wasn't trained but was given the barest of instruction from one of the senior boys. I just muddled along and worked it out as best I could.

The dairy team invariably came down late for breakfast, when everyone was finishing up or had already left the dining hall. Before going to Nuffield Hall we would wash up, take off our muddy, shitty workboots and perhaps put on some dry clothing. We got a cooked breakfast, and usually more. The cook usually understood how hard our work was and allowed us to eat breakfast cereal, which was usually reserved for staff, rather than the awful and by now cold porridge. We could also go up on the stage to the staff dining table and drink the left-over staff tea and coffee, which was normally forbidden to the Fairbridge children. It was just as well, because our cooked breakfast was by now very cold. David Eva recalls:

We'd get down there about eight o'clock and then we'd have our breakfast and, of course the bloody eggs were like rubber. If they got poached, you could throw them up in the air and they'd bounce all over the place and your porridge sat stuck in the bowl.

Derek Moriarty remembers getting special treatment in the village kitchen when he was working as a trainee at the dairy:

> When we were on dairy it was the done thing for us to go down to the kitchen at half past two in the morning before you went to get the cows in and have a bowl of five or six Weet-Bix with white sugar . . . because you knew somebody from the kitchen would be there doing the stoves or whatever.

After breakfast the horse and cart were taken to the back of the kitchens and the cart loaded up with food scraps to be taken up to the piggery and boiled up in the big coppers. We had to return to the dairy by about eight-thirty, or risk the wrath of Begley. On most mornings I worked by myself in the piggery while the other boys in the dairy gang cleaned the yard, washed the milking equipment and fed the poddy calves.

At the piggery I cleaned out the sties and boiled up the food that would be fed to the pigs the following day. There were two big coppers. I lit the smaller one for the food scraps from the village kitchens and in the bigger one I boiled up wheat from the silo with the meat offcuts and guts from the sheep killed in the slaughterhouse behind the dairy.

The dairy gang killed twice a week, on Monday morning and again on Thursday morning, usually ten to fourteen sheep in each kill. We rarely killed lambs: the Fairbridge diet was overwhelmingly old mutton. Fairbridge kids used to say that the lambs had either two teeth or four teeth, and an old sheep had a full mouth, but at

Fairbridge we killed them only when their teeth were broken and falling out.

Again, at the slaughterhouse we received little training. You learnt to kill from the more experienced, older boys in the gang. The first time, the most senior boy put the knife close to hand and pulled the sheep over on its side. I had the job of holding the sheep's rear legs while he pulled back the head of the sheep over his boot and plunged the knife into the throat, cutting outwards, then breaking the beast's neck. I was surprised there was so much blood and totally unprepared for the strength of the sheep. It kicked its rear legs free as I rolled around in the blood on the floor, trying to hold it down, while the older boys cursed my incompetence. By the time I regained control, the sheep stopped kicking and fell silent, dead.

Lennie Magee also remembers learning to kill the hard way:

> We were told – not taught – how to cut the sheep's throat, cut the jugular and break its neck. My first concern, however, was not the sheep's welfare but to make sure that I didn't stick the knife through the sheep's neck and into my boot. My initial attempt found me chasing a half-dead sheep down the hill with a knife sticking out of its neck.[9]

David Eva recalls being the new boy in the slaughterhouse:

> Then they said I had to get the brains out of the bloody sheep. A new boy – that was their first job. And of course you've got a cleaver and there was a wooden block and you had to belt and break the bloody skull open . . . Nobody helped me of course . . . You'd never get them all out; they'd all be mashed, you know.

We cut off the lower legs while the beast was still lying on the ground, then hung it on a hook, 'punched' (skinned) and gutted it, and cut off its head. The heart and the liver were put in a bucket and the remainder of the guts sat in a big pile on the floor until they were picked up – with great difficulty, usually by the boy considered to be the least competent of the gang – and taken in a wheelbarrow to the manure heap. The same boy would cut open the intestines and empty the grass inside them onto the manure heap. I would pick up the remains and take them across to the piggery to go into the big copper. The sheep's guts would slop around in my wheelbarrow like giant spaghetti as I wheeled it across the road to the piggery. No one ever seemed to come up with a better system of picking the sheep's guts up than by the armful, with slippery intestines sliding through your arms and down your legs.

The slaughtered sheep hung in the hanging room next to the slaughterhouse overnight. The next day the beast was sawn up, wrapped in meat cloths and laid in the back of the dairy cart to be taken down to the village kitchens, where the meat was butchered by one of the boys on kitchen duty.

On about my second day on piggery duty I was filling a bucket of water and, feeling dog-tired, I leant on the tap for support. Unbeknown to me, Begley had crept up behind me. He kicked me between the legs, up into my balls. As I lay writhing in the mud he grumbled something about going to sleep on the job, then wandered off. I had never met Begley before this incident but knew of his reputation from the other boys and wasn't surprised.

We usually finished in time to walk back down to the village, wash up and have lunch with everyone else in Nuffield Hall. Two of the boys in the dairy gang had the job of getting the cows into the lucerne paddock before the afternoon milk, but the rest of us could have a nap for an hour or so. On one of the days when I was 'on cows', I had herded the cows into the lucerne paddock before the afternoon milking and laid myself down and dozed off. I was woken abruptly by Begley kicking me in the head. Fortunately he was wearing rubber Wellington boots.

At three o'clock we had to start the afternoon milking, which took a couple of hours plus clean-up time. We didn't get back to the village before dark, always after everyone else in the cottage had finished their tea. Although hungry, I was almost too tired to eat. I had been working for nearly seventeen hours and would be lucky to get six hours' sleep before Goofy woke me again to go and find the cows for the next milking.

Another tough roster was working in the village kitchens. A paid cook lived in small quarters behind the kitchens and supervised the work of two trainee boys in the kitchens and two trainee girls who worked as waitresses for staff in the dining hall. The trainee boys started before the rest of the village was awake. They were responsible for ringing the village bell, which was outside the back of the kitchens.

One of the first duties each day was to 'riddle' the big Esse slow-combustion stoves that operated twenty-four hours a day. The boys rattled out the overnight ash, opened the dampers and put in more fuel so that breakfast could be prepared for almost 200 people.

One of the two trainees had to slice some 200 pieces of bread for breakfast, before two of the secondary-school-age children came to use the slicer to make the sandwich lunches for the children who would be going to school.

The second trainee boy on kitchen duty would move the five-gallon saucepan from the back burner, where it had sat overnight, to the hot plate. He would boil the water and add salt and oats to make a huge tub of porridge. In the early days, Fairbridge used grain grown on the farm for the porridge but some time in the 1950s began to buy cheap oats from Wright Heatons store in Molong. The oats came in big flour sacks and were invariably infested with weevils.

Around 5.30 a.m. the cook would come in to prepare the breakfast for the staff, visitors and the trainee boys. After breakfast the trainees confronted a mountain of washing up. Then most of the morning was spent preparing and cooking lunch, which usually involved hours of peeling potatoes and butchering meat.

Despite the long, hard workday some of the boys liked the kitchen roster, including David Eva:

> I didn't mind kitchen, because you got a good feed down there. We used to start at five o'clock in the morning and get those big bowls that they used to put the sugar in, fill them up with rice bubbles and take the cream off the top of the milk can.

The vegetable garden wasn't a bad roster and I worked there during one of the summer holidays when the gardener was Kurt Boelter, husband of our cottage mother. The roster was fairly civilised. At the morning bell we went down to begin work in the garden, where Boelter, an early riser, was already working. We came back up for breakfast in Nuffield Hall with everyone else, and were permitted a mid-morning and mid-afternoon break, at each of which we got a big mug of tea with milk and sugar, which was something of a luxury at Fairbridge. We returned to the village for lunch and finished work in the afternoon in plenty of time for a shower and the evening meal with everyone else in the cottage. We also had Saturday afternoon and Sunday off to play sport, go to church and have a free afternoon like everyone else.

Much of the work in the garden involved ploughing, planting, using the rotary hoe to keep the beds clear, watering, weeding and finally harvesting. We grew many crops, including potatoes, turnips, carrots, pumpkins, cucumbers, peas, beans, cauliflower, cabbage, spinach, tomatoes and corn. For many years all the ploughing and clearing was done entirely by a horsedrawn plough, but in the mid-1950s, following his visit to Fairbridge, the Australian governor-general, Sir William Slim, persuaded the Ferguson Company to donate a tractor. But Boelter felt that the plough drawn by old Blossom the horse did a better job and continued using it until he left the farm in the early 1960s to return to Germany.

Over the years there were a number of garden supervisors, most of whom the kids thought were okay. But in the early 1960s Ted Roach, an awful character, came to Fairbridge and became the village garden supervisor while his long-suffering wife became Canonbar's cottage mother. Roach was the opposite of Kurt Boelter. Ill-mannered and perverted, he would grab at the boys' genitals as a sick joke that made us all feel dirty and uncomfortable. He would sit at the Canonbar dining table for the evening meal with filthy hands that he had not washed since coming up from the garden, and roll and smoke cigarettes at the table while we were eating.

The trainee boys usually spent their last few months at the farm school working up on the wheat and sheep section of the farm, which was up beyond the dairy and accounted for about 90 per cent of the Fairbridge property. It was here that the trainee boys learnt to drive tractors and trucks, to plough, sow and harvest, and to farm sheep. The sheep required a lot of work around the year, including drenching and shearing; lamb marking, castrating and tail docking; treatment for footrot; scratch immunisation for scabby mouth; and crutching to prevent them from becoming flyblown.

John Wolvey, who arrived as a nine-year-old in 1940 and stayed at Fairbridge for seven years, remembers working on the farm before mechanisation:

> My God, it was hard work. We used to hate even the hay carting. All the hay was stooked . . . And the wheat was the hardest because they wanted it bagged and put on spring carts. And it was this high – one and a half metres. So what we did, we used to put half a bag up and then put another half bag up, fill it up and ram it up there and sew it once it was up on the spring cart. The dray wasn't so high. But the spring carts are higher.

At fourteen, Peter Bennett was assigned to the dairy as a trainee, in the days before the milking machines had been donated to Fairbridge:

> I went straight to the dairy on the farm . . . We hand-milked the lot. It was very hard for sure, the cleaning and the scrubbing and everything else you had to do. We were also killing about eighteen sheep a week at this stage and we did a steer once a month and a couple of pigs now and again.

Peter was to become one of the longest-serving trainees at Fairbridge:

> I got there in August 1940 as a six-year-old . . . I was supposed to leave in November 1950 but the dairy manager by the name of Jack Armstrong – he'd won a Soldier Settlement block and so he left and Woods

kept me back to run the dairy for three months . . . It was unfair. It put me three months behind on my apprenticeship.

Another long-serving trainee was Stewart Lee. In the later years of Fairbridge, when there were no more children coming from Britain, the younger children were forced to do the milking before and after school. Stewart remembers being so tired at school that an understanding teacher allowed him to sleep on his desk until lunchtime, knowing that he had been up since three in the morning and would have to go back up for the afternoon milking as soon as school was over.

The girls at Fairbridge received an even more limited range of training than the boys. Essentially they were trained to be domestic servants. They too were rotated to different jobs every twenty-eight days: in the principal's house, the village kitchens, Nuffield Hall, the deputy principal's house and Gloucester House, which provided accommodation for visitors and former Fairbridge children who were visiting. But the jobs involved doing very much the same things: cooking, sewing, serving food, cleaning, and washing, hanging out and ironing clothes. Much of it was drudgery, as Gwen Miller recalls. 'Oh, I just think it was plain slavery,' she says. She feels that the kind of heavy lifting they were required to do – for instance, of laundry baskets full of wet clothes – was inappropriate for young girls, who were still growing. 'The work we did. . . really was horrendous for our ages. I mean, scrub, clean. I can remember the laundry because it was so heavy for me and I was never a big girl.'

Gwen Miller and Marina McMahon were both trainees at Fairbridge in the late 1950s. Both remember that the jobs on their roster were much the same, but that their stints in the village kitchen and Nuffield Hall were the hardest. Work in the dining hall started at 6 a.m., when they had to set the big table on the stage for breakfast for staff, visitors and visiting Old Fairbridgians. They also set places with small tablecloths for the cottage mothers at the head of each cottage's table. In the kitchen, the two trainee girls would set up a tray with a full English breakfast for each cottage mother, and a child from each cottage would come and take it to her.

After breakfast and cleaning up, the trainee girls spent a large part of the morning sweeping and polishing the floor of Nuffield Hall. The hall was so big that after sweeping the floor they would polish only about a quarter of it each day.

Christina Murray was seven when she arrived in Australia in 1939; she remembers working as a trainee in Nuffield Hall when she was older:

> The dining room was very hard because we had to wait on the tables; we had to polish the floors. We had great big buffers that were a mile long; they were so heavy you couldn't move them. And the polish, it was terrible. We didn't have polishers or anything; we had to do it with big buffers. We never had machines. A big block of wood it was, with a handle nailed into it and it was just wrapped up with rags.

At lunch the cottage mothers ate up on the stage with the other staff so the trainee girls set extra places on the top table for them. After lunch, it was time for the girls to wash the napkins and tablecloths, and hang them on the washing line at the back of the principal's house. After a rest for an hour or two, the girls were back at Nuffield Hall by 5 p.m. to prepare the evening meal. As all the children had their evening meal in their cottages, only the odd staff member and visitor to the farm came down in the evening to eat in the hall. By the time the meal was over and the washing up and cleaning finished, the girls knocked off around seven-thirty.

The trainee girls worked and lived at the principal's house for the last few months of their time at Fairbridge, often two at a time. The principal's house, a grand timber building, was the only two-storey structure at Fairbridge. Downstairs there was a kitchen, bathroom, lounge room, dining room with a dining table large enough to seat twelve, and a sitting room where the principal's family gathered in the evening to listen to the wireless, and where Ruth Woods had her desk. Toward the back of the house was Woods's untidy office, where he would spend some time during the day and many hours at night clacking away with his two huge index fingers on an old Olivetti manual typewriter that sat in the middle of his vast desk. Most of us Fairbridge children never went beyond the office, which was just inside the back door – and when we went that far it was often only to be caned for some misdemeanour.

Upstairs there were seven bedrooms – enough for Mr and Mrs Woods and their four children when they were home from boarding school, and for special guests, including the chairman of the Fairbridge Council who came fairly regularly to the farm. One of the upstairs bedrooms was shared by the two trainee girls, but the girls were not allowed to use the upstairs bathroom.

One of the girls would have to bring the boss a cup of tea in bed early in the morning. Some remember it as an uncomfortable experience as Woods customarily slept in the nude and was completely unabashed about his state when any trainee girl came into his room. Gwen Miller remembers being shocked: 'I had never seen a man before.'

Marina McMahon had been forewarned and wouldn't

go into the boss's bedroom with the tea. 'I would leave it outside the door,' she says. 'He would call out for me to bring it in but I would just say I'd left it outside and would hurry away.'

The former trainee girls who were rostered to work at the deputy principal's house during the years that Harry Harrop and his wife were there say they enjoyed it. Marina worked at the Harrop house and says that when she and other former trainee girls found out about his crime: 'We didn't feel bad about Harry stealing because he was the one who treated us all well.'

Despite doing the work of adults, the trainees were not paid adult wages but got pocket money. For most of the farm school's history the trainees were paid one shilling a week at fifteen years of age and two shillings a week at sixteen. By comparison, the full adult wage of a farm labourer working on a sheep station in the district was around £12 a week plus board and lodging. By defining the children's work as 'training', Fairbridge was able to circumvent the labour laws, which guaranteed a minimum wage. Smiley Bayliff was one of many Fairbridge trainees who were unimpressed by the arrangement:

> Any way you look at it, it was slave labour. Looking back you can hardly believe they did that. How could they work fifteen- and sixteen-year-olds that hard anyway? How did they get away with it? Some of the jobs were sixteen hours a day, seven days a week. And for no wages. We were paid a couple of bob a week. Enough for one ticket into the pictures at Molong on a Friday night.

While Fairbridge children felt they were underpaid, by the early 1960s some members of the Fairbridge Council in Sydney thought the children were being overpaid and treated too softly. They felt they were being paid too much pocket money, and that this pampering and indulgence had contributed to irresponsible and criminal behaviour in Fairbridge children once they left the farm.

In response to queries by the Fairbridge Council, Woods advised that in addition to their base pocket money, children could be paid more for personal achievement or for undertaking extra duties. He reported that a child received an extra sixpence or shilling for such things as working as a barber in the evening cutting the other children's hair; being a Boy Scout patrol leader, hockey team captain, office bearer for the Junior Farmers Club or school prefect; or passing the Intermediate Certificate. (At the time, sixpence was enough to buy a small bar of chocolate at the Fairbridge tuckshop.) He reported that of the 265 children who had received pocket money in 1961 and 1962 eighty-one were paid sixpence a week, sixty-four were paid eight pence, fifty-five were paid a shilling, twenty-four were paid two shillings and forty-one were paid four shillings.[10]

Dr R. L. Raymond O.B.E., B.A., M.B., F.R.A.C.S. and member of the Fairbridge Council was appalled that Fairbridge children were allowed to eat sweets once a week: 'I think sweets should only be an occasional treat. Teaching self restraint is better than indulgence and having a whim satisfied.' He described an 'atmosphere of indulgence' at Fairbridge and said, 'Our duty is to educate and take care of the children, not to pamper them and bring them up as irresponsible spoilt children with a sense of easy come easy go about money.' He went on to say:

> Then these pampered and irresponsible children go out from the school . . . and fail in their responsibility

. . . roll up in motor cars and cycles. Add this to the number of O.F's who have got in to trouble with the police, or have joined bodgie gangs and I feel they have not been brought up nearly tough enough.[11]

'Indulgence', 'pampered', 'not tough enough'? Hard physical labour is the only thing most of the children at Fairbridge Farm School ever experienced. The typical child would leave with little or no education, no money and no skills – other than those acquired labouring on the farm – and was destined to spend his or her working life as an unskilled farm hand or a domestic.

8

SUFFER THE LITTLE
CHILDREN

Fairbridge was a harsh environment where children had no one to turn to and no way to seek redress. The youngest children were the most vulnerable, the least protected, and the most regularly beaten and abused. Much of the ill treatment of the children was inflicted by some of the cottage mothers.

Kingsley Fairbridge had recognised the importance of well suited and qualified staff, and the need to pay high enough salaries to attract them. However, the organisation in Australia never paid the high salaries originally promised by Kingsley Fairbridge and as a result, the standard of cottage mothers was low and turnover of staff was high. The cottage mothers were the lowest-paid staff at Fairbridge; they were paid less than the going rate for an unskilled farm labourer. In the 1950s, when a farm labourer was being paid more than £12 a week, a Fairbridge cottage mother was paid less than £10. Once tax, board and lodging were deducted she was left with £8, two shillings and sixpence a week. The situation did not improve over the years. By 1970 (and after the introduction of decimal currency) a farm labourer was being paid about $40 a week but a Fairbridge cottage mother only $25 a week.

The obstacles to attracting good cottage mothers to Fairbridge were the same faced by most other children's institutions in the postwar years: poor pay, unsociable hours of work, low job status, geographic isolation and very modest accommodation. A cottage mother's quarters – two small rooms and a bathroom attached to the end of the children's cottage – were hardly salubrious. The little apartment had a bedroom that was just big enough for a double bed and a lounge room that could fit a lounge suite and a few other small pieces of furniture.

It was a lonely existence for a single woman. While Fairbridge had for many years recognised that 'the desirability of employing married staff as far as possible is self evident',[1] it was quite rare for a married woman to take on the job of cottage mother because Fairbridge could not normally offer her husband employment.

Among the cottage mothers who stayed at Fairbridge the longest were the 'widows of Empire'. Typical of them was Kathleen Johnstone, who was at Fairbridge from the early 1950s till the mid-1960s. We knew her as 'The Witch' because of her fearsome treatment of some of the smaller children in her care. She was also known as 'Fag' Johnstone: not only was she a chain-smoker but she would leave the cigarette hanging out of her mouth until it burnt down almost to her lips. The boys in Lady Gowrie Cottage, where she ruled for many years, lived with cigarette ash everywhere; it fell from the side of her mouth as she wandered from room to room. Johnstone also had a perennially runny nose and the children used to watch to see if the snot would reach her mouth before she wiped it away. She was very short, standing only a little over five feet tall, had a slightly hunched back, always dressed in black or dark clothes and carried a huge bunch of keys on her belt.

For the first couple of years of Derek Moriarty's time

at Fairbridge his cottage mother was Miss Jenny Barr, whom he remembers with great affection:

> She was just one of those very rare people that you come across in your lifetime . . . She was a lovely old lady and lots of the kids went and saw her after they left [Fairbridge] and after she left. I know lots of kids visited her even when she got sick and was in hospital.

When Barr left and was replaced by Johnstone, Moriarty said his 'world tumbled upside down'.

> She was just a wicked little old lady . . . She never had a cigarette out of her mouth except when she was coughing and even then half the time she still had one. And she used to walk around the cottage and it gives me nightmares thinking about it . . . She would walk around with a cigarette dangling out of the side of her mouth with her nose running like a tap. It was just sickening to look at it.

No one knew a great deal about Johnstone's past or her family, but she was believed to be a widow, having been married to a British Indian Army officer. The boys in Gowrie Cottage remember that she kept a sheathed Nepalese Gurkha knife hanging on the wall of her quarters. We all knew of Johnstone's cruel treatment of children. I simply kept out of her way; if I saw her in the village I would quickly turn and head in another direction.

Vivian Bingham was unlucky enough to have Kathleen Johnstone as her cottage mother. Vivian arrived at Fairbridge in 1959 at four years of age. She was first sexually abused when she was five. By the age of six she was regularly beaten. At eight she was sexually abused by her older half-brother.

She had been a happy little four-year-old girl when she arrived at John Howard Mitchell House at Knockholt in Kent, prior to sailing to Australia. The matron's reports at the time describe her as 'a dear little girl', 'attractive and amusing', 'a loveable little girl – never lost for conversation'. According to the matron, Vivian asked 'many questions', was 'very popular with other children', and had a 'carefree' attitude. In one of the reports the matron also recorded that she regularly wet her bed, 'but this will quickly clear with care and training I feel sure'.[2]

When she arrived at Fairbridge in 1959 she was less than one metre tall and weighed 24 kg. Within months her reports began to include comments such as 'intellectually dull', 'quiet and rather nervous at times', 'lacks ability to concentrate' and 'Vivian does not seem to show any progress at all.' When she was only six years old the local school headmaster reported, 'Vivian is a real problem child.'

She remembers the early days:

> I missed my mother . . . I felt really alone and scared
> . . . because I was such a tiny thing and there were big
> cottages and all these kids around me and . . . I felt
> scared and lonely.

For the first few months she was too young to attend the local primary school and, like other children who arrived as four-year-olds, was sent out after breakfast to spend her day wandering around the village and the wood piles picking up twigs for lighting the cottage fires.

After terrorising the boys at Gowrie Cottage for many years, Kathleen Johnstone had moved to the girls' Rose Cottage. 'I was about four and a half or five when she started flogging me because I wet the bed. You know, I couldn't help it, I was only a child,' says Vivian. She explains how she was further punished when she wet the bed at the age of six: 'I had to wash the sheets. And then she put me under a cold shower and at one time she put my head down the toilet and flushed the chain.'

She remembers the bigger girls in Rose Cottage trying to take care of her but they were powerless to stop Johnstone.

> They used to look after me . . . She'd hit me and they would be upset but they didn't want to say much to her . . . 'Here's this little girl getting bashed and we want to stick up for you and we want to say something but if we do, we'll probably cop worse than what you just did' – so, they shut up.

Vivian's claims of maltreatment were corroborated in a report that followed an investigation by the New South Wales Child Welfare Department. The report has remained secret and restricted for more than forty years.

The investigation followed complaints made in 1964 to the child-welfare authorities by Mrs Jeanette Bradfield, whose children – thirteen-year-old Clair and ten-year-old William – had gone to Fairbridge under the One Parent Scheme. When she came to Australia she was alarmed at what she witnessed when visiting the farm school. While Mrs Bradfield's complaints were not substantiated by the inquiry, many other children's allegations of cruelty were.

The results of the inquiry were communicated in a letter from A. C. Thomas, Under Secretary, Child Welfare, to the Fairbridge Council in Sydney and a copy of the letter was sent to the Fairbridge Society in the UK; they remain in the Fairbridge files.[3] In the letter Thomas wrote:

> In the presence of Mr Woods, Mrs Johnstone, one of the cottage mothers, admitted that on one occasion

she had put Vivian Bingham's head down the toilet with the object of correcting the child's habit of bed wetting. Mrs Johnstone claimed that she had been informed by children that this method had been successfully applied by a previous cottage mother. She agreed that in the instance in which she was involved the child's habit had not been corrected. She argued however, in favour of this method taking the view that the end justified the means. She claimed further that this incident had occurred about three years ago. Mr Sheriff [the investigator] felt there was every likelihood that it had in fact occurred more recently, and indeed children told him that it had occurred within a few months prior to his visit.

The investigation also found that Johnstone regularly whipped the smaller children with a riding crop, which we at Fairbridge had all known about for years.

There were also complaints concerning Mrs Johnstone caning of children. Mr Woods informed Mr Sheriff that only he, or in his absence his deputy has authority to administer corporal punishment. He did state however, that more cottage mothers have the right to resort to 'domestic punishment', which was interpreted as to allowing them to give the children a smack with a stick. Mrs Johnstone did produce a thin plastic cane, which she said she used in punishing children. She claimed that she just gave them a tap about the legs or on the buttocks but denied that she had done anything more than leave a temporary red mark. In the course of complaints made earlier to Mr Sheriff it had been stated that a whip was being kept by Mrs Johnstone for the punishment of children. He asked permission to look behind the wireless where the children said the whip was kept, and Mrs Johnstone then produced the handle of a riding crop from this position. She stated however, that the children had played with this stick and denied having used it to beat them. Here again Mr Sheriff was left with the impression that punishments by Mrs Johnstone may have been more severe and frequent than she was prepared to admit. There was at least part of a whip in the position indicated by the children.

Despite the fact that the report of the investigation was sent to both the Fairbridge Council in Sydney and Fairbridge Society in London, no action was taken against Johnstone by the Child Welfare Department or Fairbridge, other than to tell her to stop whipping the children. There is no record of Johnstone having been told to stop stuffing children's heads down the toilet. She continued working at Fairbridge for several more years.

Many former Fairbridge children recall savage punishments dealt out by various cottage mothers to little children who wet their beds. As a ten-year-old, Gwen Miller witnessed the treatment of a nine-year-old girl in Lilac Cottage who wet her bed.

I remember one young girl wetting the bed, the one and only time I ever heard of her doing that . . . The cottage mother thrashed her, stripped her off and made her stand over the tub and wash them [her sheets]. Another time I can clearly remember a girl having her head bashed against a wall not once but several times.

She [the cottage mother] would hit us with a large wooden spoon on the legs, hands or even the head. Other times, if she heard us talking in the dormitory at night she would get us out of bed and make us stand for hours in the dining room.

Jimmy 'Tubby' Walker, who arrived as a five-year-old and was to spend twelve years at Fairbridge, recalls a boy being punished by his cottage mother in Brown Cottage for wetting his bed.

> I remember Tom Bates was only five or six and used to wet his bed – minus five degrees and he'd have to hang his bloody sheets out and he'd be absolutely blue. You couldn't see anything of him and she'd make him hang his sheets out on the line. He'd be absolutely blue with cold, poor little bugger.

Another of the 'widows of Empire' was Margaret Hodgkinson. Like her friend Johnstone, with whom she played bridge, Hodgkinson had been in India. She was the widow of a knighted judge named Routledge and, though her husband had died, thought she was entitled to be called 'Lady', which would have been hopelessly out of place at Fairbridge. She then married a colonel in the British Indian Army and was widowed a second time.

Michael Walker remembers Hodgkinson:

> She had a photo of Colonel Hodgkinson who had a large sweeping moustache and a turban on his head. She was imperious, superior, upper-class. We were just little bits of flotsam. We were there to do her bidding; slaves and lackeys on tap. We weren't thought to have any intrinsic value. 'Fetch this, do that, I'll have a cup of tea on the verandah,' etc. She had a drinking problem. Sherry was the grog she preferred. In her cups we were 'the scum of the English gutters'.

Lennie Magee recalls meeting Mrs Hodgkinson, his cottage mother, the day he arrived at Fairbridge as a seven-year-old. He was to be the subject of her abuse for the next six years:

> She tottered in reeking of tobacco and perfume, took one look at me and swept me into her heaving bosom. In a voice I could actually taste, she croaked, 'Ah, a cuddly boy, just what I've always wanted.' I couldn't have replied if I had wanted to. I was being suffocated by tweed and powder. She always dressed in tweed. Tall and thin, she looked as if she'd just appeared out of a 1930s *Vogue* magazine. She wore thick tortoiseshell glasses over a long nose . . . rouge powder and lipstick had been smeared thickly to cover a corrugation of wrinkles, folds and even whiskers. She could panic a cat . . . As a leftover from the Indian Raj where she had strutted with arrogance and wealth she still lived her life expecting everyone to wait on her, hand and foot. Her husband had escaped by dying and now as a refugee from society, Hodgkinson was masquerading as a 'mother' on a farm in the Australian bush where she walked slowly along a dirt road with 'a cuddly boy' hanging on to her ruby clad hand.[4]

Lennie also remembers her cruelty:

> And she was a very brutal woman, very brutal . . . She would beat the children – ironing cords, I've still got scars on my legs from ironing cords . . . She was very cruel. We had to get up very early in the morning, even as a little child, even when it was winter [and get] into the cold shower . . . And she would stand there and watch.

Jimmy 'Tubby' Walker is still angry:

> [She was] fucking shocking . . . She'd say, 'Bend down and say your prayers, you little heathens.' And we'd have these pyjamas on with no tops and she'd come round and flog us all with the ironing cord, you know, the ironing cord doubled over was her favourite weapon. Or the riding crop that she had.

Ten-year-old Gwen Miller's younger brother was regularly beaten in Brown Cottage by Hodgkinson.

> My nine-year-old brother went into a cottage that had one of the most cruel, sadistic cottage mothers out. She had a whip with which she used to whip the boys; she didn't care for the boys at all . . . I felt very sorry for siblings. You saw what was happening but when you are only a small child yourself you know there is nothing that can be done.

The victims of the abuse and cruelty had no one to turn to. They certainly saw no point in appealing to the principal for justice or redress: whenever Woods was faced with a situation where he had to side with either a child or a staff member, he invariably sided with the staff member.

Derek Moriarty recalls a morning in Gowrie Cottage when he stopped the cottage mother, 'Fag' Johnstone, from beating his younger brother Paul with a steel poker during the early-morning shower time:

> We had to get in and have a cold shower and it was just a case of run in and run out sort of thing; it didn't make any difference, as long as you got wet . . . And one day my younger brother got in there and he just

did the same as I did, in and out, and she said, 'Get back in there, you're not even wet,' and of course he objected.

At that point, Johnstone made a lunge for the steel poker that was used with the 'donkey' water heater in the bathroom.

She grabbed that and she was flailing into him with this poker. Now, he's stark naked. I was . . . in the locker room which was next door and I was in there getting dressed and of course he started screaming. And I hit the panic button and I just raced in to see what was going on. And I raced in there and she's got the poker up over her head . . . about to flail him again; I made a lunge for it and I got it.

. . . And to this day, I will never know why I didn't bring it down on the back of her head because that was the mood I was in.

. . . I went out the back and I threw it as far as I could up the backyard. And of course she went straight to the boss and that was it. I got every punishment I could get. There was no pictures, there was no pocket money, there was no dances, no nothing. And plus the usual six of the best.

She could have very well killed him. If she hit him the wrong way one more time, you know, he could have been dead.

What distressed Moriarty for a long time afterwards was that there was no one to turn to.

I had nightmares over that for a long, long time. Not so much the fact that she could attack him like that, but the fact that the authorities just turned a blind eye to it. They didn't believe me and, if they did, they turned a blind eye anyway. And it sort of gave me the feeling of what it would take for them to listen to a kid with a genuine complaint.

Billy King also recalls there was no one the children could turn to:

Of all the years that I was at Fairbridge, not one government official had ever come to me and said, 'Now, are you happy with your life? Are you getting enough food?' Not once. And everyone that I've talked to, they've said the same thing. They can't recall anyone coming.

Lennie Magee remembers being struck on the head by Harry Harrop in Nuffield Hall after an argument about the food. It was unusual for Harry to hit the kids but he never liked Lennie.

Harry hit me on the side of the head so hard . . . my right ear popped and began to buzz . . . Then the whole hall fell silent and every person turned and gawked in my direction. It's hard to pretend you're not hurt when everyone's staring at you. I'd been physically attacked and emotionally violated and I was still standing in a situation where I was completely unable to comprehend just what and why this was happening to me.[5]

We were totally unaware that much of the punishment meted out to us at Fairbridge was illegal. The law relevant to us was the New South Wales Child Welfare Act 1939. To prevent the abuse of children in institutions, Part XI, Section 56 of the Act states that the corporal punishment of 'inmates' should not exceed 'a maximum of three strokes in each hand' and that 'it should not be inflicted in the presence of other inmates'.

It is incredible that no one seemed to take any interest in what was happening to the children or that punishments were carried out in breach of the child-welfare laws for decades. On occasions the governing Fairbridge Council was made aware of the abuse of children at Molong but dismissed the claims and defended the offending members of staff.

In 1958 two fifteen-year-old boys, Nobby Stemp and Fred Southern, ran away from Fairbridge when they were taken with a group of children to Orange to do their Christmas shopping. Hitchhiking and sleeping in parks, they made their way to the Pyrmont wharves in Sydney, where the S.S. *Strathmore* was berthed and preparing for a return voyage to England. They told the drummer in the ship's band that they were unhappy and homesick and wanted to work for their passage back to the UK. The drummer suggested they go and talk to the British consul, whose office was in the Prudential building in Martin Place. They went there, and met a Mr Condon of the UK Information Service, who contacted the New South Wales Department of Child Welfare.

Fairbridge was notified and the boys were put on the overnight train back to Molong. Before the train left they were interviewed at Sydney railway station by a child-welfare officer.[6] The boys made a number of serious complaints about cruelty, including several about their cottage mother, Mrs Da Freitas, who regularly whipped the small boys in her cottage. They also complained about the excessive hours of hard work the children at Fairbridge were obliged to undertake as trainees on the farm.

The under secretary of the Child Welfare Department, R. H. Hicks, wrote to the chairman of the Sydney Fairbridge Council, W. B. Hudson, saying: 'I am particularly concerned as to the reasons which prompted the absconding.'[7] Hicks told Hudson that a number of issues needed to be investigated, including the suitability of Da Freitas to have care of children; what punishments were authorised and administered at Fairbridge; whether a proper log of punishments was kept; and the working hours of the children. Most importantly he asked: 'Are the children free to complain of injustices to the principal or other authority and is each complaint properly investigated?'

Hudson would have none of it. In a reply sent two months later he dismissed Hicks's concerns, saying he was satisfied the children were well treated. 'The cottage mothers discipline their children by giving them small penalty chores, sometimes a handslap or, on very rare occasions, a light caning,' he wrote, 'but the principal is always advised.'[8] Hudson went on to give Da Freitas a glowing character reference.

Smiley Bayliff, who had Mrs Da Freitas as a cottage mother, recalls that she owned a number of sheep and earnt a bit of extra money from the fleece. She kept the flock in the paddock behind Blue Cottage.

> She used to bring sixteen to twenty sheep into the kitchen when it rained and she would make the children keep the cooking stove going at night so the sheep would stay warm and dry. We kids were down in the dormitory with all the windows kept permanently open and no heating. Next morning there would be sheep droppings and urine all over the kitchen floor and we would be made to clean it up.

The chairman of Fairbridge thought this was acceptable. In his response to Hicks, W. B. Hudson supported Da Freitas:

Now I come to my own personal opinion of Mrs Da Freitas. Her children are well turned out, they are fond of her, they appreciate her interest in their various activities but she may be a little inclined to place too much importance on the Junior Farmer aspect of the work, but she only does this at her children's urging. I think it is possible that her interest in animals, particularly sheep, may result in her cottage not being quite as clean as some others, but I am not at all sure that what she does is not in the best interests of the children.

The children were far from fond of Da Freitas. As Smiley Bayliff remembers:

She was the most despicable person you could ever – she's dead now – I'll tell you this now – I don't know where she is . . . if I knew where her grave was, I'd go and find it and work out where her head is, and I'd piss on it. And I tell you what, I'd have to hope she died with her mouth open. And I'm not the only one – I'd be in a long line if I ever found it.

[It] was absolutely miserable; it was absolute hell. Any instances in my life, not just Fairbridge, I can forgive but one person I'll never forgive is Da Freitas, because she was such a sadistic person. Not just to me, to everybody. It didn't matter what she picked up – she used to wield a riding whip, or an electric jug cord – and she used to slash and belt you on the bare backside.

Smiley became sick shortly after arriving at Fairbridge but Da Frietas would not believe he was ill.

I got to the stage where I couldn't walk to the hospital. She called me a malingerer. And I just couldn't walk, and I could always remember David Morgan, he had a broken arm, he piggybacked me to the hospital because I was that bad. I got acute rheumatic fever and was taken to Molong Hospital, where I had my ninth birthday. I was there several months when they eventually said, 'You have to go back now.' I bawled my eyes out. Not many people bawl their eyes out when they go home from hospital.

Barney Piercy came to Fairbridge as a five-year-old with his eight-year-old brother. He remembers Da Freitas when she became the cottage mother of Canary Cottage:

> She had forty cats with a cat pan in each room of the cottage. She used to feed them our meat. Spaghetti bolognaise had meat but we'd have spaghetti without meat and the meat was going to the bloody cats. She was another ratbag, belted you for nothing. Abuse you and scream at you and swear. We were only kids, for Christ's sake. We didn't ask to be there. They seemed to get away with it. There was no one to tell . . .

While some of the former Fairbridge children think the food we were fed was adequate, it got the thumbs down from a nutrition expert in 1953. Sydney Hospital's Molly Baker, B.Sc., was asked by the Fairbridge Council in Sydney to investigate the diet of the children and she compiled a five-page report after a week-long visit to Fairbridge. She was scathing in her criticism of the food and food management. In the report, which was never made public, she claimed the children were not given enough to eat, that the food lacked sufficient nutrition and that much of it was contaminated.[9]

She observed 'maggots floating in stewed mutton', 'moths in the porridge', 'flies floating in the custard and cream' and numerous 'live flies on food and fly-blown meat' and 'decomposing organic matter on the kitchen floor'. Her further remarks on hygiene included: 'The kitchen walls are dirty'; 'Garbage cans have no lids and are left standing in the alleyways outside the dining hall windows'; and 'Almost without exception, *all* kitchen utensils were dirty. Milk cans bringing milk from the dairy, and those sent from cottages for the evening milk, are frequently improperly washed, having a sediment of grit and gravel in the bottom.' Regarding nutrition, she reported: 'The food served is monotonous, unpalatable and lacking in essential nutrients' and 'does not constitute an adequate diet'. Baker criticised the lack of covers on food and the absence of soap and towels.

Baker also claimed that the cottages were not allocated enough food and cottage mothers had complained to her that their rations 'were exhausted days and even weeks before the next issue could be expected'.

The meat, Baker said, was badly butchered by the boys: 'Meat served [was] unattractive and unpalatable.' The chops were more than half fat so that when they were stewed 'the liquid fat makes the dish most unappetising'.

Other criticisms included that the milk was sour on four occasions during the inspection; while cream was plentiful it was only 'issued to private families' and not to the children; the variety of vegetables from the Fairbridge garden was 'very limited', particularly in winter, when children were served 'parsnips, turnips, cabbage and cauli-flower for a period of about a month without change'; and for months of the year there was no fresh fruit.

Baker said the breakfast for the trainees was 'unsatis-factory' and always a 'hashed meal of the previous day's dinner' and that the school lunch sandwiches were 'dry and badly wrapped', the fillings 'neither nutritious nor attractive'.

Baker did not agree that the staff should be served a wide range of food while the children's diet was limited:

> The distinction between staff and children, in the matter of food, is very great. I feel this distinction is both unnecessary and undesirable. The cottage mother has an egg for breakfast every morning and this is eaten at the table with her cottage children, to whom an egg for breakfast is unknown.

Baker made a number of recommendations to improve the food, which could be introduced 'efficiently and quickly' and be achieved with 'very little added expense'.

Notwithstanding Miss Baker's assurance that she did 'not think individual officers can be held responsible' for the poor standard of food at Fairbridge, the cook and his wife immediately quit following the submission of the report. Principal Woods was livid. Rather than accept the report and its recommendations, he attacked Miss Baker. In a seven-page response laced with sarcasm he said:

> This cook and his wife have in fact now resigned as a result of this report from Miss Baker, since they felt that more has been asked of them than was in reason. Miss Baker has offered to help us in the matter of food and kitchen work. Perhaps she would be able to find us a cook and an assistant who can do all that she feels they should do.[10]

While Woods wrote in his response that he agreed with some of Miss Baker's recommendations, he made it clear there would be no significant changes at Fairbridge. He was unconcerned about the contamination of food caused by 'young and inexperienced' trainees. He acknowledged that they sometimes failed to wash the vegetables thoroughly enough, resulting in 'slugs and snails' in the greens, or 'overlooked' sheepskin finding its way into the stew. Nor did Woods dispute that the kitchen utensils were dirty:

> As to the kitchen utensils being dirty, the cook agrees that they probably were so, since he had a weak team of trainees to help him, and he just could not do his and all their work as well.

Nor did he refute Baker's claim that the kitchen walls were dirty. He said they would not be fixed in the foreseeable future, because the painting of the kitchen was 'fairly far down on the list of maintenance work to be done in the village'.

In response to the suggestion that cottages were given insufficient food rations, Woods demanded that Baker name those cottage mothers who had made the claim:

> I personally questioned seven of our eleven cottage mothers, and none of these seven admitted to have made any such statement, and all expressed themselves as satisfied with the rations, and preferred to have them given out monthly.

Woods explained that the chops had been fatty because the boy doing the butchering that morning was 'very new to the work'. The stronger and more experienced boys were up on the farm helping with the harvest and the cook was having his day off.

He rejected the suggestion that the children should be served eggs or the same cooked breakfast as the staff, on the basis that it would cost too much:

> The children do not normally have eggs in the main

dining hall, since the inception of the school the children have only had porridge or cereal and bread and butter etc . . . Should it be desired to serve the children with a second cooked dish as well, the budget will have to be considerably increased to allow for the increased consumption of food.

While Woods agreed that the milk was sometimes sour, he suggested Miss Baker may have been mistaken because in November, when she was conducting her inquiry, the cows had been fed on fresh green lucerne pasture, which gives milk a 'sharp tangy flavour which to the uninitiated is always taken for sour milk'.

Woods did not accept Baker's claim that there was too little variety in the fresh vegetables served to the children, calling it 'a gross misstatement'. It was 'senseless', he added, to expect tomatoes in winter or cauliflowers in mid-summer.

He said that flies had always been a problem at Fairbridge:

This cook, and all previous cooks before him, have every year had to wage the battle of the flies, and as the present cook is a New Australian, he had still to learn the menace that the Australian blow fly can be.

The fly problem, he suggested, was made worse by the design of the village kitchen, which provided numerous ways for flies to get in:

These include the vegetable door, the coke yard door, the bakery and store door, the milk and meat doorway and two servery doorways. Added to this, numerous children come in and out of the kitchen before and during meals.

Finally, Woods disabused anyone who thought the Baker report would result in more or better food at Fairbridge:

> I fear that many of our staff had presumed – quite wrongly – that Miss Baker's findings would necessarily result in everyone getting more food supplied them in all forms, and so there was the very evident attempt made more or less surreptitiously to paint as black a picture as they could for Miss Baker's benefit . . .
>
> I had forewarned the staff not to attempt to do this in a written instruction to them before I went on holiday, but had asked them all to observe the status quo, and in no way to attempt to prejudice or bias Miss Baker's mind and opinions.

In any event, the Baker report did not result in any significant changes, and the range of food and the way it was managed remained virtually unchanged for the next twenty years.

The first principal of the Fairbridge Farm School at Molong, Beauchamp, was criticised for not enforcing sufficient discipline. It was not a criticism that could be levelled against Principal Woods.

Woods, whose temper was legendary, wouldn't hesitate to strike a boy down in a fit of rage – something he had been ordered not to do some years before. Most punishments were administered in his office. You had to bend over his desk as he brought the cane down across your backside with as much force as his huge frame could muster. Lennie Magee remembers one of the occasions he was caned in Woods's office:

> I could hardly breathe. Fear like a vice had squeezed all the air out of me. He rose up to his full height . . .

'Bend over, you scoundrel.' ... Then thwack. The pain was brilliant white and jagged and it shot from your backside to the top of your head, rebounded off the inside of your skull and sprang straight down to your feet. 'Stand still, you scoundrel.' Whack. Because I'd lost my grip on the desk (and life itself) the combined force of twenty stone wielding a stick drove me over the desk and onto his wooden chair.[11]

Eddie Baker went to Fairbridge as a six-year-old in 1948 and speaks quite positively about his experiences there. He remembers that Woods was so busy running the farm he sometimes caught up on a backlog of punishments by going round the dormitories caning children in the middle of the night.

I quite admired him, because he was a man that probably got along on two or three or four hours' sleep, if that – and he would be in his office at early hours in the morning doing reports and so forth. But if he had to chastise a child, he would have it in his notebook ... Eventually he'd get round to it and it didn't matter whether it was midnight, one or two in the morning ... He'd get everybody out of bed in the dormitory, simply because he had to catch up with what he had to do in his notebook ... He brought the canes in under his arm. You'd all be shivering a bit, not knowing which one was going to get it ... Then when you were all out of bed ... the particular child would be dealt with and then you could get back into bed.

A very special status was afforded those children at Fairbridge who defied authority, and being beaten or having your privileges suspended was considered a badge of honour. This was particularly so for boys who received a public thrashing in Nuffield Hall. Public thrashings, which were illegal, were conducted for particularly serious offences, such as running away from the school, and in cases where Woods wanted to set an example for everyone else. His intention was also to humiliate the child. The public thrashings probably did deter us from misbehaving but they did not humiliate those being punished: to the children of Fairbridge, being publicly thrashed was like winning a special bravery award.

Billy King, who was about the same age as me and came out to Fairbridge on the S.S. *Strathaird* in the same party of children, recalls the public floggings:

> What put the fear of God into me was when Woods announced there would be a public thrashing ... I still have flashbacks over those episodes and [how] everyone used to gather in the [hall], because I'd never – even over in England – I'd never been beaten or hit or anything like that. And when you came out and had to see something like that – I just couldn't cope with that at all. I was absolutely terrified.
>
> I often used to think, I'm going to run away from this place, and then the public thrashings used to come into it and that used to stop me from ... It was fear; it was just . . . I just couldn't handle it. I just couldn't cope at all.

Michael Walker also remembers being upset about the public thrashings.

> When a public thrashing was announced it had a terrible effect on me. All boys had to attend. We all gathered at Nuffield Hall at our cottage tables. Then he [Woods] made each boy [being punished] bend over, hands on knees, while he gave them six of the

best. When he had finished, he was breathing heavily and he was a big man anyway, looked ferocious.

I was publicly flogged once, because four of us were caught stealing fruit from the Fairbridge orchard one Thursday afternoon on our way home from school. The Orange High School bus had dropped us off below the farm, on the Mitchell Highway, and as we walked up Amaroo Road we helped ourselves to some overripe pears that hadn't been harvested. We should have been more careful. Across the paddock, up at the sports field, Woods was sitting on an upturned petrol tin umpiring a game of cricket. He spotted us and within minutes a boy was sent, panting, down to intercept us. As we came through the village gate the boy met us and told us we had to go and see Woods.

The boss went into his customary rage, called us 'scoundrels' and said we were to be punished. Usually Woods inflicted punishment pretty soon after the offence, so I was filled with a sickening dread when a couple of days went by. That Saturday at the village lunch he announced that for our dastardly crime we were to be punished that night in the hall, in front of all the boys.

I never fully understood why Woods was so upset about us scrumping a bit of overripe fruit. There were far worse crimes at Fairbridge, such as running away and being brought back by the police, or being caught break-ing in to a building and stealing. I had been caught smoking numerous times and been caned, but almost always in Woods's office. I thought it ironic that I should be punished for doing what the Fairbridge salespeople in England had told us we could do when they were paint-ing Fairbridge as the Promised Land: eating plentiful fruit from the tree.

Woods faced a problem with this particular public flogging: he could belt only three of us. The fourth was a boy named David Newell, the son of a cottage mother who was a tough old bird. Woods would never hit a child of one of the staff members – and certainly not this one's.

When Woods announced at lunch that the three of us were to be disciplined, my older brother, Dudley, who was never to forget or forgive the incident, was outraged. At the end of our lunch he dragged me to stand and wait with him at the foot of the stage until the boss, who was sitting at the head of the staff table, finished his meal.

'Would David Newell be given the same punishment, Mr Woods?' demanded Dudley. I shrank in fear, believing that the confrontation would only make Woods angrier. It did.

As was customary for Woods when he was angry, perspiration appeared on his top, quivering lip. He bawled out my brother with exclamations such as 'How dare you?' and 'Impertinence!' But Dudley wouldn't accept Woods's line, which was that David Newell would be punished by his mother. He insisted that Woods should apply the same punishment to each boy.

I just wanted Dudley to shut up because an angry boss would only hit me harder. I spent an uncomfortable, unsettled, gut-wrenching afternoon anticipating the beating I would be getting that night.

After the evening meal all the boys shuffled over to Nuffield Hall. I remember the silent understanding on the faces of the other kids forced to witness the event. In the hall, Woods lectured everyone about what a terrible crime we had committed and said we now had to be severely punished. When it came time for Woods to flog the three of us I was anxious to get it over with and pushed in front of the others, even though the conventional wisdom was to wait until last because Woods put so much effort into his striking that we thought he would begin to tire himself out. God it hurt. There was an unwritten law that you weren't to scream out. While many kids let out involuntary yelps, I was so proud that I didn't make a sound. It also helped that Woods only gave us four cuts each rather than the regular six, which suggests that my brother Dudley's intervention may have helped after all.

We were lucky to be hit with a big stick or a cane. Woods beat Fairbridge kids of earlier years with a sawn-off hockey stick. Henry McFarlane, who arrived at Fairbridge in the first party of boys in 1938, remembers when eight boys who had run away were publicly flogged with a hockey stick. There were so many boys to be beaten that the work was shared by Woods, the deputy principal and the headmaster of Fairbridge Primary School.

> And they caught them and they gave them a public flogging. To me that was wrong . . . He [Woods] was a pretty brutal bloke . . . and he was about twenty-one stone – whoosh, whoosh . . . It was brutal. And it was wrong. They wore themselves out beating those boys. And what was the headmaster of the local school doing getting involved? It had nothing to do with him.
>
> . . . And you'd always see the kids, when they were having their shower, and when the bruise comes out, it comes out purple and after a while it goes sort of yellow, you know, on the outer. It wouldn't be allowed today.

In 1948 Woods was banned from using the hockey stick by the chairman of Fairbridge, after allegations of child brutality were made by Commander P. O. L. Owen. Though the New South Wales Department of Child Welfare investigation of the allegations found that the charges against Woods 'could not be substantiated', it did note that Woods regularly used the hockey stick to beat children, and that he had been ordered by Fairbridge not to do so in future. Woods was also ordered to cool down and not hit children in a fit of rage, and told there should be no more public floggings. The Fairbridge Council minutes recorded that:

> The principal was then instructed that corporal pun-ishment was to be given to the children only with the cane, only after several hours had elapsed from the time of the misdemeanour giving rise to the punish-ment and only in the presence of a third person of responsibility and that each caning was to be recorded.[12]

But many Fairbridge boys, including Lennie Magee and Smiley Bayliff, remember Woods occasionally using the hockey stick even ten years later. The public thrashings continued and Woods continued to punish children when he was in a fit of rage.

While Woods meted out excessive punishment, at least he only physically struck children when he felt it was warranted. Ted Begley, the dairyman, was much worse. Nearly every boy who worked for Begley has bitter memories of his savage and brutal behaviour. As David Wilson recalls:

> Oh mate, he was a shocker . . . He seemed to do it just for the pleasure of it . . . There was no complaining. If you went to Woods, he'd cane you. So you didn't want two punishments.

Former Fairbridge boy John Harris speaks highly of Fair-bridge and many of the staff, but has bad recollections of Begley:

Ted Begley was out and out low life. He'd whack you, he'd kick you, knee you. If you were bending over doing up your shoelaces you'd get a number nine up your bum. You know, he'd just kick you as he went past. He was just an out-and-out bastard. Absolutely the lowest order.

Derek Moriarty remembers being beaten and kicked by Begley on his first day working as a fifteen-year-old trainee on the dairy.

He kicked me off the stool and then kicked me when I went under the cow, where you had no escape anyway. That's exactly what happened to me on my first day on dairy . . . I was on hand-milking. And I think I was in the second hand-milking bail . . . And naturally, I've got my knees in front of me and . . . I start to get a bit of an ache, so I just went and put my foot out and as I did the kid in the next bail was walking past with a bucket of milk and he tripped. And he went one way and the bucket went that way. I didn't know Begley was there even . . . Anyway, I'm sitting back there and I'm milking away and the next minute, whack! Fair in the ribs. Off the stool, on the stool, under the cow, where could you go? He just kept kicking.

Billy King says the boys were so frightened of Begley that they would buy him Christmas presents because it might save them a beating.

He was an absolute bloody bully. Yeah. I can remember even at Christmas time, all the kids, we used to have to chuck in to buy him a Christmas present. And we didn't have any money, and to this day, I think the only reason the kids bought him a Christmas present is [that they thought they] might save themselves a bloody hiding for a fortnight or something.

I was not aware of sexual abuse while I was at Fairbridge, though many former Fairbridge children say they were victims.

Mary O'Brien, who came out in the same party as me, says she was regularly sexually abused at Fairbridge and kept it to herself for decades. At fourteen, she was moved out of her cottage and assigned to live and work in Gloucester House, where visiting Old Fairbridgians and other visitors stayed. It was also the home of the after care officer, Mr W. Phillips, and his family.

> That was considered a privilege, to go and live with these people in Gloucester House. I went to live there with them and I shared a bedroom with their daughter, but really I was just a domestic there. I was expected to clean up for them and serve them and their visitors.
>
> . . . But it was the most degrading part of my life, the most humiliating part of my life. They treated me – he [Mr Phillips] treated me – like shit, sexually abused me.
>
> He would wait until his wife was asleep and then come into the bedroom I shared with his daughter when she was asleep and regularly abuse me. I would then be expected to serve him breakfast and clean up after him next morning.
>
> I didn't mention it to anybody because I thought it was just happening to me. I had no idea whether other children were having problems.

Vivian Bingham recalls as a five-year-old being sexually abused in the vegetable garden sheds by Jack Newberry, who was the garden supervisor at the time.

I managed to get down to the veggie patch – I don't know how I got down there – and they had a shed down there and I managed to find the shed and also managed to find Mr Newberry too.

He didn't – well, he didn't actually penetrate, you know, he didn't actually – he touched me, you know. It's hard to talk about it – it has to be talked about but it is very hard to talk about that part. And I couldn't go and tell anyone. I was a scared little rat and plus, you know, he said, 'You tell and you get it worse.' Well, you're a child. You're just scared. So I just shut up and got on with life.

Liz Sharp, who went to Fairbridge as a nine-year-old in 1962, has spoken out about being sexually abused by a number of older males while she was at Fairbridge, including Jack Newberry when he was the principal.

Jack Newberry touched me up. I had three other people sexually abuse me at Fairbridge other than Jack Newberry. I must have been just one of those people that had 'victim' written on their forehead . . .

We were in Molong Cottage and we were allowed in to her [the cottage mother's] quarters to watch a movie on television with her and her husband. It must have been winter and there were blankets over everybody and I was sitting near my friends and he was sitting next to me and I mean, he even shoved his hands up inside me then . . . She must have known what he was like and she must have known he had me. Who do you tell? Because no one wants to know anyway. And then they don't believe you and then you're accused of being a liar.

Christina Murray is another who did not tell anyone about being sexually abused at Fairbridge for many decades. Christina arrived in Australia in 1939 with the Northcote child-migrant scheme and was transferred to Fairbridge in 1944. It was not until she was in her seventies – almost sixty years later – that she discussed the abuse. She says, 'Well, I won't mention that man's name, but I was sexually abused at sixteen at Fairbridge and I thought it was the law [of the place].' She didn't tell anyone at the time as 'There was nowhere to go because they wouldn't believe you'.

While some former Fairbridge boys say they were aware of sexual abuse of boys – often by older boys – few are willing to say that it happened to them. One exception is Derek Moriarty, who recalls being molested by an older boy and has finally spoken out about it.

> I had two occasions where he interfered with me and I've never told anybody this in my life. And I thought I was going to take it to my grave. I just . . . it haunts me every now and again, and I never mentioned it to anyone before because I'm embarrassed about it. Even though it wasn't my doing.
>
> Well, what I've seen and heard in the last couple of years, you know, it's really sort of sickening and I thought to myself if everybody's embarrassed and nobody says anything, it will go on. And it has to be stopped. It may never be stopped but certainly an effort has to be made. So, while we've all been in denial, I bet there's a lot more people besides myself that are in the same denial – and I've stated it publicly many, many times, you know: 'It didn't happen at Fairbridge.' It did and I don't know to what extent. But it happened to me and I would say I'm probably too embarrassed about it. I shouldn't be but I'm probably more embarrassed now that I've kept it under my hat for so long.

Robert Stephens, who arrived by himself at Fairbridge as an eight-year-old, is still upset by abuse he suffered from an older Fairbridge boy:

> Look, there was a guy . . . who used to go around taking underwear from the [girls'] cottages and it was put on me and I had the most terrible time for months and months afterwards. And it never left me.
>
> I was just that stupid young kid, and it traumatically – I mean, it just left me numb. And the ostracism of it. And later on, he admitted it. And it went on for months and months. It was just for me a terrible, terrible time.

When they came to Fairbridge most of the children had expected to find a happy, nurturing place of material generosity. What made the abuse so traumatic and difficult to handle was that they had nowhere to go and no one to turn to. Many remember being confused and frightened, and instinctively looking for the protection of a parent. Their pain and distress are perhaps captured in these words from Vivian Bingham:

> Whenever I was flogged, whenever I got hurt, I used to think, Where's Mum? so I could run to Mum. And my mum wasn't there . . . I couldn't run to Mum.

9

RETARDS

If the absence of anything resembling parental care was hard enough for kids to deal with, another harsh reality of Fairbridge was its failure to live up to the promise of providing a better future.

A big factor in many parents' decisions to let their children go to Fairbridge was the assurances they received that their children would have greater educational opportunity there. It was certainly an important consideration for my mother. Yet Fairbridge Farm School children were denied a decent education; they did not even receive the same level of schooling given to other Australian children. Almost all Fairbridge children were forced to leave school at the minimum school-leaving age to work on the farm and half of the Fairbridge children left school without completing the second year of secondary school. If a Fairbridge child turned fifteen in the term following a holiday, they didn't have to go back to school after the break, which meant some became trainees when they were still only fourteen years of age.

The practice of pulling students out of school to work on the farm began with the first party of children and continued throughout the life of the farm school. Henry

McFarlane, who was an eight-year-old in the first group
of boys to arrive at Fairbridge in 1938, recalls:

> We left at fourteen: we had no choice. They'd just say,
> well, everything on the farm had to be done, the
> harvest is coming on. Big strong blokes, you'd better
> go up there and help with the farm.
>
> See, what happened, being illiterate and that sort
> of thing – couldn't read or write, you know – I just
> used to, when my mother sent a letter, I just used to
> go on what they'd read out to you.

Joshin Richards arrived as part of the third party of
twenty-three boys and six girls on the S.S. *Orama* in
1939. He was forced to leave school at fourteen years and
four months old, and says: 'One weakness there was:
anyone who was qualified to go higher in their education
was pulled out of school to help run the farm.'[1]

Joyce Drury, who also arrived at Fairbridge in 1939,
remembers:

> At fourteen and a half I left school . . .and then I
> became a trainee . . . learning to be a farmer's wife.
> We were doing things with the boys like hobbling up
> horses to go and fetch wood; and it wasn't only clean-
> ing and ironing and washing and looking after babies
> and learning how to sew and cook . . . if you were
> going to be a farmer's wife. You know, stooking hay,
> going up for rabbits, doing all kinds of things like that.

Nearly thirty years later Fairbridge children were experiencing the same thing. Ian Dean, who went to Fairbridge
as a ten-year-old with his older brother in 1961, turned
fifteen in July 1965 and was forced to leave school even
though he wanted to continue.

I wanted to stay on at school and sit for the School Certificate at the end of fourth year but Woods just laughed. He said my marks weren't good enough and that I was needed as a trainee.

Ian spent the next two years working as one of the declining band of trainees. When he turned seventeen he left Fairbridge to work as a labourer in a dry-cleaning shop in Molong.

In the early 1950s a financial crisis had forced Fairbridge to again cut back the children's schooling. In February 1953 the chairman of the Sydney Fairbridge Council wrote to Principal Woods instructing him to shed paid staff and replace them with children, who should be taken out of school at the earliest possible date. The policy of giving every child the chance to reach the Intermediate Certificate was abandoned. The chairman told Woods: 'For the present only children of exceptional mental ability should be left at school after the compulsory age'.[2]

Fairbridge kept this a secret in the UK and continued to promote educational opportunity when recruiting children. As late as 1959 Fairbridge claimed in its annual report: 'The Fairbridge children who qualify for higher education and wish to carry on are encouraged and permitted to do so.'[3]

Evidence that Fairbridge forced children to leave school against their wishes survives in some official files. In 1954, four Fairbridge boys wished to continue at Molong Central School beyond their fifteenth birthdays so that they could sit for the Intermediate Certificate at the end of the year. They were prevented from doing so by the Sydney Fairbridge Council, despite its stated commitment by Council to a policy 'that all of our children must aim to reach at least the Intermediate Certificate standard'.[4] The headmaster at Molong Central School recommended that they be allowed to stay on, writing to tell Fairbridge that the boys had been good citizens and had done a lot for the school 'willingly and in good spirit'. He said that while their chances of attaining the Intermediate Certificate were 'not good, at least they could [attempt] that goal with steady application'.[5]

Principal Woods agreed and sent the headmaster's recommendation and the school reports of the four boys to the Fairbridge Council. In his letter to the Fairbridge board he said: 'I recommend that the Headmaster's proposal be accepted since they might all achieve the Intermediate [Certificate].' Interestingly, Woods added: 'We will not be short of trainee boys this year on the farm.'[6]

The four boys were Norm Brown, Ray Tate, Joe Smith and Jimmy Neave. Their school reports from the end of 1953 show that Ray Tate had the highest marks, having come thirteenth in the class of twenty-four. However, his conduct was described as 'indolent and inattentive'. Joe Smith, who was to commit suicide at Fairbridge later in 1954, had come eighteenth and his conduct was described as 'good'. Jimmy Neave had come nineteenth and his conduct was also described as 'good'. Norm Brown had come fourteenth and his conduct was described as 'fair'.

The chairman of Fairbridge, Hudson, initially responded by saying that he thought extra schooling for the boys would be 'a waste of time'.[7] On 21 January Woods was told only Jimmy Neave would be allowed to sit. He then withdrew Norm Brown's application but appealed again on behalf of Joe Smith and Ray Tate. (It was not unusual for Woods to question the decisions of the Fairbridge Council.)

> I would like to make a further plea to Council on behalf of the boys who were recommended by the headmaster and myself for continuation of their schooling to enable them to write the Intermediate Certificate at the end of the year.[8]

He said Ray Tate showed 'a very keen desire to continue with his school, and was very disappointed at being put to trainee work'. Of Joe Smith he said, 'He has it in him to make the grade and get through at the end of the year with encouragement.' Woods added that of the fifty Fairbridge children at the secondary school in Molong that year only three would be sitting for the Intermediate Certificate.

The Fairbridge Council was unmoved by the appeal. Two months later, Woods was notified of the decision of the Child Welfare Committee of the Fairbridge Council. Only Jimmy Neave could stay on.

> The committee has considered your request . . . They have decided that J. Neave should be permitted to sit . . . They have decided that J. Smith and R. Tate should not be permitted to sit as they have only a remote chance of passing and the Sub Committee feel that they have not made the best of their opportunities.[9]

Fairbridge's failings were compounded by the New South Wales Education Department, which kept many of the Fairbridge children out of mainstream classes at school. A high proportion of Fairbridge children who were sent to Molong Central School were put in a General Activities, or GA, opportunity class designed for children who had learning difficulties or were intellectually disabled. The students were in a composite class known as 1G-2G, crammed together into a tiny classroom. Nearly all of the Fairbridge children who spent their secondary school in this class have struggled through life with problems reading and writing.

Stewart Lee, who arrived at Fairbridge as a four-year-old, remembers being one of the Fairbridge children crowded into the little 1G-2G classroom:

> [It] was known as the 'dumb class' . . . 1G-2G. We were in one little segregated mob . . . Their idea is that you're basically waste, you've probably been kicked out of your home or you're from broken families.
>
> We weren't expected to pass, put it that way. That's basically why you were in 1G-2G . . . Being Fairbridge, you were automatically put in there. So if you had any potential whatsoever, you weren't going to go nowhere anyway. Fairbridge was exactly the same. They didn't let you get to the top of your own potential. Like, there were kids that were artists and everything else there – they wouldn't let them get to their potential.

Daphne Brown arrived at Fairbridge as a six-year-old in 1939 with her nine-year-old brother and feels that she was not given the help she needed to address learning difficulties. She says her stay at Fairbridge wasn't all bad, but as a result of her poor schooling she has struggled through adult life unable to read or write properly.

> My education was very poor . . . They should have picked up on a lot of us . . . We were in a class at Molong School called an 'opportunity class' and out of that class, all of us were from Fairbridge except for two children. Now, that should have told them something – we needed help. We missed out on that basic education when you were a child.
>
> We had to write compositions. It was all in my mind but I couldn't spell – no one could understand

what I wrote. So, therefore, I was disadvantaged right through life ... I tried to learn but I'm probably dyslexic in some way. So, I was a bit resentful in later life that I wasn't given a good education. Maybe they could have helped me a little bit there.

It remains a mystery why so many Fairbridge children were locked up in this class until they were old enough to leave school and become trainees at Fairbridge. A 1951 Department of Education report that assessed fifty-four Fairbridge children who would begin going to Molong Central School from the next year suggests that a staggering number of them were incapable of a normal school education and needed to be placed in 1G-2G. The report claimed: 'The existing intelligence scatter shows that approximately 40% of Fairbridge children will require Opportunity ... type of teaching and courses.'[10]

However it is not clear what was used to measure the 'intelligence scatter'. It could not have been IQ, the widely used measure in those days, because the IQ test results for the same fifty-four children – which also survive in the Education Department files – show that the range of their IQs was normal, or slightly above normal. Twenty-nine registered an IQ of over 100 and twenty-five below 100. Of the twenty-nine who measured above 100, six registered IQs above 120, eleven were between 110 and 119, and twelve were between 100 and 109. Of the twenty-five below 100, fifteen measured between 90 and 99, and the remaining ten measured below 90.[11]

An IQ above 100 is considered to be above average. But Smiley Bayliff, who registered an IQ of 112 in a test in England shortly before he arrived at Fairbridge as an eight-year-old in 1955, spent all of his secondary school years in 1G-2G.[12] While in the GA class he achieved consistently high marks and favourable comments from his teachers, yet he was never placed in a mainstream class, where he might have sat for the Intermediate Certificate.

Smiley was taken out of school before his fifteenth birthday to become a trainee and when he left Fairbridge he was 'unable to write two words together'. It was only in his thirties, at the prompting of his wife, Kerry, that he went to evening college to learn to properly read and write English.

David Eva spent two years at Fairbridge Primary School from the age of ten, and attended Molong Central School for two years.

> I was in classes 1G-2G which was the lowest secondary-school [level] and I stayed there all the time. As I turned fifteen, they kicked me out . . . You couldn't stay on at school. When you got to that age, you were told you had to do two years as a trainee . . . Education-wise, it was shocking. I think that a lot of children that went through that place – if they'd had a decent education, I think a lot of them would have done better.

One of the Fairbridge children who successfully worked his way up and out of 1G-2G and into the mainstream Molong Central School classes was Laurie Reid:

> Well, I went into one class there, it was the sort of class where you sort of entered into it but that's as far as you went, right, 1G-2G. But it happened that I topped the class, two exams in a row, right. So I got out of that and got put into the next class up. But they were short on the farm, so they decided at fourteen and a half they were going to pull me out. So I had to do work on the farm then.

> My [older] brother went down and saw F. K. S.
> Woods and said that he wanted me to stay on. Even
> my teacher said he wanted me to stay on. And I was
> starting to get on top of the problems I had with
> mathematics and all that, you know ... And they
> said, 'No, you're coming out; we haven't got enough
> trainees to run the farm; you're coming out.' So, I was
> put out of school.

Their poor education was to be reflected in the lives of
Fairbridge children when they left the farm school. A
record of the occupations of former Fairbridge children in
the mid-1950s shows that of the fifty-nine boys and girls
surveyed, almost all worked in unskilled or semiskilled
jobs: they were farmhands, labourers, domestics, shop
assistants or factory workers. A few were in the military,
only one had pursued 'further education' and none were
employed in a profession.[13]

Fairbridge was made aware of the serious failure of its
education programs early on in its history. In 1944, in
anticipation of the resumption of child migration after
World War II, the British Government asked for an assess-
ment of the child-migrant schemes in Australia. An investigation of the Fairbridge Farm Schools at Molong and
Pinjarra in Western Australia, and the Barnardo's Farm
Schools, was undertaken by Mr W. J. Garnett, the official
secretary to the British high commissioner to Australia.

Garnett reported that there was no real prospect of
Fairbridge boys becoming owners of farms, one of Fairbridge's stated aims. He recommended:

> In order to achieve this objective the standard of edu-
> cation provided at the farm school will need to be
> improved, certain additional facilities will need to be

provided, and the farm schools must be in a position
to send children to outside education institutions for
higher education or special training.[14]

While the Fairbridge Society in London accepted
Garnett's report it blamed the Fairbridge administrations
in Australia, at Molong and particularly Pinjarra. The
basic farm trainee scheme would continue unchanged at
Fairbridge for another three decades.

The local Fairbridge Council in Sydney was aware
from a very early date that there was a problem with the
education of its children. In February 1944 Sir Percival
Halse Rogers, a member of the Sydney Fairbridge
Council, wrote to the London Fairbridge Society chairman, Sir Charles Hambro, to express concern about the
failed education program at Fairbridge. Halse Rogers was
the chancellor of Sydney University and a New South
Wales Supreme Court judge, and had been a Rhodes
scholar at Oxford at the same time as Kingsley Fairbridge.

> We have been conducting a review on our own
> account and after a consideration of results to date
> have left some of us with a definite feeling of disap-
> pointment and a desire to inquire whether our failures
> are due to ourselves or are due to defects in the selec-
> tion and methods in Great Britain – or to both.[15]

In the late 1940s, after the resumption of child migration,
the population of Fairbridge began to grow again. The
little Department of Education school at the back of
the village, which taught both primary and secondary
students, was soon too small for the number of children.

Fairbridge wanted a new and larger school built on site
but the Education Department wanted Fairbridge children to attend Molong Central School. Classified as a

junior secondary school, it provided three years of secondary schooling to the level of the Intermediate Certificate, and taught a limited number of subjects. The Education Department argued:

> Educationally Fairbridge secondary children would benefit. A broader social experience so necessary to migrant children would be available to them. They would be eased into the general community rather than as now happens, thrust into a social scheme different entirely from that developed within the Fairbridge farm community.[16]

Fairbridge resisted the move: it wanted the children to complete their entire education on the farm. It mounted a raft of arguments, including that the children would no longer be able to have a hot midday meal and that Fairbridge could not afford the bus that would be necessary to transport the children to Molong each day. Notwithstanding Fairbridge's ongoing protests, the Education Department ordered them to send all secondary-school-age children to Molong Central School from the beginning of 1952.

But even within the Education Department there had been reservations about Fairbridge children going to school in Molong. Two years before the change, the superintendent of Secondary School Education had reported:

> I was impressed by the general high standard of the dress and personal neatness of the school children at Molong and by the fact that the Fairbridge Farm children suffer much by comparison. Until such time as the Fairbridge Farm authorities recognise the importance of training their children in personal

hygiene and neatness, and until they provide them
with clothing and footwear appropriate to secondary
school pupils with due regard to neatness and care of
hair, the Fairbridge children will look out of place in
a normal public school.[17]

Even after 1952 Fairbridge agitated for years to have the
Education Department build a bigger school on Fair-
bridge. Nearly three years after the children began attend-
ing Molong Central School the chairman of Fairbridge,
W. B. Hudson, wrote to the director of education in New
South Wales, Cyril Wyndham:

I may say that we are negotiating with the Federal
Government and state Government (at the moment
with every prospect of success) with a view to grants
being made to Fairbridge and they on their part
asking us for an undertaking that we will build the
school up to 200 children.[18]

Had Hudson been successful, Fairbridge children would
have spent their entire childhood and youth till the age of
seventeen on the farm school. As it was, children usually
went to Molong Central School for only two or three
years, which meant many children, particularly those who
went to Fairbridge at a very young age, hardly ever set
foot off the farm school for years. Stewart Lee, who came
to Fairbridge as a four-year-old, recalls that prior to going
to Molong Central School he hardly ever left the farm
school:

The only times was when Woods took us in to the
Molong swimming pool – and one Sunday a month
they had the church service in Molong. That would be
another one. And the thing about it is – and this is

what a lot of people don't seem to realise: that's why we kept our English accents for so long, because we were still only talking to other English kids. And we weren't talking to Australian kids. Simple as that.

In 1955, in the absence of any improvement in the academic achievement of the children, the Fairbridge Council in Sydney established an inquiry to look at education at the farm school.[19]

A copy of the report, which was never made public, has been locked away in a file in Fairbridge's Sydney offices ever since. The inquiry was prompted by the high level of academic failure of the children, and a concern that this was reflected in problems such as children running away from the farm, being involved in crime and antisocial behaviour, and failing to hold down employment after leaving Fairbridge.

The preamble to the confidential report lists ten reasons to be disappointed by the outcome of Fairbridge children's education and training: their poor scholastic record; 'the limited number who seriously attempt to further their education when they leave the school'; their failure to settle down in steady jobs after they leave; 'the bad reports on Old Fairbridgians from certain responsible quarters' (presumably respected members of the society); their standard of behaviour while at Fairbridge, including their 'sexual habits and relations'; abscondings; police offences and near offences; illegitimate children; the discontent evident in Old Fairbridgians' replies to questionnaires; and, finally, a rebellious attitude of Old Fairbridgians to some Fairbridge staff members.[20]

The inquiry found that the educational record of Fairbridge was poor, homework was not being done, children from Fairbridge did fewer tertiary courses than other school leavers and they could not hold down jobs. It also made the observation that happy children would not run away from the school.

Fairbridge in Sydney became even more starkly aware of its poor education standards when it compared the 1954 school performance of children who had left Fairbridge at Molong with that of children who had left Fairbridge at Pinjarra in Western Australia. Fairbridge Molong's results were much poorer than Pinjarra's. Fourteen per cent of the Pinjarra children left school before completing the second year of secondary school. Twelve per cent did not complete the first year and the other 2 per cent did not complete the second year. In contrast, half the Molong Fairbridge children who left school did not complete the second year of secondary school. Thirty-six per cent did not complete the first year and the other 24 per cent did not complete the second year.

In 1955, Mr G. S. Le Couteur, a member of the Fairbridge Sydney Council, made a number of suggestions aimed at improving the poor educational performance of Fairbridge children.[21] One of his suggestions was that they be encouraged to take up hobbies like other Australian children, and that Fairbridge make facilities available for the children to do this.

Woods said that while it was a good idea, it would require significant additional funding. A bigger problem, he added, was that unlike the children who attended Knox, the private school in Sydney that Le Couteur had used as an example, Fairbridge children worked too hard and had too little time for hobbies. He said:

> The Fairbridge child must make his bed every day . . . chop and fetch in a load of firewood . . . clean, set and light a boiler fire and fetch coke for it . . . dust, sweep and polish the dormitory . . . do the same for

any other room in the cottage . . . fetch milk, meat, stores, vegetables . . . take down mail, messages to the office and elsewhere . . . help do the ironing, mending, washing of clothes . . . gardening, working bees on the village and the farm.[22]

Woods said it was even harder for the trainee boys because they had to rise early in the morning and by the evening they didn't have the energy to give much time to activities.

To illustrate how inappropriate it would be to encourage hobbies among the children who could not read or write properly, Woods provided a profile of the boys in Gowrie Cottage as an example:

Peter Bodily, fifteen years and 8 months. He reads with difficulty and writing is an effort.
Graham Salisbury, fifteen years and 7 months. Reading and writing both difficult for him.
Glenwood Jory, fifteen years and 7 months. Reading and writing are both tedious for him.

A manual block had been built on the Fairbridge grounds around the same time as the little school was built by the New South Wales Department of Technical and Further Education, and twice a week a teacher came out to the farm to teach metalwork and other trades to the trainee boys of fifteen and sixteen. The teacher wrote to Fairbridge complaining that most of the boys had left school but were unable to read or write. Hudson wrote a letter to the Department of Education's regional head in Bathurst saying:

The point I am coming to is that the new agriculture teacher finds that the Fairbridge boys he is handling are so backward in reading and writing and arithmetic that it is exceedingly difficult for them to absorb the work.[23]

Hudson went on to ask that the local headmaster be allowed to vary the school syllabus to allow the children to be taught basic reading and writing skills. The Education Department replied that the headmaster already had the authority to vary the syllabus to meet the reading, writing and arithmetic needs of these underprivileged pupils, 'however he is maintaining an educational program which provides for the spiritual, cultural, social and other needs of the child'.[24]

Stung by this rebuff, Hudson shot back:

> I differ from you a little in your comment on the spiritual, cultural and other needs of the child, as actually a child gets a great deal more of this at Fairbridge than he or she would in her own home.[25]

The episode did not change the education of Fairbridge children.

From our party that arrived in June 1959, the four primary-school-age children started the next day at the primary school on Fairbridge. Of the secondary-school-age children, two of us, Billy King and I, were sent to Molong Central School, but interestingly, the others, including my brothers Richard and Dudley, were sent to Orange High School. Never before had so many children from a newly arrived party been sent to Orange High School, which offered a wider range of subjects than Molong Central and taught five years of secondary school to matriculation level, rather than stopping at the Intermediate Certificate.

What we didn't know was that the Education Department had appointed a new local school inspector, Keith Morton. It appears that he had instructed Fairbridge to give more children the opportunity of a high-school education.

After attending Molong Central School with the other Fairbridge kids for a couple of weeks I was pulled out of the classroom by two inspectors from the Education Department and taken to sit on a bench in the playground. One of them asked: 'Do you want to go to Orange High School to be with your brothers?' I didn't. I had found settling in to Fairbridge very difficult and was at last starting to make new friends among the kids I caught the bus to Molong Central School with each day. Despite telling the inspectors 'Thanks but no thanks', I was off to Orange High School.

Those of us who went each day to Orange High School were different from the other Fairbridge children. Not only did we leave breakfast early and miss most of the after-school work and other village activity, we also dressed and looked different. Mary O'Brien, who went to Orange High School with me, remembers being regarded as a snob by the other Fairbridge kids.

> Well, it was harder to feel part of the group because the other kids either went to the local primary school, or they went to Molong. I was considered a snob, but really I wasn't a snob. I wasn't. I was just very shy. I felt very inhibited; the whole experience made me very self-conscious.

If at Fairbridge I felt set apart from the other children because I went to Orange High, at Orange High I felt like an undesirable social outcast from the 'institution' out on Molong Road. Until we Fairbridge kids were able to somehow get hold of second-hand Orange High School black blazers with gold trim, and long grey trousers, we stood out from the thousand other students at the school in our grey woollen coats and short grey trousers.

Derek Moriarty, who had arrived at Fairbridge eight years before me, recalls that he enjoyed going to Orange High School:

> Apart from the fact that I felt like an outcast, and apart from the fact that I was still wearing little grey flannel pants at the end of fourth year when every other kid in high school had long pants after first or second year – I felt a bit out of whack there.

Laurie Field, who arrived at Fairbridge as a fourteen-year-old, describes how difficult it was being a Fairbridge kid and going to Orange High School:

> We seemed to cop it both ways because the Orange High School kids sort of looked on you as being a little bit below them because: we're from Orange and you guys are from Molong and Fairbridge Farm School, little Pommie migrants, you know, that sort of thing. And of course, from Fairbridge: oh, they're too good for us; they're going to Orange High School. It was fairly noticeable, actually.

Mary O'Brien has similar memories.

> Going to Orange High . . . I felt like [we were] the poor relatives. I think my feeling of stigmatisation goes back to even before going to Fairbridge because we came from a single-parent family in a day and age when there weren't many single-parent families, and

then going into an institution like Fairbridge just increased that feeling.

My school results at the end of the first year were a disaster but Orange High School and Fairbridge made allowance for the fact that my year had been disrupted by migration from England, and the challenges of settling in to a new school and a different education system. However, over the next year my school marks continued to plummet and I became less and less engaged by schoolwork. I was far from alone: many Fairbridge children's school performance declined the longer they were there. Bob Stephens is still upset about it:

> What irritates me now: when I look back at my Fairbridge records and I see the school results and you see I'm up within one or two of the top academically, and then after two years, it deteriorates to where I'm at the bottom of the class; and I think that's a reflection of my not being able to cope with Fairbridge and the whole situation of Fairbridge.

Mary O'Brien says, 'I had done well in school until I went to Australia.' At Fairbridge her school results slipped, and she feels that this damaged her self-esteem, which was already suffering at Fairbridge. 'It was just another sort of nail in the coffin of damaging my self-esteem, which took years to recover from.'

At Orange High School I became increasingly rebellious and antisocial. I regularly played truant with a few other Fairbridge boys, even though we had no spending money so there wasn't much to do. We hung around the parks in the town until it was time to catch the school bus back to Fairbridge. Meanwhile, both my brothers were making a better go of it. They were fitting in, developing friendships and performing better in exams and extracurricular activities, particularly sport.

At the start of my third year at Orange High I was summoned to see the legendary principal Leo 'the Lion' O'Sullivan, whom I knew well from my regular visits to his office for a caning. He seemed to enjoy telling me that I was being thrown out of the school. 'We deem you to be uneducable,' I remember him saying.

'Don't you mean "uneducatable"?' I asked, not realising that 'uneducable' was correct.

I hitchhiked back to Fairbridge Farm that morning, to be confronted by an angry Woods, whom O'Sullivan had phoned with the news. Woods was waiting to berate me for the huge and wasted cost to Fairbridge of sending me to the high school for the best part of the last two years.

Because I was only fourteen, still below the minimum school-leaving age, Woods couldn't put me to work full-time on the farm as a trainee. The next day I was back at Molong Central School.

I didn't feel like such a social outcast at Molong Central, where the Fairbridge kids had security of numbers. David Wilson, who was close to my age and went to Molong Central with me for a while, remembers how we Fairbridge kids stuck together there and kept pretty much to ourselves: 'I always remember we had what we called "the pub". It was a corner of the playground and that's where all we Fairbridge kids sat at lunchtime.'

Molong Central School was less challenging than Orange High; I swapped French, physics and chemistry for woodwork, art and biology. Later that year I passed the Intermediate Certificate, which I remember the Fairbridge deputy principal, Harry Harrop, discounting as 'something they hand to you on a plate'.

But I was luckier than most other Fairbridge children

because I had been allowed to stay at school a few months beyond my fifteenth birthday to sit the Intermediate Certificate exams. Looking back, I think Fairbridge was more generous in regard to the education of those children who had parents following them out, or whose parents were already in Australia.

Ultimately, Fairbridge would blame the poor education results on the children – whom they would officially describe as 'retarded' – and on their deprived backgrounds and failed education in Britain before they came to Australia.

At one stage the Sydney Fairbridge Council invited the headmasters of Fairbridge Primary School and Molong Central School to their meeting to discuss the continuing poor education results of Fairbridge children. The minutes of the meeting record:

> Mr Mott and Mr Heyes gave very enlightening and instructive addresses on the educational qualifications and scholastic ability of Fairbridge children, from which it was learnt that generally these children are educationally retarded, but in the last two years or so the standard appears to be improving.[26]

The description of Fairbridge children as 'retarded' is a continuing theme in the explanation of their poor educational results and was at one stage included in the annual report of Fairbridge Farm School Molong.[27] This explanation is difficult to reconcile with the fact that the children who fared better at school while at Fairbridge tended to be those who came out to Australia at a later age, having spent more of their childhood in England and less time at Fairbridge. The children who left Fairbridge with the poorest education tended to be those who had come to

Fairbridge at a younger age to spend a larger part of their childhood and schooling at Fairbridge and a shorter part of their childhood in Britain.

In its ongoing campaign to recruit British children Fairbridge gave no hint of the unhappy state of its education record. At the end of the 1950s it was still promoting education and career training. In 1959, the New South Wales Fairbridge Council said:

> The Fairbridge children who qualify for higher education and wish to carry on are encouraged and permitted to do so. They continue their education at High Schools, Technical Colleges, Business Colleges and such like establishments and if they qualify further and wish to continue, are helped to attend Teachers' and Agricultural Colleges and would be helped even to University if they win scholarships.[28]

The pledge to help Fairbridge children who earned scholarships to university was a fairly easy promise to keep since, at that time, none of them had.

The failure of Fairbridge to deliver on its promise of a decent education was one of its most serious shortcomings. Having already endured years of social isolation and a childhood of emotional privation, the typical Fairbridgian also had to contend with leaving the farm school at seventeen years of age to confront the world with no educational qualifications.

10

THE CHILDREN'S WORLD

Beneath the strict routine and discipline at Fairbridge we did manage to build our own world, whose value system was at odds with the official order. Particularly among the boys, misbehaviour, smoking, stealing, defiance of authority, bullying and absconding (with police in pursuit) were all part of life on the farm.

We gave one another nicknames, usually based on physical characteristics or distinctive behavioural traits. 'Stumpy' was squat and nuggety; his younger brother 'Runty' was small for his age; and I was 'Faddy' because I was overweight when I arrived at Fairbridge. Other fatties at Fairbridge included 'Tubby' Walker and 'Fatman' Sinclair. No one was actually overweight at Fairbridge so they too probably acquired the epithets when they first arrived. 'Muscles' had a body builder's physique and 'Shark' had fine, shiny teeth. Gwen Miller was known as 'Mini' and Geraldine Winn as 'Jellybean' because they were so tiny. 'Whoopee' could fart at will, 'Bean' had an extremely long nose and 'Swagman' was extremely untidy. As a little boy, 'Bubbles' had bubbles of snot coming out of his nose and 'Goggs' had big round eyes. 'Snowy' and 'Flossy' both had mops of very blond hair and 'Smiley' simply had a happy face. One boy was called 'Maggot' because from the time he arrived at Fairbridge as a four-year-old boy, he ate anything and everything he could. 'Whopper' was notorious for telling lies and 'Eggy' had a pronounced egg-shaped head.

The most enjoyable times were when we were able to escape from the farm and its strict routine. On Sunday afternoons it was possible to seek special permission – first from your cottage mother and then the principal – to leave the farm and go down to Molong Creek. As a treat you could take a small ration of tea-leaves and sugar and some milk, light a fire and boil a billy. In the warmer months we would strip off and swim in the creek, although at the risk of getting a nasty bite from a yabby, or attracting leeches. On a typical Sunday afternoon there might be half a dozen fires alight along Molong Creek below Fairbridge Farm.

Rabbit hunting was also very popular, especially before myxomatosis was released in the 1950s to cull the rabbit population, which had reached plague proportions and caused terrible damage to farming land across Australia. By the time I arrived in 1959 the disease had dramatically reduced rabbit numbers. When we were out hunting we could easily tell which rabbits were infected because they were so sick it was easy to run them down and they had ugly red sores, particularly around their eyes.

Rabbiting was more than recreation: the catching of a rabbit meant a nice stew back in the cottage that evening, which was a delightful change from the monotony of mutton. Before the 1950s rabbiting was also a way for Fairbridge kids to earn a bit of extra pocket money. Peter Bennett recalls the rabbit plagues before myxomatosis:

> The rabbit plagues were so bad that Woods would be able to tell a farmer that he'd be able to get all the kids to go on a rabbit drive . . . What we had to do: all the

kids would go right across the paddocks, right back
for miles. They'd have one paddock right up the end
with the wire turned up and all the trees and bushes
thrown in there, so we'd drive the rabbits and hares
all the way into there. And the kids would get five
shillings a drive. They'd be gutted and paired – they
wouldn't be skinned – and put on a truck, two at a
time, and they had these pipes down the truck and
you threw the pairs over the pipe and of course they
weren't refrigerated . . . and they'd be on the markets
the next day in Sydney . . . We got up to two and a
half thousand pairs at one stage. And the older kids
could stay behind and do the gutting, and they'd get
an extra five shillings to work, all the way through the
night, to get the rabbits away, because the skins were
going to the felt factories, where they were making all
the hats and things.

In the early days guns had sometimes been used for rabbit
hunting but were forbidden following the suicide of two
boys, Peter Johnson and later Joey Smith, who both used
guns to take their lives. Rabbiting would have been easier
with dogs but dogs were also forbidden at Fairbridge. For
a while a few of us secretly kept one in the paddock down
behind the village school but it became increasingly difficult and dangerous for us to steal the meat for its food. In
the end we had no choice but to let it go; we released it
out of the farm to fend for itself and had no idea if it
managed to survive.

For a while some of the boys kept ferrets, hiding them
in the wooden lockers that ran around the wall of each
cottage dining room. The increasing smell forced them to
get rid of the ferrets before it became too obvious to their
cottage mothers. In some other cottages the boys had permission to own ferrets, and they were kept in special little

On the steps of Nuffield Hall with the local vicar after the Sunday morning church service: the one occasion when everyone wore shoes.

Boys chopping wood.

The moment of the kill. Blood splatters as a trainee cuts a sheep's throat at the Fairbridge slaughterhouse.

Bringing eggs down to the village from the poultry.

The dairy was the boys' toughest job, involving milking at 3 a.m. and again at 3 p.m., seven days a week.

Tony 'Fishy' Bates and Bob 'Blob' Wilson baking the village bread.

Old mutton: preparing lunch in the village kitchens.

Garden supervisor Kurt Boelter, a former German tank commander, working with a trainee boy.

Most of the Fairbridge boys loved the boy scouts and the chance to go camping in the bush.

Waiting to see the village nurse on the back verandah of the Fairbridge village hospital.

Some cherished free time on a Wednesday afternoon: boys from Blue Cottage and neighbouring Canary Cottage play marbles.

John Brookman spent thirty years trying to find his mother. When he finally tracked her down he discovered she had died the year before.

Malcolm 'Flossy' Field (second row, second from right). One of the few Fairbridge children who did not come from a deprived background. He migrated to Australia twice in the same year.

Sports afternoon. Some boys played rugby league in bare feet.

A junior Orange High School rugby league team of 1960. David Hill is in the back row, third from the right. His twin brother, Richard, is the first on the left in the back row.

The former World War II Fairbridge Farm School bus, which became a famous sight around the west of the state for several decades.

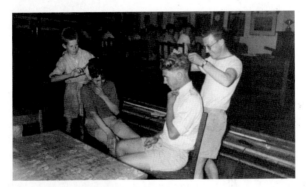

Fairbridge children cut each other's hair.

Tuesday afternoon's cottage gardening. The annual cottage gardening competition was fiercely fought out among the longest-serving cottage mothers.

Fairbridge children were officially described as 'generally educationally retarded' and most were forced to leave school at the minimum legal age.

The Governor-General of Australia, the Duke of Gloucester and the Duchess of Gloucester on a visit to Fairbridge in 1946. The Duke became the president of the London Fairbridge Society when he returned to England.

pens a safe distance from the cottages.

Michael Walker, who was at Fairbridge for ten years after arriving as a six-year-old with his five-year-old brother in 1950, remembers the joy of free afternoons and going rabbiting.

> I liked free afternoons and a favourite way of spending it was rabbiting, usually with a friend. We would head for a spot where there were known to be lots of rabbits. You would take a digging tool and dig, then put your arm down a burrow until you eventually got to the nest at the end. It was a thrill to feel the animal down there and pull it out by its back legs, give it a swift chop across the back of the neck and that was that. There was no sense of death as I remember. You were trying to earn a little money in your free time. Rabbits could be sold for their carcasses and skin in Molong.

A lot of Fairbridge kids were taken in by local families for part of the Christmas holidays and a number of them had a wonderful time, going back year after year to the same family. Many kept in touch with their adopted holiday parents for decades after leaving the farm school.

However, those of us who were not sent to stay with an Australian family felt no loss, because the highlight of the year was the annual summer holiday, when we were taken camping for a fortnight at Gerroa beach on the coast of New South Wales, south of Wollongong. The yearly trip to Gerroa was regarded by Fairbridge kids as one of life's great adventures. Sand, flies, mosquitoes, sunburn, heat, humidity and sleeping on the hard ground in old canvas army tents may sound unpleasant but we loved every minute of it.

As Michael Walker recalls:

> We all loved going to Gerroa. The freedom of Gerroa
> was exhilarating. There weren't the usual restraints.
> No school, no cottage gardening, no cottage mothers!
> There were rock pools to explore – fascinating to a
> country boy – and endless beaches to wander.

At the start of the holiday we loaded the tents and marquees, pots and pans, food and clothing into the old Fairbridge bus, then drove 200 miles, over the Blue Mountains. On the steepest slopes we were ordered to walk behind the overloaded bus. Once we had crossed the mountains we stopped at Penrith, on the outskirts of Sydney, where the local Rotary or Lions Club put on a lunch; we would eat town bread and enough free ice-cream to make ourselves sick. Then we headed south through Wollongong, Kiama and Gerringong to Gerroa, where we set up camp.

In those days, before Gerroa became a popular and crowded caravan park, we had most of the campsite to ourselves. In contrast to the regimentation of Fairbridge, we could do pretty much what we wanted, with a minimum of supervision. We all have memories of the boss when we were at Gerroa because he became far more relaxed and better humoured than he was back at Fairbridge. Almost every day there were organised events but they were not compulsory and most of the time we preferred to do our own thing. Within about a week, in the absence of enforced rules, we began to become increasingly feral, taking on the appearance of the choir-boys in William Golding's *Lord of the Flies*.

We were particularly excited about going out to play at night-time, either canoeing on the lagoon or sneaking up on other campers hoping to catch sight of any young girls who might be staying there, although at thirteen and four-teen years of age and socially clumsy we wouldn't have known what to say to them if they had spoken to us.

We had very little money to buy ice-creams, soft drinks and sweets but quickly discovered a way to get some. In those days you paid a deposit on a bottle of soft drink and were given a refund when you returned the empty bottle. There was a little kiosk on the campsite and all the empty soft drink bottles were stored behind a high wooden fence at the back. Notwithstanding the barbed wire on top of the fence, we managed on most nights to scale it and cart off as many empty bottles as we could carry, returning the next day to collect the refunds.

Kids above the age of about twelve were rostered to help with the preparation of the food and the washing up, though most of the work was done by the girls. Lennie 'Moon' Magee and I were assigned to make sure our campsite had enough fresh water for drinking, cooking and washing up. At least twice a day we would take a ten-gallon milk urn that had been borrowed from the Fairbridge dairy about half a kilometre to the camp tap. Bringing the water back was incredibly difficult for a couple of thirteen-year-olds. We staggered only a few feet before having to put the heavy urn down for a rest – and it would have been much harder for Lennie, who was nowhere near my size.

We spent most of our days playing around, mostly without hats or sunscreen, swimming in the notoriously rough surf of Seven Mile Beach, or fishing off the rocks. There were no lifesavers there then and it is a wonder that no one was lost in the sea over the many years Fairbridge children went to Gerroa.

The boys and girls had separate tents, and we slept on the ground. It was too hot at that time of year to sleep under any covers, and we would roll up the flaps on the side of the tent in the hope of attracting a little breeze. The camp was pitched close to the lagoon and many of the kids were covered in mosquito bites, but nobody seemed to mind.

We were happy at Gerroa and were very sad to leave. The long trip home up over the mountains taxed the Fairbridge bus, and the return journey was never without incident, as the old machine huffed and puffed and overheated. On one trip back to Fairbridge something snapped in the gearbox and we were all left in a bushland park at Lawson in the Blue Mountains in the searing heat, with no water, for four to five hours while they went to Bathurst to find a new part.

At Fairbridge most of the boys joined the Wolf Cubs and later the Boy Scouts; the girls joined the Brownies and then the Girl Guides. Though not compulsory it was expected of the children and actively encouraged by Woods, who was the Scoutmaster and Wolf Cub pack leader while his wife Ruth ran both the Guides and the Brownies.

The Scouting and Guide movements reinforced Fairbridge's association with Britain and the Empire. Their founder, Baden-Powell, had been a champion of the Empire, serving in the British Army in India, Afghanistan and South Africa, where he became every British boy's hero for his leadership in the seven-month siege of the British-held town of Mafeking during the Boer War. The Scouts' Oath, which we were expected to recite at every meeting, was:

On my honour I promise,
To do my duty to God and the Queen
To help other people at all times
And to obey the Scout Law

In the Wolf Cubs we recited:

*I promise to do my best, to do my duty to God and the
    Queen*
To keep the Laws of the Wolf Cub Pack
And to do a good turn to somebody every day.

To most Fairbridge boys the Scouts provided an opportunity for adventure and an escape from the drudgery and routine of the farm school. While normal Boy Scouts earnt merit badges for such things as stamp collecting, cooking or even gardening, the Fairbridge troop – with encouragement from Woods – was hardy, outdoorsy and tough. Most of us only acquired one merit badge, the 'Backwoodsman'. To earn it you had to survive in the bush for a couple of days with limited food, build and sleep in your own bivouac, cook a meal without utensils, and kill and eat some wild animal.

The Fairbridge kids loved getting this merit badge because it meant a weekend at Molong Creek, where it was easy to collect branches and bark to build a shelter, fresh water was plentiful, and the yabbies were easy to catch using a bit of old mutton tied to a line of string as bait. Some of the kids who couldn't catch rabbits caught magpies instead. They propped up a box with a length of wood that had a string tied to it, and placed a bit of mutton on the ground underneath the box. When the bird went under the box to eat the mutton they pulled the string. Woods would come down on Sunday afternoon to inspect our endeavours, so we had to be careful to hide any cigarettes and contraband food.

The boss was proud of his Scout troop and was always looking for ways to demonstrate that we were better than the many other troops in the district. He had the Scouts and Guides thoroughly practise marching so that when we attended the annual cherry blossom parade or the ANZAC Day memorial parade in Orange we would be the smartest of all the outfits. We normally felt like second-class citizens when we went to local towns so we were happy to show we could do something better than the town kids could.

Before the Orange Country Show one year, Woods took us into the bush west of Larras Lee, where we camped and cut down gum trees. We constructed a big bridge over the local creek with the wood, held together with diagonal and square rope lashings. The following week we turned up at the Orange Show with a truck full of tree trunks and ropes, and within a few hours were able to construct the bridge again in front of a large, admiring crowd.

Camping out was the most enjoyable part of being in the Scouts. Typically in winter, we would load up the old Fairbridge bus or a truck with all our gear and head off for the weekend to some remote spot. A particular favourite was out near the old nineteenth-century gold-mining site of Ophir, where we would pan for alluvial gold. At night on these camps patrols would be pitched against one another in what Woods called 'wide games'. The object of the game varied but always involved securing or holding some territory or some object against the other patrols, and always involved a physical contest between the boys, which Woods loved, as did we.

In addition to the Scouts and the Guides many of the children were members of the Molong Fairbridge Junior Farmers Club. One of the functions of the club was the preparation of an exhibit of all the produce of the farm that would be displayed at the annual country shows in various towns around the district. Some of the kids took the Junior Farmers seriously but most of us saw it as an opportunity to occasionally get off the farm to travel to some country town, assemble our exhibit and have a good time. The Junior Farmers Club gave out certificates for various things and I remember being given a Lamb and Sheep Breeding Certificate, although I had absolutely no idea what any of it was about.

Most of us loved sport and there was a lot of it at Fairbridge. We played every Thursday afternoon on the Fairbridge sports fields and again on Saturday or Sunday afternoons against competition in the surrounding towns. The main winter sport was Rugby League for the boys and hockey for the girls, although the boys also played hockey. Quite often we would travel to Orange to play one sport in the morning and another in the afternoon, when Fairbridge children fondly remember each being bought a meat pie from the Golden Key café for lunch. We also played soccer at Fairbridge and each Easter staged the inter-cottage Fairbridge athletics carnival. In summer we played cricket and competed in the inter-cottage swimming carnival.

Horse riding was popular but there was only a handful of horses available at Fairbridge. A few of the children were members of the local Molong Pony Club. The trainee boys did most of the serious riding when they worked on sheep mustering at the farm.

An annual sporting highlight was the Forbes football carnival, a day-long knock-out Rugby League tournament for hundreds of boys' teams from all over the west of the state. The Forbes football carnival was a major event on the New South Wales bush calendar for most of the twentieth century. The teams were not determined by age but by weight. Teams in the lightest weight division, whose players were under five stone seven pounds, were known as the 5.7s. Then there were the 6.7s, the 7.7s, the 8.7s, the 9.7s, the 10.7s, and finally the open weight division. Forbes was about one hundred kilometres from Fairbridge and we would leave in the early-morning darkness to drive the back bush roads through Eugowra to be weighed and have our weight limit stamped indelibly on our foreheads. Woods liked to have all the Fairbridge children weighed in early before taking us to the local Mum and Dad Café, where we were allowed to gorge ourselves on a huge cooked breakfast of sausages, bacon, egg and baked beans. Any advantage from playing with a bit of extra weight was offset by the fact we staggered out to play our first game of the day with a stomach full of undigested food.

We never did that well at the carnival because at some stage we would meet a well-organised team that had been properly coached while we had only ever been told to grab the ball and run hard when we were in possession, and run and hit the other guys hard when they had the ball. Some of the Fairbridge boys, however, remember their teams doing well at Forbes. John Wolvey recalls playing at Forbes in a very successful Fairbridge team in the early 1950s.

> We won it for the five years I was in it . . . The 10.7s never got beaten because, you know, they were up there [at Fairbridge] lugging wheat. Those other fellows were going to school – they were big fellows but they were going to school. The Fairbridge boys . . . they were men . . . they were working as men.

Winning at sport was important to most Fairbridge kids – particularly against 'town' kids, to whom we felt socially inferior.

Most former Fairbridge children say that the best thing they remember about their experience was the bond they had with other children; and for many this camaraderie has survived since they left the farm school. Asked what were the highlights of Fairbridge and what he enjoyed the most, David Wilson, who spent ten years at the farm having arrived as a six-year-old in 1951, says:

> I think the kids we were with – the camaraderie – it was just that. I suppose it was mainly the kids we were with. Because that's the only life we ever knew when I was a kid. Never knew anything else.

Cigarette smoking was one facet of bonding at Fairbridge. Nearly all the boys and many of the girls smoked, even though it was a serious offence that would attract a severe caning and the loss of privileges. Woods absolutely detested smoking and it seemed to flourish in almost a direct inverse proportion to his determination to stamp it out. Most of the children began smoking regularly at around twelve or thirteen years of age and typically left Fairbridge at seventeen years of age with an addictive habit.

Woods's efforts to stamp out smoking were all the more in vain because smoking was not then considered socially undesirable and it was perfectly acceptable for women and men to smoke in just about any social situation. Woods's added difficulty was that practically every staff member, including the cottage mothers, smoked, some of them very heavily.

Given the shortage of money on the farm, cigarettes became valuable in their own right as a currency with which you could buy almost anything from other children. We smoked when we thought we were safest from detection, often sneaking out of our cottages at night, in defiance of the village curfew. Most of the Fairbridge children had worked out the habits of their cottage mother and had a fair idea when she was likely to have settled down in her quarters and be less likely to be patrolling the kids' end of the cottage. But Woods would often patrol the village at night and, being a nonsmoker, in the clean country air could smell a cigarette from a long way off.

Amongst most of the children at Fairbridge it was also acceptable to be a thief. You could steal money, food, cigarettes or whatever you could from wherever you could, so long as it wasn't from another Fairbridge kid. We would break in to buildings if we thought there was something worthwhile to steal.

Once, on the way back from church in Molong on Sunday morning some of us discovered that we could slide out a few glass louvres at the back of a service station, crawl in and steal cigarettes and chocolates. It was a lucrative source and we never got greedy, only ever taking a few packets of cigarettes at a time so that it would not be too obvious to the owner when he opened the store on Monday morning. Eventually, other Fairbridge children found out and went overboard, killing a good thing. The owner couldn't miss seeing that so much of his stock was missing and reported it to the Molong police, who in turn notified Woods. From then on the store was made more secure and a watch was kept on it over the weekends, making breaking in a more dangerous proposition.

Those of us who attended Orange High School were acutely aware that the Orange kids always had money and we had none. To generate a bit of extra income we worked out how to break in to the stationery store at Fairbridge, which was a tiny room at the back of the small guesthouse next to the principal's house. We would load up our school cases, which we called 'ports', with purloined pens, pencils and pads until they were bulging and then sell them to the Orange High School students at attractively discounted prices. The enterprise meant that we could supplement our unpalatable Fairbridge sandwich lunch with a cream bun or something else exotic from the Orange High School canteen. Unfortunately, the Fairbridge bursar, Harry Harrop, could not but notice the dramatic shortage of stationery in the store and moved to make it more secure. We were lucky it was Harry and we escaped the inquisition and retribution that would normally follow such a discovery.

For some years a number of Fairbridge kids were aware of a small hole in the wall that separated the bake-house from the village store. The hole had been deliber-ately made into the back of a locked store cupboard that housed the chocolate and other sweets that were brought out on Saturday afternoons for sale at the village tuck-shop. The hole was kept secret from the staff, hidden behind the big bakehouse trough in which the yeast, salt, flour and water were mixed to make the village bread. By moving the trough away from the wall we could reach through, stretch and just manage to get our fingers on the booty.

To start with, access was limited to the boys who were rostered to work as trainees on the bakery, but over time more and more of us used it, provided the trainee on duty would let us into the bakehouse. Over time the hole in the wall was made bigger and bigger as boys tried to reach further and further into the cupboard. Eventually, Harry noticed that whole shelves were bare – and then he noticed the hole. Legend has it that the day he found the hole in the cupboard a hand belonging to bakehouse trainee Brian Osbourne was groping around in the cup-board and Harry grabbed it, and that was the end of that.

One of the boys' biggest thievery campaigns continued for some years and the target was the village pocket money supply. Every Saturday after lunch in Nuffield Hall the boss came round to each cottage table with a little notebook and a metal cash box filled with coins. He would put the cash box in front of one of the older boys, stand behind him and call out the names of the other cottage children one by one, and the amount they were each to be paid. As Woods called out a name the boy with the cash box would take out the designated amount of pocket money and pass it down the table to the grateful recipient. At the same time, he would steal as many coins as possible and pass them under the table to the boys sitting alongside him. Outside after lunch they would divide the spoils. The scam, involving a number of cottages, seemed to go on for years and could only have continued undetected because Woods was a careless administrator who never attempted to reconcile the little notebook with the money left in the box.

Occasionally boys – and on the rare occasion, girls – would run away from Fairbridge. It was practically impossible to escape for long because the police would immediately be alerted. Eventually the boys – with no money and, more importantly, nowhere to go – would be found, brought back to Fairbridge, punished and have their privileges withdrawn for long periods. Nonetheless, some of the boys would run away again – and the more they were punished the higher they were regarded by the other children.

Usually someone ran away every few months. As in a jail full of prisoners, the whispers would swirl around the dining hall at breakfast the next morning that such-and-such a cottage mother had reported that so-and-so had not slept in his bed and couldn't be accounted for. The news that someone had escaped caused great excitement and we would all speculate on where they had gone, which direction they were heading and how long they might be able to elude their captors for.

Derek Moriarty ran away from Fairbridge on a number of occasions.

The first time I ran away, we hitchhiked, and got to Brisbane. There was four of us – Bob Wilson, Jimmy Grundy, and I think Brian Wilkes was the other one. But we got split up in Brisbane when the coppers started chasing us. And Grundy and I went one way and Bob and Wilkes another. And of course, we eventually got caught and we all finished up back at Fairbridge. And then, sometime down the track we ran away again, just Bob and I. And we finished up down the South Coast; we finished up at Milton because Bob had a good mate from Fairbridge that was living down the coast at Murchison in Victoria, and we were heading down there. But we got a ride with a guy and he dropped us off at Milton and politely went and rang the cops and told them we were a couple of escapees from an orphanage.

And of course they took us and locked us up and that and we went to children's court and the judge asked us why we'd run away and I said – we both said basically the same thing: 'We're sixteen years of age now; we're old enough to be out in the world working for a living and saving taxpayers plenty of dollars' and one thing and another. And he was a nice old magistrate actually. He said if the authorities can find us a job in the occupation we want to work in, and suitable accommodation, he'd release us, and if they couldn't, he would put us in Mount Penang [juvenile prison] or one of the other institutions.

When runaways had stolen food, money or a car they would end up in the children's court, where they might be sentenced to serve a period in the boys' prison at Mount Penang at Gosford, north of Sydney. Even when a child had not committed a criminal offence he was sometimes sent to the boys' prison simply for running away and becoming a 'neglected child' under the Child Welfare Act.

Generally children ran away in groups of two or three. Once, six boys ran away and somehow stayed together till they were all caught north of Sydney more than a week later. Sometimes a boy ran away on his own, such as Alan 'Eggy' Taylor from our cottage. He was away for about a week and when he returned he fascinated us with his stories of survival in the bush. He told us that when his meagre escape rations ran out he survived on bush tucker; he didn't even have matches with which to light a fire to cook on. We didn't believe him when he said he had caught blue-tongue and frill-necked lizards and eaten them raw, so the next Saturday afternoon he brought back to Canonbar Cottage a live lizard to prove his point. With all of us standing around in a circle in the cottage bathroom he swung the lizard by its tail and smashed its head on the laundry tub, sliced open its belly, turned it inside out and nibbled at the meat inside. I believed everything Eggy told us after that.

Another aspect of the children's value system at Fairbridge was respect for brawn over brain. Bookish kids who showed an interest in schooling were spurned and the Orange High School kids were resented. The big and physically strong ruled over the small and the weak. Fairbridge was a pretty tough place where little emotion was shown. As Lennie Magee remembers:

> [Fairbridge] was marked by the absence of tenderness and emotion. It was considered manly to be stoic, and uncaring. Boys were told in no uncertain terms that only little kids, girls and sissies cry. Consequently, when kids were hit by machetes, or scraped off

a horse by an unyielding tree branch as I was, or suffered broken arms, legs, wrists or collarbones as often happens, the result was either a slight limp or a glazed look – rarely were there tears.[1]

Although few former Fairbridge children talk about it, there was a system of bullying, particularly among the boys. The little boys were called runts and expected to take orders from the older boys. Barney Piercy remembers being beaten by an older boy shortly after his arrival.

> It must have been the next day, the second day, I woke up in this strange land and I started calling for my mum and I got a bit upset and frantic and that's when I shit myself and I was still carrying on and this bloke came along and gave me a crack between the eyes – 'Shut up you little cunt' – and I thought, I'd better toughen up here. I did nothing after that. I just shut everything off. Once I got belted up the second day I was there, I just became hard as nails and I just got on with it basically.

Eric 'Chook' Fowler always felt a bit of an outsider at Fairbridge. He was one of ten children and was only four years old when his mother died. His father was an officer in the Royal Ulster Fusiliers based in Ireland and when he remarried he sent Eric, aged twelve, out to Fairbridge. Eric says his father thought he was going to a 'young gentlemen's school'. For the whole time he was there Eric was frightened to step out of line.

> I haven't always got on with boys but I get on with girls . . . I was worried that first day at Fairbridge that I might get into a fight – which I never did – but that's the only thing that worried me when I first got there

because I had no one to turn to . . . It was the survival of the fittest really . . . I was straight down the line. I was very careful what I did. Kept out of trouble, you know.

Malcolm Field, or 'Flossy', who had migrated twice from Britain in one year because of his feckless mother, did not come from a typical Fairbridge background either, and he did not become a typical Fairbridge kid when he reached the farm school. Malcolm explains that he got a 'lucky break' at Fairbridge.

I was just eleven . . . The governor-general, Sir William Slim, came up for the weekend . . . in his Rolls Royce and the chauffeur took the kids up and down the hill the whole weekend in the Rolls . . . On the Sunday there was this Communion service on the front lawn in front of Nuffield Hall conducted by Roland Bigrigg, an Old Fairbridgian.

After the service there was a reception in the dining hall and a number of the children were picked to show guests from around the district the village and the farm. Flossy was to look after Mr and Mrs Glasson from the neighbouring property, 'Gamboola'. A few months later the childless Mrs Glasson invited Malcolm to stay at Gamboola for Christmas. 'So I went for Christmas,' he says, 'and they have a beautiful old homestead and I lived there as a member of the family.'

Malcolm was regularly invited to spend weekends and school holidays at Gamboola. He was also one of the few who attended Orange High and remembers the Glassons helping him get a second-hand Orange High School jacket. When he finished school he went to live and work with the Glassons and boasts that he was probably the only Fairbridge boy never to have worked on a village muster or as a trainee.

> They took me in to live with them in the homestead. And I worked on the farm because I wasn't a bludger on Gamboola. So I did the harvesting, mustering, all those sorts of things, milked cows. And they paid me. It was wonderful and I would say that it was probably very rare for anyone to live with a family. Probably almost unique. So, I was very, very fortunate.

Malcolm accepts that his good fortune put him at odds with the other Fairbridge children.

> So you found a way to survive. You had to. I rose above it, a lot of the time. Because otherwise you would have gone under, and a number of kids did. Didn't cope very well at all
>
> . . . What I had to be very careful of was not only that I was going to Orange High School, and there were only five of us going at that stage out of about 200, but I was also going to Gamboola.
>
> I never mentioned to anyone what Gamboola was like because that would have been worse.

Fairbridge children were generally regarded as social undesirables by the local townspeople. Years later I was told by one of the Molong girls who was in my class at school that when the old Fairbridge bus full of kids arrived at the Molong swimming pool on a hot Sunday afternoon in summer, many of the parents would gather up their children and immediately leave.

After leaving Fairbridge, when he was working on the railways, Laurie Reid remembers going out with a nice local girl. When her parents discovered he had come from Fairbridge they put a stop to it.

> I met a girl. She was a nursing sister in Orange. Anyhow, a girlfriend, and we were going like a house on fire for a couple of months then and she said, 'Come and see Mum and Dad, they want to meet you.' So we went to see them. And they asked me what my father had done and I said he used to be in coalmining. And they said, 'In Newcastle?'
>
> And I said, 'No, over in Great Britain.'
>
> So, 'Are you a Fairbridge boy?'
>
> I said, 'Yes', and that was the end of the relationship.

Despite Fairbridge being coeducational, the lives of the boys and the girls were highly regulated and separate, and there were rarely any sex scandals. Occasionally kids had boyfriends or girlfriends, but it rarely became too serious. As Gwen Miller remembers:

> I didn't know anything about the world. I mean, we had boyfriends at Fairbridge but boyfriends to us were somebody you went with to the pictures. You know, you might kiss them behind the bush on the way home but that was the extent of a relationship with a boy.

For many years Fairbridge had an arrangement whereby Legacy girls came to stay at the farm school for a couple of weeks during the mid-year school holidays. Legacy was a big charity that assisted the families of servicemen who had died as a result of war and the Legacy girls were daughters of deceased servicemen. Their arrival created great excitement among the Fairbridge boys. I remember quivering with the thrill of having a Legacy girl as a girl-friend for a couple of weeks. We got to hold hands in the darkened back of the Fairbridge truck and I can still feel her breath now as she leant over and kissed me on the cheek.

Lennie Magee remembers as teenagers at Fairbridge in the late 1950s how clumsy and unsure we were with the girls.

> To put your arm around a girl required for me the same courage needed to stick your tongue in a light socket. I would sit for the whole movie thinking about it, obsessed with the thought. If I could just reach out in a sort of one-armed yawn and place my hand on the back of the seat, then I could just touch her soft slender shoulder . . .
>
> A few times each year, all the tables and benches were moved to the far end of Nuffield Hall and some elderly musicians were brought in so we could enjoy a Social. The band played all the hit songs from their experiences in the Crimean War, while we stood around in small groups hoping the hall would catch on fire.[2]

The girls were every bit as naïve about sex as the boys – possibly even more so. Daphne Brown, who arrived at Fairbridge as a seven-year-old in 1948, recalls:

> I never heard of anyone getting pregnant. I can honestly say if there was, I don't know of anyone. And they were pretty strict because, I mean, I got caught kissing a boy and Mr Woods took me down the office and was telling me all this stuff of what would happen and I didn't know what he was talking about because we didn't have much sex education. We did have a

movie once. Mr Woods brought it from Sydney. It was about our reproductive organs and it was quite funny because it then showed you what would happen if you were 'a lady of the night' and it showed you this lady standing up against a pub bar, with a cigarette, and then she ended up with a venereal disease and she went mad. So when I left Fairbridge, I thought anyone who stood at the bar of a pub and smoked ended up mad, so I used to walk very quickly past pubs.

Joyce Drury remembers being frightened of kissing a boy:

I can remember one boy trying to kiss me and I ran for my life . . . And I always thought, I'm not going to get married; I'm not going to have babies – and I probably thought kissing made babies in some way – because of having come from a poor, big family, and probably in my mind I thought, I don't want that to happen . . . So when someone tried to kiss me, I would run for my life.

While the children may have tried to create their own world, most had no other life experience to fall back on other than their years at Fairbridge. When they finally left the place they went out into the world alone with no family and no network of support.

11

LEAVING FAIRBRIDGE

Most Fairbridge kids as seventeen-year-olds out in the world found themselves physically and emotionally isolated, often living entirely by themselves, working by themselves and coming home to empty barracks. They had to live with something frighteningly new: loneliness.

Having a mum made my brothers and me different from other Fairbridge kids, because we knew we belonged somewhere and Fairbridge was not our only family. I will always remember one of the toughest trainees coming over to me when I was hanging out washing one afternoon behind Canonbar Cottage. When he was sure no one was near, he asked, 'What's it like to have a mum?' I had no idea how to answer the question and he left disappointed when I said words to the effect that I thought it was okay. Even though the fact we would be together as a family again made us different, I didn't feel the kids treated us any differently – we were all in it together, trying to cope with life at the farm school as best we could.

Even after the introduction of the One Parent Scheme in the late 1950s, Fairbridge discouraged parents from having too much contact with their children. Following a visit to Australia, a member of the UK Fairbridge Society, W. L. Sandover, reported to the London Fairbridge

Society that 'A lot of trouble arises when parents follow the children to Australia.'[1]

Single parents such as my mum were told that once they arrived in Australia they would be encouraged to make regular visits to see their children. A brochure explaining the One Parent Scheme made the claim that the parent:

> will follow the children to Australia at a later date. The parents will be found employment and accommodation in the same state, so that they may be kept in touch with the children and visit them.[2]

But my mum complained that from the time she arrived in Australia late in 1959 she was provided with no assistance and no guidance in finding a home or a job. At one point Mum applied for a job as a cook on the neighbouring farm Gamboola, owned by the Glasson family. Mum was at Fairbridge visiting us and was to be picked up after eight o'clock that evening by Mrs Glasson, who proposed to drive her over to Gamboola, show her around, interview her for the job and then drop her off at Molong railway station in time to catch the overnight Forbes mail train to Sydney.

Nearly fifty years later the following file note, signed by Woods, was discovered in a miscellaneous collection of papers in the Fairbridge Foundation offices in Sydney.[3]

> Phone message from Mrs Glasson.
> She has seen Mrs Hill but cannot engage her now as she already has someone coming to work here tomorrow. She has however arranged to fetch Mrs Hill tonight at 8.20 and will take her to Gamboola and then on to the train, so that Mrs Hill can see the place and the job in case she might take the job there later.

The Glassons however do not usually keep anyone very long.

Speaking generally, it is better to have parents of our children not employed very near Fairbridge as they usually become a nuisance after a time – Mrs Hill is the least likely to become so, but proximity might make a change for the worse in her.

Signed,
F. K. S. Woods

The difficulty for Fairbridge was that when parents visited the farm school they were often disturbed by what they saw. I still recall when my mother first came to Fairbridge. She was horrified.

She stayed up the back of the village in one of the two guesthouses for visitors – simple accommodation with two single beds in each guestroom and a communal bathroom and toilet at the end of the verandah. It had a common room with an electric jug so my brothers and I were allowed at certain times during her visit to go up and have a cup of tea with her.

On her first morning she was shaken by the scene in Nuffield Hall. She was obliged to sit up on the stage with the staff and visitors to be served breakfast. Looking down, she would have seen us being marched in with nearly 200 other children, largely barefoot, dressed in rough clothing and with terrible haircuts, then seen us all sitting along wooden benches, eating bread and porridge on a lino-topped table from steel bowls and plates.

She was distressed after breakfast and we tried to console her as she mumbled words to the effect of 'What have I done?' and 'It's like something out of *Oliver Twist*.'

Some parents were so concerned when they came and

saw Fairbridge that they wanted to immediately take their children away. A surviving undated report from the after care officer, W. Phillips, to Principal Woods outlines the concerns expressed by two sets of parents who were visiting their children for the first time at the farm school. After a two-day visit one of the fathers said the children 'were treated far more badly than he himself had been treated as a prisoner of war'.[4]

Phillips asked the parents to bring down their luggage to the principal's house on the day they were leaving so he could give them a lift to Molong railway station. At an early lunch on the staff table in Nuffield Hall one of the parents, Mr Royale, said very loudly, 'I wouldn't leave my kids here for anything if I had somewhere else to leave them.' When Phillips suggested to Royale that it might be better to take the children with him when he left, Royale responded by saying that he had already checked with the migrant hostel manager in Sydney, who said they could not take the children.

Royale told Phillips that he had talked to many of the boys during his two-day stay and that even though they had been 'afraid to open their mouths', they all told him they hated the place. Phillips wrote:

> He referred to an incident in which he saw a small boy pushing a barrow load of wood, 'far too large for him to handle'. He asked the boy what he was doing and the boy told him that he was carting wood for the cottage. Mr Royale then asked him what happened if he 'couldn't do it' and the boy told him that he would be caned.

Phillips's main worry was that another parent present with Royale, Mr Parker, said that the Methodist minister in Orange had described Fairbridge as a 'dreadful' place.

What I am concerned about is the truth or otherwise of
the statement attributed to either Mr Clancy or to Mr
Pierce of the Methodist Church in Orange, to the effect
that it agreed that Fairbridge was a 'Dreadful' place.

In 1961 I turned fifteen, and in the normal course of
events I would have been expected to become a trainee
working on the farm for the next two years. But by now
Mum was in Australia. After completing my Intermediate
Certificate I was going to leave the farm school to go and
live with her.

When I told Woods at the end of the school year that
my mum had arranged for me to join her, he said that
I was expected to be a trainee like everyone else. The
following Saturday, when I intended to catch the train
to Sydney, he overruled my plan and announced at the
village breakfast that I was to captain the under-fifteen
cricket team that was to play that morning at Fairbridge
against a team from Molong. I was filled with dread at
the thought of not being allowed to leave and spending
the next two years at Fairbridge as a trainee.

During the cricket game I hit a ball to the boundary
through mid wicket and heard Woods, who was umpiring
the game from his upturned oil can, shout, 'Ho, ho, Hill
leaves Fairbridge victorious,' which signalled to me that
he was not going to stand in my way after all.

At the end of the game I raced down to my cottage to
pack my belongings into a small cardboard suitcase. It
struck me how sad it was that after nearly three years
at Fairbridge I had so little to take away with me. I had
just enough time to say goodbye to my brothers, who
intended to stay on at Orange High School but would
both leave a few months later. In my desperation to catch
the train I didn't have enough time to say goodbye to any
of my friends, Woods or even my cottage mother.

It was now too late to catch the daylight train to Sydney at Molong railway station as it would already have passed through, but Paddy O'Brien, the oldest boy in our group that had come out to Australia on the S.S. *Strathaird*, now had his driver's licence and was driving a Fairbridge truck into Orange to pick up supplies. Paddy was happy to give me a lift, once I assured him I wasn't absconding and he wouldn't get into trouble with Woods. We were able to reach Orange with a few minutes to spare, as it had taken over an hour for the train to get there on the steep railway line from Molong through Amaroo and Borenore.

On the exhausting 300-kilometre train trip to Sydney I thought about my years at Fairbridge and contemplated what life now held in store. I felt strangely empty about leaving, which was similar to how Lenny Magee felt the day he left:

> As we drove through the open Fairbridge gate for the last time, I tried to feel something of what had been my absolute dream for the last ten years. Freedom, escape, pleasure. I felt nothing but stomach-churning apprehension.[5]

The train to Sydney was crowded. I was sitting next to a man who worked as a piano tuner and travelled around the countryside tuning pianos for several weeks on end, going home to his family for a few days every month. It sounded like an unappealing way to spend a life and I remember hoping that fortune would smile more kindly on me.

It was after nine o'clock when I reached Sydney and I was tired and hungry, having spent the last of my money on a bread roll from the train buffet some hours before. My mum was at Sydney's Central railway station to meet me.

It had been almost three years since she had waved us goodbye at the Fairbridge house at Knockholt in Kent. I recall her excitement, mixed with relief, that we were back together; but she would not be totally relaxed until my brothers left Fairbridge and joined us in a few months' time.

We caught a suburban train through the city's underground and over the Sydney Harbour Bridge to North Sydney. I sat, wide-eyed, in the window seat, marvelling at the harbour and seeing the bright lights of a big city for the first time. We walked down from North Sydney station to Mum's tiny downstairs bed-sitter, which was in a terrace house at 96 Union Street that had been split into five little flats, all occupied by migrants from Europe. We all had to share the one bathroom and one toilet, which were upstairs. Mum's bed-sitter had two small rooms. In one was a single bed, a bedside table, a tiny wardrobe, a small table pushed up against the wall under the window and three chairs. There wasn't room for the fourth chair. The other room was even smaller: it had enough room for a stove, a sink and in the corner a camp stretcher for me. The flat had no phone, no refrigerator, no TV and only a transistor radio.

We weren't particularly badly off since most migrants to Australia in those postwar years lived that way until they'd saved enough for a deposit on their own home, which in most cases took many years of hard work and a lot of overtime.

Mum had a boyfriend named Paul. He was an unmarried German builder and, like Mum, was in his mid-forties. They had met when Mum was working for a while at Sydney's Concord military repatriation hospital as a nursing aid. On Saturdays a group of German workers who had come to Sydney from work on the Snowy Mountains project for a weekend's recreation would phone the nurses quarters' and ask out women of a similar age to the German Concordia Club in a nearby suburb for dinner and a dance.

After my arrival Paul didn't stay on the scene long and Mum was devastated when he stopped calling around. The short period he was on the scene was the only time I remember seeing her with a man and so happy. She thought my arrival and the prospect of my two brothers arriving had frightened him off – but he had stayed around long enough to show me how to shave. By the age of fifteen I had grown a lot of facial fluff and had no idea what to do about it, as I'd never seen anyone have a shave before.

Mum was working in the Coles cafeteria in Pitt Street in the city. She wasn't earning a great deal so it was expected that I would immediately find a job and start paying my own way. The day after I arrived was a beautiful summer Sunday that I spent walking with Mum around the foreshore parks near North Sydney. The next morning Mum left early for work and I got myself ready to start looking for a job. At Fairbridge I had been taught some basic rules about turning up for an interview, including having a clean, ironed shirt, neat, combed hair and polished shoes.

I caught the number 247 bus from outside North Sydney station up the Pacific Highway to Crows Nest, where Mum had told me I would find the government-run unemployment office. I filled out a form and it wasn't long before I was called in for an interview. A nice man opened a drawer in his wooden filing cabinet marked 'Male 15–16 year old', which was full of cards recording available jobs. In those days Australia was experiencing 'over full' employment, meaning that the number of jobs outstripped the number of people looking for work. For the next few years jobs were so plentiful that I drifted from job to job and could boast that I was never unemployed for more than a day.

Of all the jobs at the unemployment office open to unskilled, inexperienced fifteen-year-olds I applied to work at Ismays' hardware shop in Willoughby Road, Crows Nest – because it was the closest to Mum's little flat. The Ismays were looking for a junior and were paying the award rate of £5, four shillings and sixpence a week (the basic full adult wage was around £12 a week).

Somehow, they knew about Fairbridge and were very tolerant and understanding, even though I was dumb-struck at the counter of the shop whenever a customer asked for even the most basic item and I had no idea what they were talking about. It was even worse when the shop was very busy and someone would yell out for me to answer the phone. I had never used a telephone before and didn't know I had to say something when I picked up the handset. After a short time they limited my duties to going out with the truck driver to help with deliveries, or sorting out nuts and bolts at the back of the shop, which I found excruciatingly boring.

I knew no one in Sydney except for Auntie Effie, Mum's sister, who had migrated to Australia in the late 1940s with her husband, Harold. They lived with their two daughters, Jan and Ann, in Panania in the city's south-western suburbs.

Because I had nothing else to do, after work on Saturdays I would often catch a train to stay with Paddy and Mary O'Brien's mum, who had a little flat in the outer suburb of Penrith. She had followed her kids to Australia, as my mother had done. Although she didn't have much she always made me feel welcome and allowed me to stay overnight. I would sleep on the kitchen table because she didn't have a spare bed and Mary, who had also recently left Fairbridge, was sleeping on the lounge.

On other occasions I would go by myself on a Saturday afternoon to watch Rugby League being played at the

Sydney Cricket Ground. On the walk back down to Central station I would treat myself to a sixpence bag of hot chips from the fish and chip shop in Foveaux Street.

Like most of the children, I experienced terrible loneliness after leaving Fairbridge. And I was one of the lucky ones – I had a mum – and things also got better when Richard and Dudley left school and joined us in Sydney, and we managed to rent a slightly bigger flat.

Mary O'Brien felt deeply for those children who had nowhere to go and no one to take them when they left Fairbridge.

> I remember arriving in Sydney and being with my mum. And a sense of freedom. Somebody that I loved was there for me and I really feel sorry for those who never had that: to walk out of Fairbridge and have their mums to go to. My mum was poor and she was sick. But she was my mum. And she took me away from there. And that was everything.

Most of the kids had no family to go to when they left Fairbridge and were found jobs on farms in the more remote parts of the state. In many cases, in the absence of someone to protect them from unscrupulous employers, they worked extremely hard and for long hours for poor pay, living in awful accommodation.

They left Fairbridge with a little money – usually less than a week's wages – and a suitcase containing a new outfit, which for boys usually consisted of underwear, two pairs of shoes and socks, two shirts, two pairs of slacks, a jacket, a pullover and a pair of pyjamas. They were expected to repay Fairbridge the cost of the clothing from their wages. They were also expected to send half their wages back to Fairbridge, to be banked for them until they reached twenty-one and Fairbridge was no longer their guardian. Many complain they never saw the money and believe Harry Harrop may have pocketed their cash when he was robbing Fairbridge.

Fairbridge children left with few social skills and little knowledge of the workings of the outside world. As Jimmy 'Tubby' Walker observes, most Fairbridge children had rarely even been into a shop.

> I had never used a telephone when I left Fairbridge. I didn't how to bank my wages. You couldn't even buy your own clothes. Because you never did it, you know. You went into a shop – you didn't know what size you were – and they'd say, 'What size are you?' I didn't have the faintest idea.

David Wilson spent more than ten years at Fairbridge, and was then sent to a job on a remote farm in the north-west of the state.

> My first job was at Collarenebri [on a sheep property], working anything up to fifteen hours a day . . . I was a jackeroo up there. And you'd complain your hands were sore, so [the boss would] give you more to do . . . I lived in the shearers' quarters, by myself . . . it used to get lonely there, yeah.
>
> Actually, I asked Woods – and this is as true as I sit here – I wanted to be trained as a baker . . . Baking bread at Fairbridge was just a job I liked doing . . . And he wouldn't let me. He just said, 'No, you're going out on a property.'
>
> Another job they sent me to when I was seventeen and a half – and I'll never forget it – it was at Narromine. I worked for a wheat cocky. I couldn't lift up the 180-pound bags of wheat, which is what the bags were at the time. He [the boss] said to me,

'You've got to learn how to lift these bags.' He was a man of about thirty-five, forty, and he expected me to be able do the same work as him. I used to live in a shed at the back of the house and he used to just throw rocks at the thing to wake me up in the morning – about four o'clock in the morning . . . to go and milk the cow and feed all the pigs. Then I'd come in and have breakfast, and he used to give me a tractor and say, 'Come in when you can't see no more.' Luckily it didn't have any lights on the tractor. You'd be out ploughing all day . . . All day – up to sixteen or seventeen hours a day.

No one knew that the reason most of the Fairbridge children were found jobs in the remote west and north-west of the state was that a secret deal had been made by Fairbridge with Barnardo's to divide New South Wales when it came to finding jobs for children leaving their farm schools.

Barnardo's had been operating its child-migrant farm school in Picton outside Sydney since the 1920s, which was the reason Fairbridge London did not initially share the enthusiasm of the Rhodes scholars pushing for the establishment of a Fairbridge Farm School in New South Wales.

Before Fairbridge was opened a formal agreement was reached between the two organisations: Fairbridge would not seek jobs for its children in the south of the state or in Sydney, which was left to Barnardo's. Fairbridge trainees would be found jobs north of a line that ran from Port Stephens on the north coast west to Dubbo, south to Molong and then followed the railway line west from Molong to Broken Hill.[6]

Barnardo's was relieved that as a result of the demarcation of the state its children would not be sent out to lonely and remote places. A Barnardo's internal report recorded that the arrangement was more favourable to them than it was to Fairbridge:

> Though Fairbridge would have more of the remote extensive grazing areas, it would not be a tremendous advantage as these properties are not suitable for our children and are often difficult of access.[7]

Billy King remembers his first job in the remotest part of the north-west:

> It was right up near the Queensland border on a cattle station. The nearest town was Bourke, which was about ... three hours away. There was only the station owner and myself there ... I lived on the verandah ... I couldn't use a telephone. I knew nothing about banking; I knew nothing about my entitlements – they could have paid me a pound a week if they wanted to – I wouldn't have known. I was doing everything. I was fencing, working cattle, mustering, in the shearing shed, scrub cutting, killing.

Joyce Drury remembers the terrible loneliness of leaving Fairbridge to work as a domestic servant and live in a tiny attic storeroom.

> And they showed me where I was to sleep, and it was up in the attic, which was a box room, and there was a bed in there and all these boxes and boxes ... It was the loneliest part of my life I would say. That was the first time I'd been alone in a room by myself. Now, Fairbridge hadn't prepared us for those kinds of things. That was one failing I would say. Suddenly, after living for years in a dormitory, and here you are.

And also I was treated as a servant and I wasn't prepared for that either – I expected to be with a family.

[One] Sunday night Mrs Le Coutier said to me,
'Joyce, would you like to come down and listen to the
radio play?' and I thought, I've made it. I'm going to
sit in a living room and be with a family. And I came
down and she had put a chair outside the living room
door and the door was just ajar and she said, 'You'll
be able to hear it from there.' And of course, I walked
up the stairs and cried my little heart out and thought,
How could people be like that?

Gwen Miller remembers the trauma of being sent out on
her own to work as a domestic servant for a doctor and
his family in the town of Parkes, in the west of the state.

The first night I went to my room for the night was the
loneliest I have ever felt in my life – totally alone with
two sets of clothes; I remember wishing that I had died
with my mother . . . I was sixteen and three-quarters.
I hadn't turned seventeen . . . I was a domestic, a cheap
servant. And I tell you the first night that I left Fairbridge, I think it affected me deeper than leaving
England . . . They showed me my bedroom and I don't
know what I did between then and going to bed that
night. But I remember going back into that room at
night and the incredible loneliness. It was terrible.

Like all of us Gwen also recalls that she had few social
skills when leaving Fairbridge.

I really didn't know how to conduct myself or anything . . . I really didn't know anything about money
when I left . . . I just didn't know how to behave in
front of other people. Social contact. At Fairbridge

. . . you'd be half grown up and half a child still, but treated like a baby, if you know what I mean.

David Wilson was lonely living and working largely alone on remote farms. On the subject of whether he missed not having a life with his parents he says:

Did I ever think, Where's my Mum? Not as much as when I left Fairbridge. Because you get lonely out there and you think, jeez, I wished I would have had a parent.

Fairbridge children who found themselves down on their luck after they left had no one to turn to and found little comfort when they approached Fairbridge as a last resort. At one point in his late teens David Wilson was out of work and out of money and called on the chairman of the Sydney Fairbridge Council, Mr W. B. Hudson. With nowhere else to go – and with Fairbridge his legal guardian until he reached twenty-one – Dave Wilson asked Hudson for a train fare back to Molong.

He [Hudson] used to work in Sydney; he was like our father because that's the only people we ever knew. But then he wouldn't even help you in the end. I asked him for help. And he said, 'No. I'm not helping you anymore.' I didn't have a job. We were only getting, I think, a pound a week and don't forget, Fairbridge was taking some of it, too. Because that was part of the deal. All you wanted was a train fare back to Molong and he wouldn't give it to you.

Smiley Bayliff didn't wait till he was seventeen to be found a job by Fairbridge: he ran away when he was sixteen with another boy, John 'Swagman' Booty. The two boys hitchhiked to the outskirts of Sydney, where they split up. Fairbridge notified the police and Smiley was hunted for several months.

> We decided the first place we got dropped off in Sydney, which happened to be Kingswood, I said I'll go this way and he said he'd go that way. We had enough money for a train trip into town. And I never seen John from that day to this. Almost did once, when he was in the army, but I didn't get to see him because he was on duty. I still haven't seen him to this day. Dying to see him and ask him what happened.

Smiley met up with some people in Sydney he had met through the Fairbridge Boy Scouts and worked in a number of jobs under the assumed name of 'Barron', but then he had to move on because the police were getting closer.

> I went down to Bentley's Employment Agency in Elizabeth Street. They used to employ people for farms, and I said, 'I'm after a job – on a farm,' and she said, 'Ah well, we've got this one at Nyngan.' So I took the job, got on a train, went up there to a place called The Mole, sixty miles out of Nyngan.
>
> There was no house – the house had been burned down a little bit before in a fire – and I lived in the shearers' quarters. Oh, jeez, it was lonely there. It was incredible. By the same token, I was out of harm's way – or at least I thought I was out of harm's way where I couldn't get caught and taken back to Fairbridge again.

Nyngan is a small town in the remote north-west of New South Wales and a number of former Fairbridge children worked on the big sheep properties out that way. After a couple of months Smiley went into Nyngan on his day off and was surprised to find that his older brother Syd and a couple of other Fairbridge boys who worked on local farms had also gone to town for the weekend.

They were going over to Western Australia, him and Bobby Wilson and Eddy Scott. [Syd] said, 'Why don't you come?' We drove over to West Australia [in an] old 1938 Chevy, an old black one that broke down along the way, and we had to hitchhike the last few hundred miles. We wanted to catch the S.S. *Arcadia* over to England as stowaways. It was in the dock at Fremantle and we were going to hop on the ship, the four of us, and wait until the ship got way out to sea and if they found us, they wouldn't throw us back . . . But we couldn't get past the gangplank because it was leaving that night and they wouldn't let anyone on, visitors or otherwise . . . So we abandoned the plan and decided to come back to the east.

We split up and hitchhiked and got a number of lifts . . . One, the biggest lift we got, was from near Norseman and we travelled with a Yugoslav fellow who picked us up in a 1951 single spinner Ford and took us to Broken Hill, which was a long way. We shared . . . with the fuel bill and by the time we got to Broken Hill we were absolutely flat broke . . . [we only had] a few bob just to buy the very basics. Our next lift was on a mail truck that dropped us off at Wilcannia. We stayed for four days in Wilcannia near an Aboriginal reserve and they used to come and bring us a pot of tea out in the morning and some of their bread. We used to buy a tin of bully beef and that was our meal every day.

With nowhere else to go, they hitchhiked back to Fairbridge, where they were given a shower and a bed for the night. After breakfast next morning Woods told Bayliff, who had now turned seventeen, that he could come back and work as a trainee for two months and then be found a job and be provided with an outfit of clothing. Smiley says he would have nothing to do with the offer. Then, as Smiley recounts, Woods 'called me a vagrant and ordered me off the place, never to return. I think he gave me about a quid. That's all they gave me out of my bank account.'

Smiley and Bobby Wilson went down below the farm school and bivouacked at Molong Creek, and Bobby's younger brother Ronnie, who was still at Fairbridge, supplied them with stolen food.

> And then Bobby and I hit the track for three months after that, you know, just bumming about. We got the track ration and all, the swagman's special track ration. You got thirty shillings of groceries . . . you couldn't buy booze . . . it was a voucher. You could buy a tobacco pouch and papers . . . Thirty bob was a lot of money when you didn't have to pay for accommodation . . . You could get the vouchers once a week from the town police station but if you went to the police station in the next town two days later you could get another voucher.

Eventually Smiley met up with his brother Syd again.

> So I went to Wollongong and I got a job with Syd in the coalmines down at Port Kembla. It was all horse-drawn . . . Four ton of coal behind a horse. About three to four miles underground . . . I went to the steelworks after that.

When he was twenty years old Smiley was one of a number of Fairbridge boys who were conscripted into the Australian Army in the late 1960s and sent to fight in the Vietnam War. After the army Smiley worked as a coach driver, a bus conductor and a prison warder. His second wife, Kerry, encouraged him to enrol in the course that helped him read and write properly.

For many years now, Smiley has been helping Old Fairbridgians to search for information about their long-lost families and fill out the necessary forms. There are many cases where children have spent years, even decades, trying to find their parents, with a lack of cooperation and occasionally some resistance from Fairbridge.

John Brookman was sent to the Northcote home in Victoria as an eight-year-old in 1939 and was transferred to Fairbridge at Molong in 1944. He had no brothers or sisters or any other relatives in Australia. He began asking Woods about his family in the UK when he was fourteen, and started searching for relatives when he was twenty-one years old. After more than thirty years, and with the help of a genealogist, he finally tracked his mother down. She had died the year before. John complained that he received no help from Fairbridge in his quest to find his mother:

> I was the one who suffered most as I was institution-alised up to the age of seventeen years and left the institution [Fairbridge] not knowing anyone whom I could contact regarding my family. For years I tried many times to trace my family, mainly through the Fairbridge Farm School Society in London or through Fairbridge Farm School Molong, without avail.[8]

John was never to experience family life. After spending his entire childhood in institutions he left Fairbridge aged seventeen and drifted from one labouring job to another. He never married. For many years he worked as a farm labourer at Peak Hill in the west of the state and returned to Fairbridge at twenty-one to live and work as a labourer on village maintenance. He also worked as a train guard with the New South Wales railways and for many years lived in a caravan working for the New South Wales Department of Main Roads, travelling around and camping near the available work.

John was never to develop friendships or relationships outside of the Fairbridge network. He spent most of his holidays back at Fairbridge Farm because he had nowhere else to go. He stayed in Gloucester House, which had been built to accommodate visiting Old Fairbridgians. For most of his life he lived alone, although he did flat with some other ex-Fairbridge boys in Sydney for a while in the 1960s, and would sometimes spend weekends with an ex-Fairbridge boy who had married and started a family. Some boys who were at Fairbridge after John say that when they were conscripted into the Australian Army and sent to Vietnam he regularly posted them newspapers from Australia.

When Brookman, as a fourteen-year-old, first asked if Woods could find out anything about his family, Woods wrote to the Fairbridge Society in London, who in turn wrote to the children's home John had come from in 1939. They were told: 'I very much regret that we can obtain no information.'[9]

When John returned to Fairbridge to work as the village maintenance man he again sought information but was only able to track down some photos taken of him at the children's home before he left England. For the next few years he made inquiries at the church where he was baptised in Brighton in the UK, the Salvation Army Missing Peoples Office and the Red Cross, all 'again to no avail'.[10]

In 1979 he planned to go back to England with another Old Fairbridgian, Syd Lee, to carry on the search, but he was unable to obtain an Australian passport because he had difficulty tracking down a copy of his birth certificate from Fairbridge. Disheartened, Brookman let the trail go cold until he was put on to the Australian Society of Genealogists in Sydney, who in 1983 put him in touch with genealogist Peter Bennett in Southampton, England. In April 1985 Bennett was able to tell Brookman:

> I have now completed your researches, except for the difficult task of relating the story. Briefly, I have discovered your cousin and he cared for your mother until she passed on last year.

The cousin, also named John Brookman, was to provide a great deal of information, and had written a short history of the family. John Brookman in Australia corresponded with his cousin and planned to visit him in the UK. However, his cousin died unexpectedly in his London office on the eve of his retirement, so the two never met. The surviving John Brookman was given a copy of the family history written by his cousin, and it revealed his mother had an equally tragic life to his own. Dorothy, known to the family as Dolly, was born in 1895:

> A pretty child with fair hair, it would seem that of all the people her life was going to be a happy one. But unfortunately it was not so, and the tale that unfolds shows that her life was a very sad one.[11]

During World War I Dolly was a nurse. She was to marry an officer she had met at the military hospital but was prevented from doing so at the last minute by her stern Victorian father.

His main objection was that Dolly, having had TB should never marry, though the family considered this merely as an excuse so that he could tie her to the family, where she could keep house with her mother, and also look after her [mentally retarded] sister May. Dolly remained a spinster.

A decade later Dolly was helping with the running of the family's guesthouse in Cavendish Place, near the waterfront at Eastbourne, when she had an affair with a married man who worked at a chicken farm up on Beachy Head. She became pregnant and her father 'went berserk. He ordered her to get out of his house immediately and never come back, and within hours she was out'. Help came from her brother Leonard and his wife, who lived across the road in Cavendish Place and secretly took her in.

Dolly had to remain hidden inside all day every day, but could take walks out along the promenade after dark when no one would recognise her. It must be remembered that Eastbourne was a town where Victorian people and Victorian morals ruled supreme, and the shame that would have descended upon the Brookman family were the truth to come out would have been horrendous.

How could she keep the baby? Her father would never have her back home, and there was no man to support her. In the end she had only one choice – to have the baby adopted or put in a home.

And so on a cold wet day in November 1930, Leonard took his sister to a maternity home in Brighton, and on November 10 – Dolly's 35th birthday – she gave birth to a son. Six days after the birth of her baby Leonard again made the trip to Brighton and brought her back to number 3 Cavendish Place, but without the baby.

Back at No 8 Cavendish Place [the family's guesthouse], for some time Emily Palmer [Dolly's mother] pleaded the case with Thomas to take his daughter back, and at last he relented and took her back. But only on one condition, that she never spoke to him, or he to her and for eight years that condition was religiously kept.

And so apart from the father and the daughter not speaking to each other, everything turned back to normal at No 8.

And so the 1930s passed uneventfully. Dolly worked hard at No 8 Cavendish Place, managing all the upstairs rooms and also helping to look after her sister May.

During World War II, Dolly worked in a munitions factory, then moved back to the guesthouse as guests began returning after the war. Dolly's father died in 1957, May had a series of strokes, the guesthouse was sold, and Dolly and May went to live in Westbury, where May died in 1976.

Although Dolly missed the company of her sister, she took on a new lease of life, and now 72 years of age she was at last free of encumbrances. She got out as much as possible to her friends and friends visited her. For two years she continued happily in this way, but it was not to be for long. Happiness was never to be for long where Dolly was concerned.

One cold night in early December 1969 a neighbour happened to get out of bed in the early hours of a Monday morning, and looking across the road at Dolly's house noticed a white light in the front-room downstairs window. He dressed and crossed over to see what it was and it appeared to be a television set left on. When they broke in they found Dolly unconscious on the floor of the lounge, and she was rushed to hospital. A brain haemorrhage was diagnosed, and it was thought that she would not live.

But Dolly did not die then, though perhaps it would have been kinder for her if she had done so. She was taken from the little cottage hospital at Westbury to St Johns at Trowbridge, and here she lived for a further 14½ years until her death in 1984. From the time she was taken ill until her death she never spoke again, nor could she comprehend anything.

Former friends of Brookman say the revelations about his mother and a trip he took to the UK in 1988 to fit the pieces of his past together were devastating for John. 'He was never the same when he came back,' recalls Syd Lee.

It was often the case that Fairbridge children, after decades of hoping and searching, found the reality disappointing and unfulfilling. Brookman was like a lot of Fairbridge children who felt incomplete until they reconnected with their family. Yet what Brookman discovered were a couple of surviving distant cousins who had little knowledge of the family history, no knowledge of John and little in common with him. He learnt that his mother had led an altogether tragic life; and the one person who had some empathy for the story, his cousin John, had also died before he reached England. There was no one there for him.

Brookman returned to Australia, where he was living alone in a small apartment in Orange he had bought with a payout from the Department of Main Roads following an injury to his back. He was drinking heavily and died in his sleep in 1991. He was only sixty years old.

BOOK 3

12

AGAINST THE TIDE

At the start the Fairbridge scheme was enthusiastically embraced by the British ruling elite who thought it was virtuous for rescuing destitute children from their impoverished backgrounds and providing them with a fresh start, and for strengthening the British Empire by sending out white stock to populate her colonies. Its standing was further enhanced by the public and financial support it received from the British aristocracy and royalty.

Yet the day the school opened in 1938 its founding principles were already looking dated. Within five years a continual stream of internal reports and official investigations began to make Fairbridge's failings at Molong apparent.

Throughout its history Fairbridge repeatedly rejected criticism and resisted change, even where reform would have improved the welfare and prospects of the children. When confronted with evidence of brutality it ignored the information; it took no action against staff it knew were guilty of committing terrible acts against children. Whenever it was seriously tested Fairbridge was able to muster enormous power and influence in high places.

One of the early attempts to persuade Fairbridge to address the flaws in its scheme was made by E. R. Heath, who went to Fairbridge Farm as the farm supervisor when it opened in 1938 and became its principal in 1940. When he resigned in 1943 he wrote a special report highlighting the failure of the Fairbridge trainee scheme, which he said placed too much emphasis on the use of the children as farm labour and provided too little training and learning.

> After nearly five years at the Fairbridge Farm, Molong and before relinquishing control of the School there are several matters that I wish to bring before the notice of the Council. During my association with Fairbridge, its failures as well as its virtues have become apparent to me and I offer these suggestions briefly but frankly in the hope they may be of some use to the Council in future planning.[1]

The report, which has never been made public, went on to say that more adult supervisors needed to be employed:

> Too much stress has been and is being laid on the ratio of staff to children and a wrong but general feeling seems to be that all or most of the work should be done by the children. They do it now to the detriment of their training. So much time is spent in doing routine work and there are so few instructors that there is little time in which to learn. This applies to the farm as well as the village as there the stress is laid on the amount we produce rather than on the course of training we give.

No changes were introduced as a result of Heath's report; the use of trainees as cheap farm labour continued unchanged for the life of Fairbridge.

Fairbridge was again made aware of problems with its scheme a year later due to a far more substantial investigation by the British high commission in Canberra. In October 1944, Mr W. J. Garnett, official secretary to the British high commissioner in Canberra, wrote a comprehensive forty-page report titled 'Report on Farm Schools in Australia'.[2] Garnett argued that the pause in child migration caused by World War II provided an opportunity to reassess the farm-school system.

> The date when the migration of children can be resumed is still uncertain and the time is therefore opportune to review the purpose and results of the schemes and to consider what, if any, changes are desirable when they are in a position to resume operations.

Garnett studied the Fairbridge farm schools at Molong and Pinjarra, the Northcote School in Bacchus Marsh, Victoria, which was based on the Fairbridge model, and the Barnardo's Farm School at Picton, New South Wales. Most of the detail of the report dealt with the Fairbridge schools. The report was given to Fairbridge but not made public.

Garnett said there was 'conclusive proof' that Fairbridge had failed in its basic aim of converting child migrants into successful farmers and that such an aim was, in reality, unachievable anyway. He believed that Fairbridge was out of date and fundamental changes needed to be made to the future operation of the scheme.

> The experience gained from the working of these schemes in the past and the change in social consciousness in regard to the education and treatment of children suggest that some modifications in the basic principles underlying the schemes are overdue.

> Boys trained on Farm Schools cannot look forward to becoming farmers on their own account save in exceptional cases . . .
>
> At the time Kingsley Fairbridge commenced work in Western Australia [1912] farming conditions were such as to justify the hope that a boy properly trained and placed in employment as a farm worker would, if industrious and thrifty and after gaining practical experience, have a reasonable prospect of becoming a farmer on his own account . . . This hope has not been realised and only a handful of boys have succeeded in establishing themselves on their own account.

Garnett argued that the fault lay in the farm schools and that they should provide better education and training to equip children with a wider range of career choices.

> The primary aim and object of the Fairbridge Schools has been to train boys and girls for rural employment and the farm schools have not the facilities them-selves save in exceptional cases to assist promising children to qualify for and enter other forms of employment . . . The scheme should be modified so that, while the primary purpose of the Farm Schools should continue to be to train children for primary employment, it should be possible for children to exercise some choice of occupation and for boys and girls who show themselves to be specially qualified to follow the other occupations to receive the necessary training.

The report also dealt with the recurring problem of poor staff at Fairbridge, particularly cottage mothers, who in the main lacked qualifications and the sensitivity required to meet the needs of the children:

They do not appear to have made sufficient allowance for the classes of children with whom they are dealing, amongst whom a number of cases requiring patient and sympathetic treatment are bound to arise.

Garnett also highlighted the problems of isolation and loneliness experienced by Fairbridge children that arose from 'segregation in isolated communities'.

In a comprehensive point-by-point response to the report in August 1945, the secretary of the Fairbridge Society in London, Mr Gordon Green, agreed with most of the points made by Garnett and painted an even bleaker picture of Fairbridge's record.[3]

Green agreed that Fairbridge children rarely managed to become farmers in their own right and went further, suggesting that Fairbridge children tended to become underpaid labour, destined to be despised as an underclass and left to a life on the fringes of society. He admitted that on the whole it appeared that the main product of Fairbridge was unskilled cheap labour. 'For the boys, attainment of an economic status which would warrant marriage and a family, was extremely difficult . . . They have remained the underprivileged class.'

Much of Green's understanding of Fairbridge came from discussions he had with former Fairbridge children who had joined the armed services and were serving in Europe during World War II. A number of them had visited the Fairbridge offices while in London and complained to Green that they 'found themselves despised as outcasts from Britain' working for lower wages than Australians doing similar work.

Green went on to argue that the Fairbridge farm schools compared unfavourably with the Roman Catholic Christian Brothers School in Bindoon, Western Australia, which he said was 'wise as well as just and should be emulated by Fairbridge'.

According to Green, the Fairbridge Society in London, though being responsible for recruiting children for the farm schools in Australia and providing a large part of their funding, was not responsible for the failures pointed out by Garnett and were powerless to fix them. The fault, he said, lay with the local management running the farm schools. He commented that the London Society had attempted to be involved in governing the farm schools but had been defeated in Western Australia by the incorporation of the Perth committee by Kingsley Fairbridge and in New South Wales by the Sydney committee's insistence on autonomy. He conceded: 'But undoubtedly the interests of children would have been best served if no such total surrender of right of direction of a Farm School had been made by the London Society.'

Despite acknowledging the failures in the Fairbridge scheme Green rejected the need for a fundamental rethink of the 'basic principles', as advocated by Garnett. He reiterated that the basic principles underlying the Fairbridge scheme remained those established by Kingsley Fairbridge.

> Certain children are by misfortune denied the security and fostering of a normal family life. They need care and protection. The illegitimate child and the child of lawful but irresponsible parents has much to expect from Fairbridge if by the transfer to Australia or Canada it can be free of its disabilities. There is that benefit to the child and if the work of fostering and educating the child is properly accomplished, the community where the child is, in time, settled in Australia or Canada, has the profit of a good citizen, healthy, confident and stable. This basic principle remains.

So change was again resisted and Fairbridge did not embark on the fundamental reform. Over the next few years the Fairbridge Society in London was able to negotiate formal agreements with the Fairbridge bodies in New South Wales and Western Australia that clarified their respective powers and responsibilities. However, the farm school scheme continued much as before.

The next serious challenge to the Fairbridge scheme came with the Curtis report into child welfare in Britain in 1946 and the Children Act in 1948, which together caused a fundamental shift in child care away from institutions toward foster care, and away from benevolent volunteer organisations to the state taking responsibility for the welfare of children. The childcare professionals replacing the volunteer amateurs became increasingly opposed to child migration and child-migrant institutions.

Central to the change in approach was the belief that if children were unable to be properly cared for by their natural parents they should be cared for in environments that resembled homes. Fairbridge had never considered the emotional or developmental needs of the children and was modelled on the provision of discipline, hard work, only elementary schooling, a roof overhead and food. But now the days of the large, impersonal children's institutions seemed to be over: the future demanded that children be afforded affection and understanding. The British Government encouraged the volunteer organisations and charities to restructure their homes. Fairbridge was one of the institutions that resisted change the longest.

In April 1948, while the new Children Act was being drafted in Britain, sixteen British welfare organisations protested about the continuation of Fairbridge and other child-migrant institutions. They called for a government commission of inquiry into the condition of the children. The group of welfare organisations was headed by the

British Federation of Social Workers and included the Association of Children's Moral Welfare Workers, the National Association of Probation Officers and the London County Council Children's Care Organisers. They were concerned that the new life promised the children was worse than the one they had left behind and that the child-migrant institutions were more poorly run than institutions in England.

The London *Daily Mail* reported the story under the headline 'Anxiety for 300 Child Emigrants'. An official spokesperson for the group of welfare organisations told the paper:[4]

> Our members have heard disturbing reports about the children who have emigrated through voluntary organisations. Some will get nothing better than elementary education and, whatever mental ability they show, will have little chance of raising themselves above the standard of domestic servants and agricultural labourers. Our greatest fear is that the population needs of the Dominions are being put before the welfare of these children. The children must be safeguarded.

The paper reported that the organisations wanted the inquiry to investigate:

> The conditions under which these British children were selected for emigration; what happened to the children overseas; what safeguards there are for their well being; how they can be protected from 'blind-alley' jobs.

They also wanted child migrants to be selected more carefully, and offered to participate in the process, but the London Fairbridge Society dismissed the offer. In a letter to Lord Scarborough, the acting general secretary of Fairbridge, H. L. Logan, wrote:

It requires an almost inordinate amount of self-esteem not to say 'effrontery' to suggest that the mere participation of their members in the selection of children constitutes 'the first attempt in this country to create a systematic method of selection and to gain the confidence and goodwill of the child'.[5]

In 1951 the British home secretary pointed out that a number of national children's institutions in Britain had already been closed and that the Children Act recognised it 'was generally accepted' that boarding children out with foster parents was the best form of care because it 'approached normal home life'. The best new children's homes, he said, were of the 'small family type' of 'varied ages and both sexes' and most importantly, children 'brought up away from their home needed not only decent material conditions but a home in the true sense where he could find understanding, interest and affection and the security that these brought'.[6]

Other reports in the early 1950s, including the Moss report, identified a number of problems with the various child-migrant schemes, including Fairbridge. Overall the Moss report supported a continuation of child migration but it argued more children should be fostered out in Australia rather than being kept in institutions. Moss also observed that 90 per cent of child migrant were 'backward for their age on Australian education standards' and recommended further assimilation of child migrants – particularly Fairbridge children – into the Australian community.

Then in 1956 the British Government sent a fact-finding mission to Australia to investigate the child-migrant institutions that took British children. The British Government had been funding Fairbridge and other child-migrant schemes under the Empire Settlement acts since

1922. Prior to the expiry of these acts in May 1957 the government gave consideration to the appropriate levels of future funding. As part of its policy review it proposed to send a fact-finding mission to Australia to investigate the child-migrant institutions. The Overseas Migration Board (OMB) advised the British Government's Commonwealth Relations Office in July 1955 that 'The information at present available about child migrants was not sufficient on which to base long term decisions on Government assistance.'[7]

In agreeing to send the mission to Australia the British Government warned that 'Continued Government funding should be conditional on child-migrant organisations adopting more enlightened child care practices, including a shift from institutional to foster care.'[8]

> Approval for increased grants for societies concerned with the migration of children and the extension of the existing schemes beyond 1957 should be dependent upon their acceptance of the new doctrine that the selection of children for unaccompanied migration needs to be carefully done, from the psychological as well as other points of view, and the aim should be that such children are placed in family homes and not in institutions.

The British Government made the Australian Government aware of its intentions and of the fact that the British authorities had for some time been attempting to persuade the child-migrant institutions to modernise.[9]

> Australia House and presumably therefore also the Department concerned at Canberra, are aware of the difficulties about child migration as a result of a softening-up process on which we have been engaged for

some time and that they would probably welcome any mission which might lead to results which could be helpful from their point of view.

The fact-finding mission had three members: chairman Mr J. Ross, under secretary of state of the British home office, Mr W. J. Garnett and Miss G. M. Wansbrough-Jones. Garnett was, of course, familiar with child migration to Australia, having written a report on farm schools more than ten years before, when he was secretary to the British high commissioner in Canberra. Wansbrough-Jones was considered to be the childcare expert in the party, having worked in child welfare with the London County Council. The secretary of the committee was Mr E. H. Johnson of the Commonwealth Relations Office (CRO).

The mission arrived in Australia in February 1956, and visited and reported on twenty-six child-migrant centres operating in Victoria, New South Wales, Tasmania, South Australia, Western Australia and Queensland. In their report they said: 'We were received everywhere with kindness and consideration, and were given every facility during our visit to acquaint ourselves with the arrangements for the care of the children.'[10] The generosity of the comment disguised the considerable tension their visit caused at a number of institutions, only revealed in the secret addenda to the mission's report, which were never made public.

Prior to the arrival of the mission to inspect Fairbridge at Molong, W. B. Hudson wrote to Principal Woods explaining that he had met the mission in Sydney and outlining the arrangements for their inspection of the farm school. The party, which included the three members of the fact-finding mission and other government officials, was to arrive at Bathurst airport at 8.45 a.m. on

15 February and then drive to Orange. There they would be taken to Fairbridge for lunch and be shown round the village and school in the afternoon. Hudson wrote: 'I would like all seven of them to have their tea separately with the children in their cottages. Breakfast with the children in the morning and then go over the farm.'[11]

He added that the children should be instructed to wear shoes for the duration of the inspection: 'I have a feeling that barefooted children would have a very adverse effect on the visitors and suggest that if you agree it would be advisable to see that they wore their shoes and socks.'

The mission travelled around the six states of Australia over a six-week period and in March delivered a highly critical report based on what they had seen.[12]

The main body of the report did not mention any of the institutions by name: they were named only in the secret addenda.

As a starting point, the mission said that it had adopted the modern standards of child care as the basis for measuring the performance of child-migrant establishments.

> As the report is concerned with children from the United Kingdom, we have thought it right to take account of child care methods as developed there since 1948, when the Children Act was passed into law, namely, boarding out wherever possible, and failing that, residence in small children's homes in preference to large ones.

The mission argued that child migrants deserved special sensitivity.

> We think that it will be agreed generally that the desirability of enabling children deprived of a normal

home life to be brought up in circumstances approaching as nearly as possible those of a child living in his own home applies with particular force to migrant children, who, in addition to the basic need of children for the understanding and affection that lead to security, have experienced disturbance arising from the transfer to new and unfamiliar surroundings.

This sensitivity to the needs of children was totally alien to Fairbridge. Indeed, the entire thrust of the report was fundamentally at odds with the Fairbridge model. While the Fairbridge farm schools provided institutional accommodation for up to 300 children the mission recommended that child migrants be fostered out to Australian families. The report noted, though, that Fairbridge and the other establishments they visited had not given 'serious thought to boarding out migrant children in their care'. The implementation of this recommendation would have required a total reconstitution of the Fairbridge Farm School Scheme.

The fact-finding mission rejected arguments made by child-migrant institutions that their Spartan conditions were acceptable because they were comparable to some English boarding schools:

We think that this point is not a valid one; those suggesting it overlook the fact that the migrant children, unlike most children attending boarding schools, have no home for the time being other than that provided by the organisation caring for them.

Few with whom we spoke seemed to realise that it was precisely such children, already rejected and insecure, who might often be ill equipped to cope with the added strains of migration.

It found that the establishments they inspected were 'institutional in character' and that many of the children 'were disturbed by reason of separation from their parents'.

The mission was made aware of the child-migrant schemes' difficulty in attracting suitable cottage mothers. It was sceptical that: 'those engaged in the work had sufficient knowledge of child care methods to be able to give migrant children the understanding and care needed to help them adjust themselves in strange surroundings' and found that there was 'no specialist scheme of training in Australia for child care work'.

They were especially critical of the children's 'segregation in large measure from the life of the community', lack of homely atmosphere, lack of personal privacy, and the children's difficulty in adjusting to normal life on leaving the institution to go to work. They were frustrated that the establishments they visited 'were not persuaded of the benefit to the children of having all meals as a family group in their cottages'.

The report struck at the heart of the Fairbridge model by recommending that children not be kept to run the farm when they finished school but be found outside employment. In a clear reference to Fairbridge they observed:

> We gathered at one place that the work done in this way by the boys was essential to the running of the farm. It seemed to us that these arrangements were unsuitable for boys and girls who did not intend to follow farm and domestic work.
>
> Children should not ordinarily remain in an establishment between leaving school and entering outside employment, except for the purpose of receiving training for the occupation they intend to enter.

Finally, the report dropped a bombshell by recommending that in future the consent of the home secretary should be required for any child to migrate. The implications were clear: if Fairbridge did not fall into line with the recommended modern childcare practices they would not receive authorisation to send more children to Australia.

The report of the fact-finding mission caused considerable heartburn in London. The OMB, which had initiated the mission in the first place, was embarrassed by the findings and recommendations and moved quickly to distance itself from the report. In a report to the government's CRO in May 1956 M. K. Ewans of the board said:

> The Overseas Migration Board yesterday discussed the report of the Child Migration Mission. It was quite a stormy meeting and it is clear that the Board are now rather sorry that the mission was sent at all.[13]

The board indicated that some of its members wanted the report hushed up but accepted that it would inevitably be leaked if an attempt were made to keep it secret.

> A minority of the Board urged very strongly that the report should not be published but it was eventually agreed that publication was inevitable in view of the certainty of leakage in one form or another.

If the mission's report were to be made public the board wanted to have the opportunity to say that they viewed the report with 'extreme disfavour'.

Costley-White of the CRO, who received the report, told his superiors:

> The Overseas Migration Board would like the preface
> [of the report] altered so that they escape responsibil-
> ity for being instrumental in the appointment of the
> mission whose report they do not approve . . . They
> wish to put their own independent comments on the
> report.[14]

The government was happy for the OMB to criticise the
mission's report but was concerned that it would then be
forced into declaring its own opinion. An internal memo
written by a home office civil servant said:

> I see some advantage if the Board comes out, on the
> date of its publication, with a refusal, so far as they
> are concerned, to accept its terms. The trouble will be
> that as a result the UK Government will presumably
> be pressed to declare their own opinion about the
> Report.[15]

There was a continued campaign to keep the report
secret. Sir Colin Anderson, a member of the OMB and a
director of the Orient line, whose ships carried many of
the child migrants to Australia, argued against the release
of the report. His rather original argument was that the
Australian child-migrant organisations were likely to
'close their ranks to resist criticism', hence publishing the
report may in fact defeat efforts to get the organisations
to raise their standards.[16]

G. E. B. Shannon of the home office agreed and in June
wrote to the department's under secretary, Sir Saville
Garner, saying:

> I am concerned at the controversy likely to be engen-
> dered in the press and Parliament in both countries
> when the report is published. A further difficulty is

that, once the report is published, the United Kingdom Government will be pressed to say whether they accept it. They may reject the Mission's recommendations but, having sent the mission to ascertain facts, it would be difficult to maintain the facts are not what the mission says they are.

But in the face of Australian susceptibilities, it would be just as difficult for the UK Government to agree with the Mission's report on the facts. We are hoping to get around this dilemma by saying that we are consulting the Australian Government about the action to be taken on the report, without saying whether we agree or disagree with it. But we could avoid the political and public dilemma altogether if the report is not published.[17]

But far more damning and potentially damaging than the general report of the fact-finding mission were the secret addenda, which included highly critical comments about individual child-migration centres in Australia, particularly Fairbridge.

On 9 June 1956, Costley-White of the CRO sent a complete copy of the report, including its highly sensitive addenda, to R. J. Whittick of the home office. He made it clear that the addenda were to be kept secret, even from the OMB and the Australian Government.[18]

The Home Office have not hitherto received a copy of the confidential Addenda to the report of the fact-finding mission on Child Migration. A copy is enclosed herewith, which as you will see, is extensive.

These Addenda have not hitherto been seen by anyone outside the Commonwealth Relations Office. It is not our intention to publish them at the time that the report is published; we are not intending to give

> them to the Australian Government, to the Overseas Migration Board, or the Voluntary Societies. You will understand that it is therefore important that they should not be quoted or referred to in dealing with outside persons or organisations.

Keeping the addenda secret was one thing, but the government had to make a decision about further migration of children to Fairbridge and other institutions that had attracted critical comment from the fact-finding mission. Costley-White continued:

> The question arises whether in the light of the fact-finding mission report, we should continue to allow further children to go to Australia. It will evidently be difficult for the United Kingdom Government to approve children going to institutions which have been criticised by the fact-finding mission; but rather than make a complete closure on all child migration it may be considered wiser to adopt a middle course of allowing children to go to institutions provided they have not been adversely criticised by the Fact-finding Mission.

The addenda to the report became the basis of a black list drawn up by the home office.[19]

The secret addendum on Fairbridge Farm at Molong included a number of critical observations:

> Furnishing and equipment: The cottages have the minimum of furniture and little comfort. The beds consist of wire mesh, which tends to sag, on a steel frame, with very poor mattresses. There is no other furniture in the dormitories and the floors are bare wood. A typical playroom contains one large table,

with plain wooden chairs, and lockers forming seats around the walls. Bathrooms and kitchens are shabby and poorly though adequately equipped. In the dining hall, the children use plain metal plates and beakers.

Children's Activities: A considerable amount of domestic and other work is done by the older school children, who spend about two hours before morning School and another hour in the evening on their duties in the cottages, kitchen, bakery, etc., or at farm or garden work.

General comments: The children at Molong have to work hard and have no luxuries ... From conversation with a number of children it was clear that at first many of them find life strange and are homesick. [20]

The report pointed out that Fairbridge at Molong was harder for girls than boys: 'Those who leave school at fifteen have little preparation for anything but domestic work and even less opportunity than boys of seeing much of Australian life.'

The addendum on Pinjarra was also unflattering: the fact-finding mission found that it 'was complacent, and reluctant to accept new ideas' and 'showed a lack of appreciation of current thought on child care'.

The mission was relatively more impressed with a number of other institutions. Of the Clarendon Church of England Home at Kingston Park, Tasmania, the mission reported:

In this home there are good material conditions, and the children appear to receive individual affection and understanding. The home is run on sound principles, and the children seen seemed to have plenty of interests and to be happy and spontaneous.

And of the Methodist Home at Burwood in Victoria it said:

> These homes provide good material care and a high standard of comfort, in an attractive setting. The Superintendent is keen, active and enlightened, and has considerable personal knowledge of individual children. These appear to be really good homes of the grouped cottage type.

Having received the damaging addenda on the child-migrant institutions from the CRO, on 22 June 1956, R. J. Whittick of the Home Office wrote to his boss, G. E. B. Shannon to advise him on compilation of a black list:[21]

> We have, in consultation with our experts on child care, gone through the notes on the various establishments and, based on those notes alone, we have drawn up the enclosure to this letter. Establishments in category 'A' are those which we think are not fit to receive more migrants, for the present at least, Category 'C' are establishments that pass muster. Category 'B' contains those about which we do not know enough to say whether they ought to be placed in 'A' or 'C'. Some of the establishments in category 'A' are so wrong in the principles on which they run that they would need a complete metamorphosis to bring them into category 'C'.
>
> Organisations on the 'black list' would be told that their establishments had been criticised by the Mission, would be shown the reports or parts of them or given the gist of the criticism and would be asked to put matters right before you approved any more children being sent to these establishments.

It is clear from Whittick's memo that the home office was well aware of Fairbridge's influence in high places in Britain and of the political difficulties that would flow from putting Fairbridge schools on the black list.

> The reputation in which the Fairbridge organisation has been held in this country – and no doubt in Australia as well – may, we recognise, remove from the sphere of practical politics the possibility of putting the Farm Schools at Pinjarra and Molong on your black list, although well informed opinion would condemn them from the point of view of the accepted principles of child care.

Of the twenty-six institutions inspected by the fact-finding mission, ten were placed in category A and included on the black list, eight 'passed muster' and were placed in category C. The remaining eight were placed in category B.

The institutions on the black list were: the Fairbridge Farm School at Molong; the Fairbridge Farm School at Pinjarra; St Joseph's Roman Catholic Orphanage, Lane Cove, Sydney; Dhurringile Presbyterian Rural Training Farm, Victoria; St Joseph's Roman Catholic School, near Rockhampton in Queensland; the Salvation Army Training Farm, Riverview, Queensland; the Methodist Home at Magill, Adelaide; St Vincent's Roman Catholic Orphanage, Castledare, Western Australia; St Joseph's Roman Catholic Farm School at Bindoon in Western Australia; and St John Bosco Roman Catholic Boys' Town at Glenorchy in Hobart, Tasmania.

The institutions in Category C, which 'passed muster' were: Dr Barnardo's Homes, Burwood, Sydney; Dr Barnardo's Homes, Normanhurst, Sydney; Northcote School, Bacchus Marsh, Victoria; St John's Church of

England Home, Canterbury, Melbourne; Burton Hall Farm School, Tatura, Victoria; Methodist Homes, Burwood, Victoria; Clarendon Church of England Home, Kingston Park, Tasmania; and Hagley Area Farm School, Tasmania.

Category B was made up of: Maelrose United Protestant School, Pendle Hill, Sydney; Murray Dwyer Roman Catholic Orphanage, Mayfield, New South Wales; Goodwood Roman Catholic Orphanage, Goodwood, Adelaide; Clontarf Roman Catholic Boys' Town, Clontarf, Perth; St Joseph's Roman Catholic Home, Leederville, Perth; Methodist Home, Victoria Park, Perth; Swan Church of England Homes, Midland Junction, Western Australia; and Nazareth House, East Camberwell, Melbourne.

By the end of June T. H. E. Heyes, secretary to the British high commissioner in Canberra, gave the Australian Government the general report of the fact-finding mission but not the addenda.[22]

Following consultation with Mr J. Ross, the chairman of the fact-finding mission, the home office decided that it would not authorise further child migration to institutions on the black list. The Fairbridge Society in London, which was by now aware of the developments, had sixteen children at John Howard Mitchell House in Kent waiting to sail to Australia. On Monday, 2 July, Mr W. B. Vaughan, the secretary as well as the director, of the London Fairbridge Society, called on Mr Armstrong, the chief migration officer at Australia House, 'greatly concerned' that formal approval had not been given for the children to go to Australia. Six of the party were destined for Molong and the other ten were going to Pinjarra. The party's escorts had been recruited and bookings had been made to sail a little more than three weeks later, on 26 July, from Tilbury.

Vaughan, according to Armstrong, said that the board

of the Fairbridge Society was meeting at 2.15 p.m. that
Thursday – only three days away – and he wanted the situation resolved before then. There would be 'a first class
row' if he had to report to the board that approval had
been denied for the children to go to Australia. Vaughan
threatened that Fairbridge would apply political pressure.
Armstrong wrote: 'He had no doubt that a sudden suspension of child migration would lead to pressure on the
secretary of state and possibly questions in the Commons
or the Lords.'[23]

As His Royal Highness the Duke of Gloucester was the
president of the Fairbridge Society the civil servants were
all too aware of the political implications of denying
authorisation for children to be sent to Fairbridge. In a
memo to his boss, G. E. B. Shannon, Costley-White of the
CRO noted that there would almost certainly be:

> immediate Parliamentary repercussions since Fair-
> bridge has the means of making itself heard in both
> Houses of Parliament and to the public at large. The
> President of the Fairbridge Society [HRH the Duke of
> Gloucester] is known to take an active interest in its
> affairs, and it is on the cards that his intervention
> would be sought if a 'stand still' were suddenly to be
> imposed, and imposed in the first instance against the
> Fairbridge Society.[24]

Costley-White felt that it 'was almost impossible' to
resolve the matter before the Fairbridge board meeting at
2.15 p.m. that Thursday. He was starting to look at ways
to back down on the issue. Having deliberately withheld
the addenda from the Australian Government he now
used the need for consultation as a possible way out of the
impasse: 'To take what would appear to be a somewhat
high handed decision to hold up child migration without

consulting the Australian Government would appear to be dangerous.'

Shannon hastily took the lifeline and in the first of a series of backdowns sent a memo to Costley-White on Thursday morning.

> I have discussed the foregoing with Sir Saville Garner and Commander Noble. They agree that the sixteen children for Fairbridge and three others for the North-cote Fund should be allowed to go, on the understanding that we cannot guarantee approval of future applications pending consideration of the Fact-finding Mission's report and consultation with the Australian authorities about it.[25]

Later that morning Costley-White met with Mr Vaughan of the Fairbridge Society, telling him that the children already booked could go to Australia. He informed Vaughan that it was 'the general wish of the UK Government' that there be no other child migration in the 'immediate future weeks', while the British Government discussed the report with the Australian Government.[26]

So, as a result of political machinations, sixteen more children, and countless others after them, were dispatched to Australia to spend the remainder of their childhood in an institution black listed by the British Government and condemned as unfit for children.

At the meeting of the Fairbridge Society that Thursday, Vaughan described how the CRO had held up the approval for the party of children at Knockholt to sail on 26 July; he had gone to their offices and protested strongly at not having been told; and then went to Australia House, where the chief immigration officer had been very kind and added his protest to Vaughan's. The minutes finish:

I am glad to say that this combined action had the
desired effect, and that I was called to the CRO again
yesterday to be told by Costley-White one of the
Under Secretaries that without prejudice to further
arrangements the party would be allowed to sail on
the 26th.[27]

Meanwhile, the Fairbridge Society considered the published report of the fact-finding mission. It was in no
mood to reform and disagreed with most of the report's
important recommendations. In a letter to the CRO,
Vaughan made it clear that Fairbridge disagreed with
the principal thrust of the fact-finding mission and of child
welfare generally: that the days of institutions were over.

The proposal that the aim should be to provide for
migrant children by boarding them out is one of the
major problems as, apart from other important
aspects, lack of housing and the difficulty of adequate
supervision must inevitably influence such a policy.[28]

The London Fairbridge Society was supported by the
Sydney Fairbridge Council, which also criticised the fact-
finding mission's proposal to foster out migrant children
in Australia. The chairman of the Sydney Fairbridge
Council, W. Hudson, wrote to the chairman of Fairbridge
in London, Sir Charles Hambro, dismissing the idea as
impractical. He wrote that he was sure 99 per cent of the
people in Australia who would want to take in children
'would not and could not give them as good a start in life
nor be able to give them the same opportunities we can'.
He went on to express his conviction that 90 per cent of
the homes where children were likely to be boarded
'would be a poor substitute for the upbringing we give
them at Fairbridge'.[29]

The Fairbridge Society in London had been successful in getting the British Government to back down; however, the number of children being committed to Fairbridge began to fall dramatically as enlightened childcare authorities in effect boycotted the scheme. At the time of the release of the initial report of the fact-finding mission, Vaughan had warned the London Fairbridge Society that childcare professionals were turning away from the scheme. He explained that local authorities did not see any advantage in emigration for children in their care, and he didn't think it was likely that applications from them would increase.[30]

The following year Sir Charles Hambro publicly criticised those who did not recognise the benefits of the Fairbridge scheme. *The Times*, under the headline 'Negative Outlook of Local Authorities', reported that in an address to Fairbridge's annual general meeting:

> Sir Charles Hambro said he was driven to the conclusion that for the present local authorities responsible for child welfare in Britain felt that, in spite of the unhappy background and bad environment from which these children might come, they had a better chance under the care of local authorities in the crowded towns and cities of this country than they would have in Australia. This view prevailed in spite of many proofs of the great success achieved by those distressed children who had benefited under the Fairbridge scheme.[31]

Finding itself unable to attract sufficient numbers of children for unaccompanied migration, Fairbridge was forced to devise a new recruitment strategy, the One Parent Scheme. Under the scheme Fairbridge would be able to increasingly recruit directly from single-parent families, rather than from child-welfare agencies. Single parents were less likely to be aware of debate about modern child-care practices, and less likely to be critical of or hostile to the child-migrant institutions that were increasingly out of favour with child-welfare authorities. They were also unlikely to be aware of the debate raging within government and welfare circles as a result of the fact-finding mission's report.

But Fairbridge had trouble getting the British Government's approval for its new scheme. On 14 March 1957, Sir Charles Hambro wrote an informal note to Lord Home, who was then the secretary of state for Commonwealth relations. (In 1963 he would move from the House of Lords to become Sir Alexander Douglas-Home and prime minister of Britain.) In the letter, Sir Charles dismissed as 'extreme' the views of the fact-finding mission, and refuted the suggestion that Fairbridge had something to answer for. He acknowledged the help that Lord Home had given Fairbridge as secretary of state, and asked if he realised that Fairbridge's work had been frustrated during the last two years:

> . . . by the comings and goings of semi-official fact-finding missions to Australia. These people have adopted what seems to us to be a very extreme view on child immigration, which we have proved to be so successful over many years.[32]

Hambro explained that the new One Parent Scheme was being held up by the British Government, although it had been 'enthusiastically supported by the federal and state Governments of Australia and by all our subscribers over here'. He finished with a request: 'If you can do anything to expedite action and give us the all-clear to go ahead, we shall be everlastingly grateful and many hundreds of human beings will benefit.'

The lobbying worked and Fairbridge was able to launch the One Parent Scheme later the same year, without making any changes to the way the Fairbridge farm schools operated. The London Fairbridge Society became resigned to the fact that childcare professionals were in effect boycotting its scheme. At a special meeting in 1958 the Fairbridge Society in the UK was told by Sir Charles that no amount of political lobbying would change the situation.

Hambro expressed in a letter to Hudson in January 1959 his belief that the council and executive of Fairbridge in Sydney were under the impression that Fairbridge London could pressure local authorities into sending children to the farm schools in Australia. He explained that even members of parliament had achieved no tangible result from approaching the local authorities in their constituencies. He wrote: 'I put these facts before you, as I feel that there is no hope of a change of attitude, and this should now be realised by everybody connected with Fairbridge.' He demonstrated how out of step Fairbridge was with contemporary childcare thinking, saying he believed that 'in nine cases out of ten a good children's home is better than boarding out'. He lamented that in Britain:

> The authorities and the new hierarchy of children's officers have convinced themselves to the opposite policy of what you and I advocate and we are compelled for the present to bow before them.[33]

In the last year of the old recruitment scheme, 1958, the number of children migrating to Fairbridge in Molong fell to only eight, down from an annual average of thirty in the previous few years.

While Fairbridge was taking a battering in Britain, it was

facing – and resisting – official criticism in Australia, too. In the 1950s the New South Wales Department of Child Welfare made repeated requests that Fairbridge investigate a number of allegations of maltreatment of children

After sending numerous letters to Fairbridge, in February 1958 the director of Child Welfare in New South Wales, R. H. Hicks, wrote to the Australian Department of Immigration, which was technically the legal guardian of Fairbridge children, to complain about the unwillingness of Fairbridge to respond to complaints. He said 'generally good work is being done at Molong by Fairbridge', but also said:

> Fairbridge does not welcome any suggestions for improvement and apparently resents any inference that there may be matters which require attention. Dr Barnardo's Homes on the other hand act very promptly when any matter is brought under notice. The executive is objective in its inquiries and very frank with the Department. No doubt with such a wide and lengthy experience executive officers realise that with even well managed institutions occasionally situations arise which require investigation. It is a pity Fairbridge does not adopt the same approach.[34]

The One Parent Scheme provided Fairbridge with some temporary respite. In 1959, the first year of the new scheme, fifty children went to the Fairbridge Farm School in Molong; eighty-three went in 1960; and ninety-seven went in 1961. By the end of the 1950s Fairbridge had developed an elaborate network of representatives spread throughout Britain promoting and marketing the scheme directly to single parents from poor families.

In 1960 Fairbridge announced a new Family Scheme, under which both parents could come to Australia at

the same time as their children. The children would be
left at Fairbridge while the parents found a job and
accommodation, and eventually they would all be back
together as a family.

Fairbridge faced a problem with the One Parent
Scheme, though. On leaving school at fifteen years, children were extremely unlikely to work on the Fairbridge
farm for two years for only a bit of pocket money when
they could join their parent, immediately start work and
earn a wage, as I did. As early as 1961, when I was still
at Fairbridge, Woods expressed his concern in a 'Special
Memorandum' attached to his regular principal's report
to the Sydney Fairbridge Council:

> Firstly, by the end of the year we will have too few
> trainees to run all the various sections of our Farm
> Training in the manner we have done for several years
> – that is the Dairy, Piggery, Slaughter yards, Vegetable
> Garden and Orchard, General farm work, Laundry,
> Bakery, Main Kitchen, Stores, Gloucester House,
> Village maintenance, and all the other general domes-
> tic chores of the community.[35]

Woods noted that it would be necessary to reduce the
range of 'general training' Fairbridge provided, to elimi-
nate a number of aspects, 'such as baking, gardening and
main kitchen, and employ staff to deal with some of the
work'. Alternatively, they could employ additional staff
and the work could be shared by staff and trainees.

> Secondly, there seems now to be a probable cessation
> or at least a lessening in the flow of children to Fair-
> bridge even under the 'Family' scheme. It is very
> necessary for future planning to know how many
> children we may expect here, say in the next twelve

months, since if we do not get many more, or our
numbers continue to fall at all appreciably, we should
reduce our milking herd, thereby reducing the amount
of work to be done by the reduced number of trainees,
we should cut down much of our garden area, and we
could reduce the number of cottages we have open.

The loss of trainees was critical to Fairbridge since child
labour had enabled the farm to function. The Family
Scheme caused even more problems for Fairbridge. Many
parents who were supposed to leave their children at Fairbridge while they were setting up their new lives in Australia were dissatisfied when they saw the farm school and
would not leave their children there for one day longer
than was absolutely necessary. During 1962, for example,
a total of 144 children arrived at the farm school under
the Family Scheme but ninety-three had left by the end of
the year to be with their parents.[36]

For the next two years the number of children coming
out to Australia under the Family Scheme was maintained, but the children tended to be older and stayed for
a shorter period of time. The number of children at the
farm school continued to rapidly fall. By the middle of the
1960s the situation had become critical and the director
of the London Fairbridge Society, General Hawthorn,
travelled to Sydney to tell the local Fairbridge Council
that the last party of children would be arriving from
Britain early in 1966.

To help shore up numbers the Sydney Fairbridge
Council began taking Australian children. In the late
1960s Fairbridge placed ads in newspapers promoting the
Molong farm school as a good boarding school: children
could attend one of the local schools while paying to
board in the Fairbridge village. By 1970, almost all the
British children had reached seventeen years of age and

left Fairbridge, and there were only sixty-seven children still there, including thirty-five paid boarders.

Ian Dean was one of only a handful of British children when he left Fairbridge at the end of 1967.

> You could see the decline going on around you. It was falling to pieces. There were only half a dozen original British children still there. Most of the children at Fairbridge at that time were the Australian kids. There were only about four children's cottages still open. The rest were closed. There were no village musters, little cottage gardening and hardly any sport. No one seemed to be in control. It was very different from the feeling at the place when it was full of people.
>
> The rot set in after Woods left. Indeed the rot seemed to set in before he left. After his wife died. He didn't seem to have the same sense of purpose after that.

Toward the end Fairbridge supplemented its numbers by accepting children who had been 'committed to care' by the children's courts.[37] The offences committed by the children sent to Fairbridge included stealing, break and enter and 'uncontrollability'. The farm school had, in effect, become a children's prison.

Even in the early 1970s the authorities were still trying to persuade Fairbridge to make the cottages more 'comfortable and homelike'. In 1971 the New South Wales Director of Child Welfare, Bill Langshore, called on Fairbridge to have the 'cheerless' cottage dining rooms (which he called 'common rooms') furnished with some comfortable chairs, bright curtains and floor coverings, and for each child to be given a bedside locker in which to keep personal effects. He also wanted bedside floor rugs in all the cottages, plastic shower curtains in the girls' bathrooms to give them some privacy, and for the laundries and bathrooms to be separated by partitions. He called for smaller tables to 'improve the atmosphere of the dining room'.

In 1972, Langshore's appeals produced results. Fairbridge announced that partitions had been erected in the big cottage dormitories, shower curtains had been installed to give a little privacy, lino tiles had been laid on the cement floors of the kitchens, and the long dining-room tables had been cut down into smaller tables that each accommodated six children. The school had managed to successfully resist all of the attempts to make it reform until now – two years before it closed.

Fairbridge made its last, desperate – and ultimately unsuccessful – attempt to save Molong as a farm school by trying to arrange a financial bail-out from the Isolated Children's Parents Association.[38] In 1973, all efforts to financially salvage the farm having failed, Fairbridge threw in the towel and announced it was going to sell the farm school. Its annual report said:

> This decision had been made after the most exhaustive investigation by Council and with extreme regret because of the support received over the years particularly from local services. However, the increasing rate of erosion of capital accompanying operations at Molong forced the decision and the sale of the property was negotiated in November 1973 to T.A. Barrett Pty Ltd.[39]

The last British child at Fairbridge was Vivian Bingham, who had arrived as a four-year-old in 1959. She remembers being sad as the other children gradually left the farm and she became the last British child migrant there.

> I felt terrible . . . I felt like, everyone's leaving me . . .
> as they started to go . . . it was like part of my family
> was disappearing. I felt very lonely and sad and scared
> because I was on my own again.

She finally left the farm in March 1973.

Fairbridge closed in 1974 and became a chicken farm. Some of the cottages were sold and moved from the village to become country homes around the west of New South Wales. The remainder of the village fell in to disrepair. In 1988 the property changed hands and continued to be used for a variety of farm activities. A number of the children's cottages that remained at Fairbridge were rented out to locals; the rest of the village increasingly resembled a ghost town. The Fairbridge Council became the Fairbridge Foundation and invested the money it earned from the sale of the property. It distributes the dividends and profits from these investments to other children's charities.

13

LEGACY

Every childhood lasts a lifetime. For many who spent their childhood at Fairbridge the experience has had an enduring impact throughout their adult lives. But despite the difficulties they have faced there are a number of inspiring stories of former Fairbridge children who have turned their lives around.

Typical Fairbridge children had no one. They arrived in Australia alone, and later left to go out into the world still completely on their own. When these kids left the farm school at around seventeen they were likely to be poorly educated, socially and emotionally incomplete, lost, alienated, poor. Some went on to suffer mental illness, spend time in prison or commit suicide.

When I embarked on compiling the histories of former Fairbridge children, I had no idea of the extent to which so many of them had suffered from the experience, and how they have carried the pain and the memories all their lives. Even though I had been at Fairbridge at the same time as many of the people I interviewed, I had little comprehension of what they were going through. I was a boy at the time, and I had a far more fortunate experience than most of the other Fairbridge children. I was older when I arrived and came with a twin and an older brother, and we did not suffer the abuse that many of the other younger children did. My brothers and I spent less than three years there, whereas the majority spent their entire childhood at Fairbridge. Most importantly, we belonged to a family who had temporarily been split up in the process of migration and would get back together later. We had a mum. Consequently my story is in no way comparable with the awful childhoods experienced by typical Fairbridge children.

I asked one of the former Fairbridge girls why it had taken more than forty years for her to be prepared to tell her story; why she hadn't spoken out about the awful things she experienced as a child. 'To who?' she replied angrily. 'I never had anyone to speak to about this.'

I went on to ask her if she had talked it over with her family. She said that while she'd wanted to, it had always proved to be too difficult, which means that her husband, children and grandchildren will first learn of her story from reading this book. She found it easier to talk to me – and through me the whole world – rather than tell those closest to her about her experiences at the school.

I hope those who have found the courage to tell their stories will find strength in the stories of others. Many of the former Fairbridge children thought their horrible experiences were unique. A number expressed surprise that others had also been sexually abused. Many didn't know that other Fairbridge kids have struggled through life with unresolved issues similar to their own.

Gwen Miller, who arrived at Fairbridge as a ten-year-old in 1952, feels that Fairbridge robbed her and her sister and brothers of their childhood, and that the experience has affected her throughout adult life.

My children missed out on the most important thing in a child's life. I didn't know how to show them that

I loved them, apart from when they were babies. I didn't kiss them and cuddle them enough as they were growing up. I didn't show any real emotion . . . I don't think they ever saw me cry.

I wish I had been able to tell them that they were the most important people in my life. I don't know, maybe it was that I don't trust or get too close because it makes one vulnerable, then you might get hurt.

[At Fairbridge] no one ever put their arm around you or touched your arm or your hand. The word 'love' was never mentioned. Fairbridge taught us to work hard from the time the six a.m. bell went until after tea. You don't show any emotion and you never let anyone know you were upset about anything.

The worst thing is there was sort of no love or attention and I don't think anybody would ever have put their arm around a child out there; even my little brother probably never had anyone's arm around him. I don't recall hearing anyone ever say to a child 'You did very well. That was very good what you did.'

Janet Ellis arrived at Fairbridge as a seven-year-old in 1954 with her ten-year-old brother, Mickey, and her eight-year-old brother, Paul, and spent ten years at the farm school. Janet also feels her childhood at Fairbridge has affected her all her life.

I can't shake it. I don't think I'll ever get over it; I know I won't.

I had a pretty unhappy childhood there. There wasn't anyone to pick you up and give you a cuddle and say it was all right. They called me scum; they said I was dirty. They said I was the lowest form of life. I don't remember anyone ever saying to me 'You did a good job, Jan. Well done.' I remember a lot of people hitting me around the head and belting me with whatever they could lay their hands on.

While at Fairbridge she was given no help with growing up.

I didn't know anything. Absolutely nothing. I remember the first time I got my periods and I thought, Oh God. I'm bleeding to death. And I went to bed. The cottage mother came in and I said, 'I can't get out of bed, I'm bleeding to death.' And then one day the cottage mother threw this huge old lady's bra at me. I didn't know what it was. It was as big as a tent and I was told I had to wear it.

Janet is one of a number of former Fairbridge girls who say they were sexually abused by Jack Newberry.

I was eleven or twelve. I still find it hard to talk about. He used to grab you and run his hands all over you. It was disgusting. He was a creep. He just thought he had a God-given right to do what he wanted. And what could you do? He used to say no one would believe you.

I was angry and then you tell your cottage mother and she accuses you of telling lies. The adults didn't want to believe you. So I went to Woods and he said the same as the cottage mother: 'You're telling lies.'

After leaving Fairbridge, Janet, like so many other girls, was sent to work as a domestic servant on a remote farm out in the west of the state, where she was lonely and felt socially inept.

Every time a visitor came I used to run and hide somewhere. We had never socialised with anyone at Fairbridge. We were unimportant. My biggest fear was fear. There was nobody. You were alone and lonely. I got married. I think it was just escape, actually. I think it was the worst thing I ever did. So violent it was unbelievable. I ended up escaping through the bathroom window. He used to flog the hell out of me.

I spent so much time in counselling and I tried to commit suicide and I've also lost babies. I suddenly wake up after so many years and think, 'If you commit suicide you're giving in to these bastards.' And it's not my fault. It's not my fault.

Life began to turn around for her when she married a second time and, in her thirties, gave birth to her daughter, Kim. But she still has trouble talking about her childhood experiences, even to her family.

It's not a thing I talked about. I don't even tell my family. You can't let people get too close to you. I still can't, to a certain degree. You just don't want to continue to be hurt for the rest of your life.

Robert Stephens went to Fairbridge as an eight-year-old and spent his entire childhood there. He believes that lack of affection when they were young is a big issue for Fairbridge children in adult life.

A huge factor. Particularly later in life. I mean, in my case . . . I never had it as a child, affection of a parent, having been in an orphanage from day one . . . I never knew how to cuddle; I never knew how to love someone, or things like that.

Now, that had huge implications further down the track . . . There was an incredible lack of affection . . . There was just a theme right through the place: you were a sook if emotions came into it.

Vivian Bingham is pleased that Fairbridge children are now speaking out, even though it is painful:

> I just kept it to myself . . . now it's all coming out . . . like, the floodgates are opening. The can of worms is just opening and . . . you know you've bottled it up so long and it's started to come out . . . And when you start to relive it, the pain . . . comes back. It's the best thing that could happen . . . to get it out . . . It really wrecked a lot of people's lives, that place.

Billy King, who sailed to Australia on the same ship as me, never experienced any family life as a child and grew up unable to express love and affection.

> Well, I had lots of problems with my kids. It's only now the kids have grown up I give them a cuddle when they come over. But it took me a lot of years to be able to do it. When the kids were growing up I couldn't do any of that . . . [As a child] I missed having a family. At Fairbridge, if you had a problem there was nobody you could sit with – all the years I was at Fairbridge . . . there was no one to turn to [who would] put their arms around me and give me a bloody cuddle and say, 'It will be right, Billy. It will be right.' There was no one there you could sort of talk to. There was no love in the place at all. It was just absolutely stone cold.
>
> I had a lot of trouble when I left Fairbridge, like, as a matter of fact, I was under a psychiatrist for quite a while, and I remember him saying to me: 'Look Bill, the problem is, if you've never been shown love, how the hell could you give it? These things have to be taught.' I remember him saying that.

Billy still holds the social worker who arranged for him to be sent to Fairbridge partly responsible for what he went through:

> She's dead now, and you shouldn't speak ill of the dead, but . . . with what she has done to my life, if she was still alive, I just would have loved to have fronted up to her and said, 'Well, look, here's me. This is what I've gone through. This is what you've done.'

A number of those who have unpleasant recollections of Fairbridge nevertheless managed to salvage something of value from the experience. John Wolvey has many awful memories, but says Fairbridge had some benefit: 'It prepared me for the hard times I had later.' Derek Moriarty is bitter about being sent out to Fairbridge – recalling stories of brutality, sexual abuse and running away and being pursued by police – but says he still has positive feelings about the place.

David Wilson was five when he arrived at Fairbridge and lived there for ten years. David was a wild young fellow and ran away from Fairbridge on a number of occasions, eventually ending up in a boys' prison.

> Honestly, I can't really put Fairbridge down. Because we got three feeds a day; we always had a bed to sleep in; and now, when I think about it, you know like, when I was in England, it would have been a lot worse.

Very few speak with unqualified support of the place. John Harris is unusual not only for his strong support of Fairbridge but also for his belief that all children should be forced to spend two years in an institution like Fairbridge when they reach ten years of age.

I would like to see every kid go through an institutional experience like that – not in Sydney but a place like Molong, or Orange or Pinjarra or somewhere. It would equip them better for life . . .

But John admits Fairbridge has left him emotionally insular and short on personal and social skills.

Quoting others, including my wife, Fairbridge, in her opinion, has made me too self-sufficient. I rely on no one – if I can't do it myself, it doesn't get done or I'll call someone in [and pay them] to do it. I will not ask anyone for help.

Fairbridge didn't allow us to go to Molong to mix with the kids other than [at] school time . . . [If they had] I'd say we'd be better for it in terms of our skills in dealing with people outside an institution. Coming from such a disciplined background – and remember, I'd been in institutions from the age of about six – I didn't know much else.

Those who are more generous about Fairbridge were mostly older when they arrived at the farm school, so spent less time there. Laurie Field arrived as a fourteen-year-old in 1952 and stayed barely two years. He thought the Fairbridge scheme to be a 'good idea', but would not like to see his children go through the same experience.

Most of Fairbridge children have overwhelmingly negative memories of the farm school. As Lennie Magee says:

So, if somebody tries to tell me what a wonderful experience Fairbridge was, I say, well that's good for you. I'm not going to knock your good memories but don't tell me that I'm exaggerating the situation when I tell you I had a dreadful time there.

Many years after all the child-migrant centres had closed the parliaments of Britain and Australia conducted inquiries that condemned the child migrant schemes for what they did to children.

In Britain, the House of Commons Select Committee for Health conducted an inquiry into the welfare of former British child migrants and its report was published in 1998.[1] It concluded that:

> Child migration was a bad and, in human terms, costly mistake . . . In many cases child migrants suffered emotional and physical hardship and abuse, of a kind which has had damaging consequences for their health and well-being for the remainder of their lives.

The committee also concluded that the former child-migrant organisations had responsibility for addressing the damage they caused to children.

> Blame must be distributed amongst all the governments and agencies who involved themselves with child migration. This imposes on them a responsibility to offer help to the surviving human casualties of the child migration schemes.

Two organisations that had been involved with child migration agreed with the House of Commons inquiry and accepted some responsibility for the damage it caused to children. The Children's Society ran a child-migrant scheme principally to Canada and later to Australia from the late nineteenth century till the 1950s. Its social work director, David Lovell, told the House of Commons inquiry that the organisation accepted responsibility for what happened to the children and had established an after-care service for former child migrants. 'We accept the responsibility for the past in the organisation and the responsibility to look at what we are doing to try to do our best to heal that'. When giving oral evidence, Roger Singleton CBE, chief executive of Barnardo's, which also ran child-migrant schemes to Canada and Australia, told the inquiry: 'It was barbaric; it was dreadful. We look back on it in our organisation with shock and horror.'[2]

In contrast, the London Fairbridge Society told the inquiry that it was now a different organisation, no longer concerned itself with the problems of former Fairbridge child migrants, and did not have the resources to care for them. Its director, Nigel Haynes, said Fairbridge was now 'a national charity which offers long-term personal development to young people aged 14 to 25 in inner cities' and that the organisation wanted to look to the future and not the past.

> Our current expenditure budget is £4.3 million a year. Previously, the Fairbridge Society, which ceased in 1982 and is now under a constitution and re-shifting of goals approved by the Charity Commissioners, operated child emigration to farm schools . . .

In its submission to the Commons Fairbridge said it could not 'provide the aftercare and counselling required' and that it was not 'economically viable' to employ a counsellor to help former Fairbridge children.[3]

During the course of giving oral evidence to the inquiry Haynes said there was no record of physical or sexual abuse occurring at Fairbridge after 1938. In his oral evidence to the inquiry on 11 June 1998, he said:

> Turning to sexual and physical abuse, we have got cases in the records of a case of neglect, it was called, and physical abuse in 1938 in a farm school called

Molong. These complaints were received in London, investigated and the staff were dismissed immediately. Molong then became semi-autonomous from 1948 although accepted funds from London. Apart from that, we have no cases of complaint or abuse on record as far as Fairbridge is concerned, other than – and I hate to go back to it – the context of disciplines relevant at that time against what was happening in this country as well.[4]

However, the London Fairbridge Society records show that in 1964 the society was advised of the child-welfare investigation that had confirmed abuse by Kathleen Johnstone, the cottage mother who regularly whipped the children with a riding crop and forced the head of a six-year-old girl down the toilet as punishment for bedwetting. A copy of the report is contained in the minutes of a meeting of the London Fairbridge Society held on 2 July 1965, which are currently stored in the Liverpool University archives.[5]

In Australia, an inquiry was conducted by the Senate Community Affairs Reference Committee, which reported in 2001. The report was titled 'Lost Innocents: Righting the Record – report on Child Migration'.[6] The Senate committee was as critical of child migration as the House of Commons's committee had been.

The child migration scheme is now universally recognised as having been fundamentally flawed with tragic consequences.

The evidence received by the Committee overwhelmingly emphasised the dark, negative side of child migration – the brutality of life in some institutions where abuse and assault, both physical and sexual, was a daily occurrence and where hardship, hard work and indifferent care was the norm. Living such negative experiences led some child migrants into a life of family and relationship breakdown and domestic violence, of crime and violence, and of substance abuse.

Loss of identity, a sense of belonging and the loneliness of being far from home affected all child migrants.

Barnardo's Australia, which is independent of Barnardo's in the UK, had similar views to its sister organisation about the failings of the child-migrant schemes. In evidence to the Australian Senate committee, Mr William Hoyles, Barnardo's youth services and after care officer, said:

> We have no hesitation in saying it was a shameful practice, that it was barbaric and it was completely against any practice that we currently uphold . . .
>
> We are able to offer an after care service, and we are doing so since the days of the first child migration to Australia . . .
>
> Our policy is not to just turn them away.

When giving evidence during the Senate hearings, the chairman of the Fairbridge Foundation, John Kennedy, was asked if he agreed with Barnardo's. He replied: 'I believe our view would not agree with Barnardo's.'[7]

In its written submission to the inquiry, the Fairbridge Foundation maintained that nothing seriously wrong happened at the farm school at Molong.

> The Fairbridge Foundation is unaware of any unsafe, improper or unlawful treatment occurring at the Fairbridge Farm School at Molong. It is also unaware of any serious breach of any relevant statutory obligations occurring there.[8]

Yet Fairbridge's own files reveal they were aware of a number of cases of unsafe, improper or unlawful treatment at Fairbridge over the years. For example, the Fairbridge council minutes record instructions to Woods in 1948 to desist from hitting the children with a hockey stick and to stop public thrashings, practices that were in breach of the Child Welfare Act.[9] And correspondence from 1957 reveals that its chairman at the time refused an investigation into child abuse sought by the Department of Child Welfare.[10]

The Senate recommended:

> That the Commonwealth Government issue a formal statement acknowledging that its predecessors' promotion of the Child Migration schemes, that resulted in the removal of so many British and Maltese children to Australia, was wrong; and that the statement express deep sorrow and regret for the psychological, social and economic harm caused to the children, and the hurt and distress suffered by the children, at the hands of those who were in charge of them, particularly the children who were victims of abuse and assault.

Fairbridge didn't agree. In its written submission to the inquiry it said:

> The Fairbridge Foundation cannot find any reason why the present Australian Government should apologise on its own behalf or on behalf of the previous Australian Governments for anything which they have done in regard to the Fairbridge Farm School at Molong.
>
> It thinks that an apology would be both unnecessary and inappropriate.

The Fairbridge Foundation also rejected the suggestion that it has any responsibility for the welfare of former child migrants and expressed its opposition to providing material support for former Fairbridge children in need: 'The Fairbridge Foundation does not believe that any reparation or monetary compensation in any form should be paid to former child migrants.'[11]

The Fairbridge Foundation has assets of several million dollars. Each year the foundation pays out hundreds of thousands of dollars to other children's charities, but continues to be opposed to spending any of the money on assisting former Fairbridge children who may need help. John Kennedy, who is the chairman of the foundation and was a member of the Fairbridge Farm School Council when the farm school was still operating, says the constitution of the Fairbridge Foundation does not allow it to help individuals.

Amendment of the constitution is unlikely because the foundation's membership is restricted to the ten men on its board. The only time a new member is invited to join the foundation is when a sitting board member retires or dies. As the foundation stated in its submission to the Senate: 'The Foundation, though open to Membership from all quarters, is in practical terms, a Council of 10 persons.'

While many former Fairbridge children have struggled through life, a number have, against the odds, overcome disadvantage and managed to turn their lives around. In many cases the turnaround came with the support of a loving partner.

Linda Gidman remembers leaving Fairbridge not knowing how to express love or affection.

> There was no nurturing . . . The cottage mother. . .
> didn't know how to come along and comfort a child

in need . . . The problem with a lot of us, especially with the Fairbridge girls, is you can't put your arms around each other, even now: 'Don't get too close because I'm not used to that sort of thing.'

I found it very traumatic. I had to basically go under psychotherapy in my twenties when I had a breakdown, two breakdowns. I just couldn't get it out of my system. I think my saving grace has been, in the last eighteen years, meeting my partner. Because my partner has taught me over these years, you know, like, family values. He's got a very close-knit family and it took me a long time to adjust to that sort of situation. And I think family values were taken away from us there. It was tough. I wouldn't wish it on anybody.

Christina Murray, whose diabetes and brain tumour went unrecognised at the farm school, says her life turned around when she received proper treatment and married in her twenties.

The turning point for me was when I was properly diagnosed and when I met my husband; when I got married and I had someone to love. Somebody that had put their arm around you . . . thinking, 'She's not a bad old stick.' That hadn't happened before. And just for him to be there, having breakfast and going out together. It was just brilliant.

Smiley Bayliff is also grateful for being able to find comfort in a loving family.

I can't complain about my life in all honesty. There's parts of everyone's life you say you wished didn't happen, but it happened, but you just move on – but

I can't turn round and say I'd change things that much. All right, it would have been lovely to have had my parents there. It would have been lovely if my parents had the money to be able to bring us up as a family unit, you know, that's fine; but I've done pretty well with my wife and kids and things like that, you know. I've got a good wife . . . I've got good kids and, you know, the oldest one, she's doing law now and the other one, she's a hairdresser by trade but she's gone back to TAFE and she's been accepted for uni next year to do psychology, actually.

Smiley's brother Syd also feels he got out of Fairbridge moderately unscathed, mainly because of a loving and understanding partner, even though their relationship got off to a rocky start after he left the farm school. 'When we first got married, we nearly got divorced in the first six months,' he says. The couple lived in a two-room flat in Marrickville in Sydney and Syd would often have about six former Fairbridge kids around. His wife did all the washing up and cooking, without help or appreciation from any of them. 'She threw them all out one night. She did her nana one night and it was nearly the end of my marriage but we've been together forty years next year.'

Barney Piercy, who spent nearly twelve years at Fairbridge, has bitter memories of the experience but feels lucky that he found great strength and support in his partner.

[It] was like getting out of gaol for something you didn't commit. I didn't steal a loaf of bread or anything. I just happened to be born. I didn't ask to be born, did I? Looking back? A feeling of loss, a feeling of anger. A feeling of all those wasted years. It's the things I can't get back – my childhood, teenage years

– and [the chance to be] a better man. I had no one to
guide me, no one to relate to, no one to love me, no
one to tell me I was a good person.

And then when I was twenty-one I came to Sydney
and that's where I met Maggie. That was my break-
through, for sure. She was my friend; she was my
lover, my wife.

Many former Fairbridge children have found comfort and
strength in their bonds with other former Fairbridge children. The Old Fairbridgians' Association was formed in
the late 1930s and helps former Fairbridge children keep
in touch with each other. It publishes a newsletter a couple
of times a year and organises a reunion at Molong every
two years. As Daphne Brown who came out to Fairbridge
as a seven-year-old, points out, other Fairbridge kids are
the only 'family' that many of them have ever known:

> The Fairbridge kids . . . have stuck together . . . We
> seem to have more of a bond . . . Most of my good
> friends are from Fairbridge and I'm on the executive
> committee of the Old Fairbridgians' Association . . .
> I feel the boys are my brothers and the girls are my
> sisters.

David Eva, who was at Fairbridge some years after
Daphne Brown, feels the same way.

> There are a lot of people . . . from Fairbridge – we see
> them and they ring us and that sort of thing. We
> see each other . . . we have barbecues and birthdays,
> so the comradeship's still there.

Religious faith has been critical in the adult lives of a
number of former Fairbridge children. What turned

things around for Lennie Magee was the discovery of Jesus many years after he left Fairbridge when his life had plunged into drugs and confusion. When Lennie left Fairbridge as a seventeen-year-old he worked on the railways in the west of the state and got involved in the rock 'n' roll – and drug – scene, becoming lead singer in a number of bands around bush towns. Ambitious to do better, he headed for Sydney. Living in Kings Cross, he joined The Cavemen and slid further into the drug scene. Of that period he says, 'I was gradually wrecking my life and I still felt incomplete. I felt that if I could find my mother I would be whole.'

To earn some quick money Lennie headed for the Northern Territory and worked on road-building gangs near Tennant Creek in Central Australia. Then he headed back to England, along the hippie trail, in the late 1960s. He recounts: 'I went from Singapore to Calcutta to Kathmandu with nothing more than a dilly bag and a flute that I couldn't play and was heavily into speed and hashish.'

Finally, after fourteen years away, he was back in London. He met up with his mother but he says the reunion was a disaster: 'I was stoned. To her I was like a ghost come back from the dead. It didn't work.'

Lennie recalls reaching rock bottom one night in Soho when he was so drunk and stoned that he collapsed in the garbage out the back of a club.

> Then there was an amazing moment. At my mum's council house I found an old black Bible in the cupboard and I started reading it. Genesis, the beginning, and I came under the conviction of sin. I knew I was a sinner, yet I knew there was a God.
>
> I slid off the bed and began to cry. You know Fairbridge kids don't cry. I cried out to God to save me. I wasn't conscious at first that it was Jesus. I was filled

with an indescribable peace, better than any drug I'd known, and I felt a sense of forgiveness. I was crying with joy because at last I had in God a father for the first time. I spent three months crying out all the bitterness.

Shortly after his epiphany he felt God calling him into the ministry. He studied for the next five years to become a full-time pastor and evangelist. Lennie started singing again and became Britain's most popular gospel singer-songwriter. He sold 150,000 albums and was in high demand, travelling around the country to preach and sing at evangelical churches.

In 1979 he was invited to visit a group of evangelical churches in Australia. He felt 'God calling me back to Australia' so he returned with his wife, Heather, and became a highly successful preacher. Lennie is at pains to say that his success is not something he achieved.

It was not of my doing. It was something that happened to me. It was a miracle.

One of the Fairbridge boys said to me recently, 'Let me ask you a question: you're a minister; do you ever feel you don't belong anywhere? That you don't fit in, that you can't settle anywhere?' I have different reasons, more Christian reasons, for none of those things fazing me today, because I had an amazing deliverance from that, a healing from that. But I look at these other dear guys today who don't know who they are and don't know where they've come from. And a lot of these guys still feel lost.

Malcolm 'Flossy' Field says that God has been his 'strength and refuge' since leaving Fairbridge. Flossy was one of only a few Fairbridge children to matriculate from

Orange High School. He then won a scholarship to train as a primary-school teacher at Bathurst Teachers College. After training, he was appointed as the sole teacher in a tiny school at Tenandra in the Warrumbungle Mountains in the remote north-west of the state. He taught for ten years then headed off to England.

In the UK he managed to track down his father's brother and became close friends with his family for the next twenty-nine years. In 1995 he returned to live in Australia and visited his mother, who had moved to New Zealand. 'Sadly, she had little involvement in my life after I went to Fairbridge,' he says. Malcolm has never married and has remained active in his local church and Bible study fellowship.

Mary O'Brien's life turned around when she was in her thirties. She has no fond memories of Fairbridge and recalls being regularly sexually abused there by the after care officer.

> My spirit was crushed, and Fairbridge did that more than anything else . . . Had somebody patted me on the back, or put their arms around me, as I was growing up and [said] 'You can do it,' I probably would have done a lot better. I lost twenty years of my life as a consequence.
>
> I was still very, very embarrassed about where I had come from and what I had been doing and I hated anyone asking me where I was from . . . It took me a long time to turn my life around.
>
> Do you want to know the experience that changed my life? Okay. I was about thirty, in my early thirties, and I was reading a *Reader's Digest* magazine and it . . . was a MENSA article. I completed this test and sent it away because it was the sort of thing that I did enjoy doing . . . even though I felt inadequate in so

many ways ... Then I sent away to them to ask if I could sit for one of their tests and they said, 'Come on in.' I went in and sat their test and it took hours; it was quite in-depth. But I did it and when I got the results a few weeks later and they told me that I had an IQ in the 99th percentile I was just dumbfounded. I sat and cried and I thought, This is ludicrous. Why have I not accomplished anything with my life? And I sat down and thought about my life and where I'd been and what happened and I thought, Well, I just never had the opportunities, and I've never had the guidance; I've never had the direction ... Nobody had ever taught me that I was worthwhile and that I could accomplish anything.

Since then, I've gone on, I got a degree in nursing and then a Masters degree in health administration and, considering the circumstances, I'm very happy with the way my life had turned around and my accomplishments. I know I should have done better had I had a better start early in my life, but I've got great kids and I'm really quite comfortable with my life and where I'm at.

I was one of the lucky few who managed to get a decent education ... after I left Fairbridge. My school record was poor and at fifteen I left Molong Central School with an unimpressive Intermediate Certificate. After my first job in the hardware store I drifted from job to job over the next few years, working as a messenger boy, mail order clerk, builder's labourer, printer's assistant, waiter, barman, pub bouncer, garbage collector, sandwich maker and driver of a dry-cleaning van. In the year after I left Fairbridge I applied to become a police cadet but failed the fairly simple spelling and arithmetic test when I sat for the entrance exam at Sydney's Bourke Street Police Centre.

After a few years of drifting from job to job, living in a rented flat with my mum and two brothers, I was driven – largely by boredom – to do something else. I enrolled in a one year, full-time 'crash' matriculation course at East Sydney Technical College. I worked as a waiter in a pub at night and on weekends and skipped the odd day at college to work as a builder's labourer, because I still had to pay my board.

The course didn't get off to a great start. I was one of a handful of students out of 120 who failed the arithmetic and spelling test at enrolment. I am still bitter about being pulled out of class in the first week by a career advisor who tried to persuade me to cancel my enrolment and take up panel beating or spray painting. I persisted and thoroughly enjoyed the year, though I had to struggle and juggle study and work. At the end I was surprised to matriculate with my first-ever strong results and a scholarship to Sydney University. After completing an economics degree, I was offered a job on the academic staff as a tutor, and completed a Masters of Economics degree two years later.

I was one of only a few Fairbridge children ever to reach university but I reject the suggestion that I am a good example of what Fairbridge kids have been able to achieve. My experience is in spite of Fairbridge, and not at all typical or representative of the far less fortunate experiences of most of the children who went there.

The best thing that can be said about Fairbridge is that it was well-intentioned. It had widespread support and was highly regarded for 'rescuing' destitute children and providing them with a 'fresh start' they would not have received had they stayed in Britain. However, no concerted effort was made to address the problems that beset the scheme from its inception and the files of the Fairbridge Society in the UK and the New South Wales Fairbridge Council corroborate almost all the disturbing episodes recalled by the former Fairbridge children who recounted their histories to me.

The Fairbridge scheme was a product of the upper classes of Imperial Britain, who saw great virtue in putting the 'orphan and waif class' to work in order that they became good and useful citizens of the Empire. Fairbridge never pretended that the children it rescued from the destitution of the lower classes would climb the social ladder, and the Fairbridge scheme only reinforced in Australia the appalling inequality of the British class system.

Many former Fairbridge children feel they were betrayed. Some feel they were betrayed by their parents – for abandoning them to Fairbridge and denying them a childhood in a loving home.

Gwen Miller had an extensive network of family in England and feels it wasn't necessary for her father to send the children out to Fairbridge when her mother died.

> After my mother died I remember a great aunt [who was a nun] telling me my mother was in heaven watching. I used to talk to her at night. I was happy about that, but when my father gave us away I didn't want there to be a heaven because if there was, my mother would look down on us and cry every day because the man she trusted gave away her babies.

Fairbridgians feel betrayed by the child welfare and education departments – for failing to ensure that Fairbridge provided for their welfare and education. They feel betrayed by the British and Australian governments, which had ultimate responsibility for ensuring the protection of the children and did not intervene even when they knew Fairbridge was failing them.

But most of all they feel betrayed by the farm school – for depriving them of a peaceful and happy childhood; for, in many cases, seriously abusing them; and for failing to deliver on the promise of a better future.

Christina Murray perhaps sums it up best:

> When I look back at Fairbridge I think, Did it happen? Did it happen? Then you think, Well, yes it did. And you think of what you've got now and you ask, Why did they do it? Why? They were there to look after children, and they didn't.

NOTES

1. Journey Out

1. By 1960 there were Fairbridge honorary secretaries in Aldershot, Alresford, Arundel, Ashvale, Barnham, Bath, Bedford, Berkhamsted, Bicester, Bolton, Boston Spa, Bramley, Bristol, Bury, Canterbury, Carlisle, Clockham Mill, Cornwall, Darlington, Eastbourne, Eton and Windsor, East Grinstead, Forest Row, Hailsham, Hampstead, Haslemere, Hawkhurst, Heathfield, Hemel Hempstead, Henfield, Hornchurch and Upminster, Hove, Kendal, Kings Lynn, Lewes, Lytham St Annes, Sturminster, Malton-Driffield, Middlehurst, Minehead, Newcastle, Newton, Oxford, Penrith, Petersfield, Preston, Sheringham, Salisbury, Seaford, Shrewsbury, Southampton and York

2. 'The Fairbridge Society: Founded 1909 to Provide a New Life for Children in the Commonwealth', *c.* 1958, Fairbridge Farm School NSW files, Fairbridge Foundation, Sydney

3. Sherington papers, box 4, ML 1781/79, State Library of New South Wales

4. Ibid.

5. *Strathaird* breakfast menu,
http://ozhoo.net.au/~strathsisters/strathaird/

6. *Strathaird* luncheon menu,
   http://ozhoo.net.au/~strathsisters/strathaird/
7. *Strathaird* dinner menu,
   http://ozhoo.net.au/~strathsisters/strathaird/

2. Origins

1. Fairbridge, Kingsley, *The Autobiography of Kingsley Fairbridge*, Oxford University Press, London, 1927, chapter 1
2. Fairbridge, Ruby, *Pinjarra: The Building of a Farm School*, Oxford University Press, London, 1937, p. 12
3. Fairbridge, *Autobiography*, p. 171
4. Sherington, Geoffrey and Jeffery, Chris, *Fairbridge, Empire and Child Migration*, University of Western Australian Press, 1998, p. 25
5. Fairbridge, Kingsley, 'The Emigration of Poor Children to the Colonies', speech read before the Colonial Club at Oxford in 1909, reprinted by the Child Immigration Society, 1930, Fairbridge Society archives, D296 A2, University of Liverpool, UK
6. Fairbridge, *Autobiography*, p. 171
7. Ibid., p. 173
8. Fairbridge, Kingsley, 'The Emigration of Poor Children to the Colonies'
9. Ibid.
10. *The Times*, 24 May 1910
11. Fairbridge, Ruby, *Pinjarra*, p. 32
12. Fairbridge, Kingsley, 'The Emigration of Poor Children to the Colonies'
13. Fairbridge, Ruby, *Pinjarra*, p. 66
14. Ibid., p. 83
15. 352 1967/13, Public Record Office, Western Australia
16. Fairbridge, Ruby, *Pinjarra*, p. 109
17. Ibid., p. 168
18. Sherington and Jeffery, *Fairbridge, Empire and Child Migration*, p. 168

19. CO 721/12 ff 8:9, Public Record Office, London, UK

20. Sherington papers, ML 1781/79, State Library of New South Wales

21. Fairbridge Society NSW annual report, 1935, University of Liverpool, UK

22. Report to the Secretary of State for Dominion Affairs and Interdepartmental Committee on Migration Policy, British Parliamentary Papers, cmd 4689, p. 48

23. Fairbridge Society NSW annual report, University of Liverpool, UK

24. *The Times*, 21 June 1934

25. Sherington and Jeffery, *Fairbridge, Empire and Child Migration*, p. 160

26. Ibid., p. 164

27. Ibid., p. 182

28. Fairbridge Farm School NSW annual report, 1938 and 1939, Fairbridge Foundation, Sydney

29. Minutes of meeting, 30 July 1936, Fairbridge Foundation, Sydney

30. DO 57/188 15330/1, Public Record Office, London, UK

31. Fairbridge Society archives, D296 J3/1, University of Liverpool, UK

32. Fairbridge Farm School NSW annual report, 1937, Fairbridge Foundation, Sydney

33. *Sydney Morning Herald*, 24 February 1937

34. Fairbridge Farm School NSW annual report, 1939, Fairbridge Foundation, Sydney

35. Tuder, Len, *A Pommie Kid*, 2003, unpublished autobiography of Len Cowne

36. *Sydney Morning Herald*, 28 November 1938

37. Fairbridge Farm School NSW annual report, 1946; the Fairbridge Family Chronicle, 1946, Fairbridge Foundation, Sydney

38. Minutes of meeting, London Fairbridge Society, 14 December 1948, D296 B1/2/6, University of Liverpool, UK

39. Fairbridge Farm School NSW annual report, 1952, Fairbridge Foundation, Sydney

40. 'The Fairbridge Society', *c*. 1958, brochure, Fairbridge Farm School NSW files, Fairbridge Foundation, Sydney

41. Report of the Care of Children Committee, British Parliamentary Papers, cmd 6922 ,1946–7

3. A Day in the Life

1. Fairbridge weekend notice (undated), Fairbridge Foundation, Sydney

4. Settling in

1. Letter from Billy King to Dorothy Watkins, 23 June 1959, personal papers of Billy King

2. Interview with author, 8 August 2006

3. Letter from John Ponting to author, 20 May 2006

4. Magee, Lennie, unpublished autobiography, 2001, chapter 13

5. Families

1. 'Child Migration to Australia', report for the British Home Office by John Moss, 1953, para 15

2. Letter from W. B. Vaughan to E. H. Johnson, 10 September 1956, DO 35 6383, Public Record Office, London, UK

3. Letter from Dora Lee to London Fairbridge Society, 5 September 1954, personal papers of Ian Bayliff

4. Ibid., 8 September 1954

5. Ibid., 15 September 1954

6. Extract from a letter from Dora Lee contained in a letter from F. K. S. Woods to W. R. Vaughan, 7 November 1955, personal papers of Ian Bayliff

7. Letter from F. K. S. Woods to W. B. Vaughan, 7 November 1955, personal papers of Ian Bayliff

8. Letter from W. R. Vaughan to E. M. Knight, 15 November 1955, personal papers of Ian Bayliff

9. Letter from E. M. Knight to W. B. Vaughan, 29 November 1955, personal papers of Ian Bayliff

10. Letter from F. K. S. Woods to W. B. Vaughan, 7 November 1955, personal papers of Ian Bayliff

11. Letter from Dora Lee to E. M. Knight, November 1955, personal papers of Ian Bayliff

12. W. B. Vaughan, file note, 6 February 1957, personal papers of Ian Bayliff

13. Letter from Dora Lee to Australian Immigration Office, Australia House, London, 28 March 1958, personal papers of Ian Bayliff

14. Letter from W. R. Vaughan to E. M. Knight, 19 November 1954, personal papers of Ian Bayliff

15. Letter from G. C. Watson to W. B. Vaughan, 28 August 1958, personal papers of Ian Bayliff

16. Ibid., 22 January 1959

17. Magee, unpublished autobiography, chapter 19

6. The Boss

1. Letter from W. D. Stewart to Sir Charles Hambro, 1 October 1940, Fairbridge Foundation, Sydney

2. Tuder, *A Pommie Kid*, chapter 3

3. Minutes of meeting, 23 October 1940, Fairbridge Society, Fairbridge Foundation, Sydney

4. Letter from Sir Charles Hambro to R. Beauchamp, 25 September 1940, D296/19/27, University of Liverpool, UK

5. Magee, unpublished autobiography, chapter 3

6. Ibid., chapter 20

7. Letter from Sir Charles Reading to Sir Charles Hambro, 5 February 1946, D296/19/25, University of Liverpool, UK

8. Letter from Ruth Woods to Miss Hart, December 1945, D296/19/25, University of Liverpool, UK

9. Ibid., 29 January 1945

10. Letter from W. B. Hudson to Sir Charles Hambro, 16 March 1948, D296/19/25, University of Liverpool, UK

11. 'Investigation at Fairbridge Farm School', report by V. A. Heffernan, 5 March 1948, D296/19/25, University of Liverpool, UK

12. An account of Ruth Wood's death and funeral are contained in a report by Jack Newberry, who at the time was the After-care Officer at Fairbridge, Fairbridge Foundation, Sydney

13. Letter from F. K. S. Woods to the secretary of the Fairbridge Council, 3 June 1966, Fairbridge Foundation, Sydney

14. Minutes of meeting of the London Fairbridge Society, 2 July 1965, D296 B3/1/1-2, University of Liverpool, UK

15. Letter from Dr Calov to Lord Slim, 22 July 1965, Fairbridge Foundation, Sydney

16. Letter from secretary of the Fairbridge Council to F. K. S. Woods, 22 September 1965, Fairbridge Foundation, Sydney

17. Minutes of meeting of the Fairbridge Council, 6 November 1965, Sherington papers, ML 1781/79, State Library of New South Wales

18. Fairbridge Farm Schools NSW annual report, 1966

19. Jack Newberry's job application, 14 August 1966, Fairbridge Foundation, Sydney

20. Fairbridge files, M1841-M1845, State Library of New South Wales

21. Letter from H. L. Kingsmill to J. Newberry, 6 April 1969, Fairbridge Foundation, Sydney

7. Child Labour

1. Tuder, *A Pommie Kid*, chapter 4

2. Fairbridge, 'The Emigration of Poor Children to the Colonies'

3. Minutes of meeting of the London Fairbridge Society, 12 July 1939, D 296 B1/2/3, University of Liverpool, UK

4. Ibid., 19 October 1948

5. Fairbridge Farm School NSW annual report, 1940, Fairbridge Foundation, Sydney

6. Ibid., 1949

7. Ibid., 1950, 1951, 1952, 1953

8. Ibid., 1940

9. Magee, unpublished autobiography, chapter 22

10. Report from F. K. S. Woods to the Secretary of Fairbridge Council, undated, Fairbridge Foundation, Sydney

11. Dr R. L. Raymond, notes on principal's report, 28 October 1962, Fairbridge Foundation, Sydney

8. Suffer the Little Children

1. Fairbridge Farm School NSW annual report, 1950, Fairbridge Foundation, Sydney

2. Vivian Bingham's reports, 16 October, 3 November and 6 November 1959, personal papers of Vivian Bingham

3. Letter from A. C. Thomas to secretary of Fairbridge Council, 17 January 1964, D296 B3/1/1-2, University of Liverpool, UK

4. Magee, unpublished autobiography, chapter 2

5. Ibid., chapter 20

6. Department of Child Welfare file note, 10/37271, State Records NSW

7. Letter from R. H. Hicks to W. B. Hudson, 30 December 1957, 10/37271, State Records NSW

8. Letter from W. B. Hudson to R. H. Hicks, 24 February 1958, 10/37271, State Records NSW

9. 'Report on the Food Service of the Fairbridge Farm School, Molong', M. Baker, 9 December 1953, Fairbridge Foundation, Sydney

10. 'Principal's Comments of Report by Dietitian', F. K. S. Woods (undated), Fairbridge Foundation, Sydney

11. Magee, unpublished autobiography, chapter 13

12. Minutes of meeting of Fairbridge Council, 25 February 1948, Sherington papers, ML 1781/79, State Library of New South Wales

9. Retards

1. Letter from Joshin Richards to the author, 5 February 2006
2. Letter from W. B. Hudson to F. K. S. Woods, February, 1953, D296 J3/2/10, University of Liverpool, UK
3. Fairbridge Farm School NSW annual report, 1959
4. Ibid., 1951
5. Letter from F. K. S. Woods to secretary of the Fairbridge Council, 11 January 1954, Fairbridge Foundation, Sydney
6. Ibid.
7. Note from W. B. Hudson to secretary of the Fairbridge Council, 18 January 1954, Fairbridge Foundation, Sydney
8. Letter from F. K. S. Woods to secretary of the Fairbridge Council, 15 February 1954, Fairbridge Foundation, Sydney
9. Report by Fairbridge Council members H. A. Henry and P. R. Le Couteur, 3 March 1954, Fairbridge Foundation, Sydney
10. Department of Education, 51/92/3158, State Records NSW
11. Department of Education, 14/7491, State Records NSW
12. Personal papers of Ian Bayliff
13. Sherington and Jeffery, *Fairbridge, Empire and Child Migration*, p. 236
14. 'Report on Farm Schools in Australia', W. J. Garnett, 6 October 1944, Fairbridge Foundation, Sydney
15. Letter from Sir Percival Halse Rogers to Sir Charles Hambro, 24 February 1944, Fairbridge Foundation, Sydney
16. Department of Education, 51/92/31578, State Records NSW
17. Ibid., 49/B73/13186
18. Letter from W. B. Hudson to C. Wyndham, 29 November 1954, Fairbridge Foundation, Sydney
19. 'Report of Sub-committee re Education and Training', undated, Fairbridge Foundation, Sydney
20. Education memorandum, Fairbridge Foundation, Sydney
21. Memorandum for Education and Training, G. S. Le Couteur,

15 September 1955, Fairbridge Foundation, Sydney

22. 'Comments on Memorandum re Education and Training', F. K. S. Woods, 20 November 1955, Fairbridge Foundation, Sydney

23. Letter from W. B. Hudson to C. M. Clayton, 1 July 1957, Fairbridge Foundation, Sydney

24. Letter from C. M. Clayton to W. B. Hudson, 3 July 1957, Fairbridge Foundation, Sydney

25. Letter from W. B. Hudson to C. M. Clayton, 9 July 1957, Fairbridge Foundation, Sydney

26. Minutes of meeting of the Fairbridge Council, 26 May 1956, Fairbridge Foundation, Sydney

27. Fairbridge Farm School NSW annual report, 1953

28. Ibid., 1959

10. The Children's World

1. Magee, unpublished autobiography, chapter 11

2. Ibid., chapter 16

11. Leaving Fairbridge

1. Minutes of meeting of London Fairbridge Society, 1 April 1954, D296 B1/2/8, University of Liverpool, UK

2. 'The Fairbridge Society: to Provide a New Life for Children in the Commonwealth', c. 1958, Fairbridge Foundation, Sydney

3. Fairbridge file, undated, Fairbridge Foundation, Sydney

4. Memo from W. Phillips to F. K. S. Woods, undated, Fairbridge Foundation, Sydney

5. Magee, unpublished autobiography, chapter 23

6. Sherington papers, ML 1781/79, State Library of New South Wales

7. P. T. Kirkpatrick, General Superintendent, Barnardo's Children's Homes, 17 August 1936; Sherington papers, ML 1781/79, State Library of New South Wales

8. Letter from John Brookman to David Spicer, 4 April 1988, personal papers of John Brookman

9. Letter from the secretary of the London Fairbridge Society to F. K. S. Woods, 18 February 1946, personal papers of John Brookman

10. Letter from John Brookman to David Spicer, 4 April 1988, personal papers of John Brookman

11. Brookman, John, 'A Potted History of the Brookman Family from 1864–1985', unpublished and undated, personal papers of John Brookman

12. Against the Tide

1. Special Report by E. R. Heath, May 1943, Fairbridge Foundation, Sydney

2. W. J. Garnett, 'Report on Farm Schools', October 1944, Fairbridge Foundation, Sydney

3. G. Green, response to the Garnett report, August 1945, Fairbridge Foundation, Sydney

4. *Daily Mail*, 5 April 1948

5. Letter from H. T. Logan to Lord Scarborough, 19 March 1948, D 296/10/2, University of Liverpool, UK

6. Rt. Hon J. Chuter Ede, M.P., opening address at the Conference on Children, Westminster, 4 April 1951, M 1841–1845, State Library of New South Wales

7. Commonwealth Relations Office files, 28 July 1955, DO 35/6380, Public Record Office, London, UK

8. Ibid., 2 August 1955

9. Memo to Sir S. Garner, 2 August 1958, D 35/6382, Public Record Office, London, UK

10. 'Child Migration to Australia: Report of a Fact-finding Mission', 28 April 1956, paragraph 7, Commonwealth Relations Office files, Public Record Office, London, UK

11. Letter from W. B. Hudson to F. K. S Woods, 2 February 1956, Fairbridge Foundation, Sydney

12. 'Child Migration to Australia: Report of a Fact-finding Mission', 28 April 1956, Commonwealth Relations Office files, Public Record Office, London, UK

13. Letter from M. K. Ewans to Costley-White, 10 May 1956,

DO 35/6381, Public Record Office, London, UK

14. Memo from Costley-White to McLennan, 11 May 1956, DO 35/6831, Public Record Office, London, UK

15. Commonwealth Relations Office memo, 9 June 1956, DO 35/6831, Public Record Office, London, UK

16. Ibid., June 1956, DO 35/6981, Public Record Office, London, UK

17. Ibid.

18. Memo from Costley-White to Whittick, 9 June 1956, Public Record Office, London, UK

19. Addenda to Fact-finding Mission Report, DO 35/6382, Public Record Office, London, UK

20. Ibid.

21. Memo from Whittick to Shannon, 22 June 1956, DO 35/6382, Public Record Office, London, UK

22. 25 June 1956, DO 35/6382, Public Record Office, London, UK

23. Armstrong's account is contained in a memo from R. H. Johnson to Costley-White and Shannon, and follows a phone call to Johnson from Armstrong, 2 July 1956, DO 35/6382, Public Record Office, London, UK

24. Memo from Costley-White to Shannon, 3 July 1956, DO 35/6382, Public Record Office, London, UK

25. Memo from Shannon to Costley-White, 5 July 1956, DO 35/6382, Public Record Office, London, UK

26. Memo from Costley-White to Shannon, 7 July 1956, DO 35/6382, Public Record Office, London, UK

27. Minutes of meeting, London Fairbridge Society, 7 July 1956, D 296 1/2/8, University of Liverpool, UK

28. Letter from W. B. Vaughan to R. H. Johnson, 10 September 1956

29. Letter from W. B. Hudson to Sir Charles Hambro, 7 September 1956, Fairbridge Foundation, Sydney

30. Minutes of meeting, London Fairbridge Society, 5 April 1956, D 296 B1/2/3, University of Liverpool, UK

31. *The Times*, 7 June 1957

32. Letter from Sir Charles Hambro to Lord Home, 2 February 1957, ML 1841–1845, State Library of New South Wales
33. Letter from Sir Charles Hambro to W. B. Hudson, 19 January 1959, D296 J3/2, University of Liverpool, UK
34. Letter from R. H. Hicks to secretary of the Department of Immigration, 25 February 1958, 10/37271, State Records NSW
35. Principal's report to Fairbridge Council, July 1961, Fairbridge Foundation, Sydney
36. Fairbridge Farm School NSW annual report, 1962
37. 'Committed to Care Cases, Fairbridge Farm School Molong', December 1971, Fairbridge Foundation, Sydney
38. Fairbridge Farm School NSW annual report, 1972
39. Ibid., 1973

13. Legacy
1. 'The Welfare of Former British Child Migrants', House of Commons Select Committee for Health report, July 1998
2. Oral evidence to the House of Commons committee, 11 June 1988
3. Ibid.
4. Ibid.
5. London Fairbridge Society, D 296 B 3/1/2-1, University of Liverpool, UK
6. 'Righting the Record', Australian Senate Community Affairs Reference Committee report, 2001
7. Oral evidence to the Senate committee, 22 March 2001
8. Fairbridge Foundation submission to the Senate committee, no. 43
9. Minutes of meeting of Fairbridge Council, 25 February 1948, Sherington papers, ML 1781/79, State Library of New South Wales
10. Letter from W. B. Hudson to R. H. Hicks, 30 December 1957
11. Fairbridge Foundation submission to the Senate committee, no. 43

BIBLIOGRAPHY AND FURTHER READING

Fairbridge, Kingsley, *The Autobiography of Kingsley Fairbridge*, Oxford University Press, London, 1927

Fairbridge, Ruby, *Pinjarra: The Building of a Farm School*, Oxford University Press, London, 1937

Gill, Alan, *Orphans of the Empire: the shocking story of child migration to Australia*, Millennium Books, Alexandria, 1997

Humphries, Margaret, *Empty Cradles*, Doubleday, London, 1994

Magee, Len, unpublished autobiography, 2004

Moss, John, *Child Migration to Australia*, HMSO, London, 1953

Penglase, Joanna, *Orphans of the Living: Growing up in care in twentieth-century Australia*, Curtin University Books, Fremantle, 2005

Rutherford, D. A., *Follow Fairbridge the Founder*, Cabonne Printers, Molong, 1983

Sherington, Geoffrey and Jeffery, Chris, *Fairbridge, Empire and Child Migration*, University of Western Australia Press, Nedlands, 1998

Tuder, Len (Len Cowne), *A Pommie Kid*, unpublished autobiography

'Child Migration to Australia: Report of a Fact-finding Mission', Commonwealth Relations Office, British Parliamentary Papers, 1955–6

'Comments of the General Secretary of Fairbridge Farm Schools on the Findings and Suggestions of Mr. Garnett', Green, W., Fairbridge Foundation, Sydney, 1945

'Lost Innocents: Righting the Record', Australian Senate, Community Affairs Reference Committee report, 2001

'Report of the Care of Children Committee', British Parliamentary Papers, 1946–7

Report on Farm Schools in Australia', Garnett, W., Fairbridge Foundation, Sydney, 1944

Sherington papers, box 4 ML 1781/79, State Library of New South Wales

'The Welfare of Former British Child Migrants', British House of Commons Select Committee for Health report, 1998

ACKNOWLEDGEMENTS

I am grateful to a large number of people for their support and assistance with the book, including my friends, colleagues and members of the Fairbridge Heritage Association, which is endeavoring to compile a comprehensive historic record of the Fairbridge Farm School at Molong.

I would like to acknowledge the support I received from a number of organisations. They include the Fairbridge Foundation, who supported the recording of Fairbridge's history and allowed me access to some of the farm school files held in their Sydney Office; the staff of the Special Collections and Archives of the University of Liverpool Library, for their assistance in accessing UK Fairbridge Society material; the staff both of the State Library of New South Wales and at State Records NSW; and the NSW Migration Heritage Centre and the New South Wales Heritage Office, who provided some financial support for the recording of the oral histories of former Fairbridge children. I must also thank Professor Geoffrey Sherington, who helped me to access his Fairbridge papers, which are held in the State Library of New South Wales.

The Old Fairbridgians' Association supported the book and provided me with assistance in contacting many of the former Fairbridge children whose stories are told on these pages. The Molong Historical Society and Museum have been very helpful and allowed me to use photos in their collection – as did former Fairbridge children Eddie Baker and Eric 'Chook' Fowler. I am also grateful to the current owner of the Fairbridge Farm, Moffat Beydoun, who allowed me access to the old Fairbridge Farm School site.

I appreciate the help I received from the staff at Random House, including Tim Whiting and Catherine Hill for their professionalism, understanding and guidance.

I am indebted to my family, including my brothers and my wife, Stergitsa, for the strength of their support; and to my son Damian, who turned five years old when I was writing the book and became an important reference point as I realised he was older than many children were when they were sent out to Fairbridge.

The most important information in the book has come from former Fairbridge children, and I am grateful to all of them for sharing their stories or supplying me with their letters, photos diaries, memoirs, unpublished auto-biographies, and other personal records and files.

Finally, a special thank you to Ian 'Smiley' Bayliff, who was a friend of mine when I was a boy at Fairbridge and with whom, some forty years later, I have renewed a close friendship. Smiley has been a good friend to lots of former Fairbridge kids. He has been collecting data about Fair-bridge for many years now and has been a valuable source of information to me, helping to fill in many gaps that have opened in the decades since I was at Fairbridge.

INDEX